COMPLETE WORKS
OF
PIR-O-MURSHID
HAZRAT INAYAT KHAN

ORIGINAL TEXTS: SAYINGS
Part II

PIR-O-MURSHID INAYAT KHAN
1882 - 1927

COMPLETE WORKS
OF
PIR-O-MURSHID
HAZRAT INAYAT KHAN

ORIGINAL TEXTS: SAYINGS
Part II

Source Edition

East-West Publications

London/The Hague

Previous volumes in this series:

Biography of Pir-o-Murshid Inayat Khan (1979)
Complete Works of Pir-o-Murshid Hazrat Inayat Khan:
1923 I, January-June (1989)
1923 II, July-December (1988)
Sayings, Part I (1989)
All books published by East-West Publications b.v., Anna Paulownastraat 78,
2518 BJ The Hague

Edited by Mrs. Munira van Voorst van Beest. Published by East-West Publications in collaboration with the Nekbakht Foundation.

ISBN 90-5340-001-X.

CONTENTS

P R E F A C E

This second volume of the above indicated series contains sayings and other words of Pir-o-Murshid Inayat Khan, which are presented here in the following sections:

Part One: the original versions of the sayings, published end 1921/beginning 1922 as the book "The Bowl of Sâki";

Part Two: hitherto unpublished sayings, mostly from Inayat Khan's Notebooks and partly from old MSS.;

Part Three: hitherto unpublished sayings, found in the handwriting of some of Inayat Khan's early mureeds;

Part Four: Aphorisms gathered by Mrs. Kefayat LLoyd, published in the magazine "The Sufi Quarterly" of 1927 - 1929, and then published as a stencilled booklet by Mr. Mumtaz Armstrong;

Part Five: the Phrases given by Inayat Khan to his mureeds.

The object of this series of books is threefold :

- To safeguard for posterity the data gathered together by Nekbakht Furnée, pupil and secretary of Inayat Khan, to whom he entrusted this task;
- To serve as the basis for future publications and translations;
- To make the original versions of Inayat Khan's words available to students and other persons interested.

Among the old documents found in the archives, those showing the original texts of the sayings and their elaborations are far from complete. For this reason it is not always possible to understand by whom, when and why different versions or alterations in the texts were made.

Key to the Presentation of Parts One and Two.

First column : "Origin and elaborations". [1]

Here is indicated where or in what form the saying first appeared and what transformations it underwent.

Each saying can be studied separately.

Each item (a, b, c, d etc.) deals with one and the same document, with a simultaneously dictated text or/ and with identical versions.

Note 1): For the explanation of signs and abbreviations see separate list on pages VII and VIII.

Cont. First Column.

a) . . . If known, the year of Inayat Khan's pocket notebooks (Notebooks) is mentioned.

. . . "Reported" means taken down in shorthand or longhand while Inayat Khan's lectures were given by him.

a) or b)

. . . "MS." ("MSS.") denotes a handwritten text taken down from Inayat Khan's dictation, or a copy of this dictated text in the handwriting of the same person.

. . . "Copied" indicates all handwritten texts other than "MSS".
A copied text may show additions, omissions and/or corrections.
There are various kinds of copied texts.
One part might be a "MS." but it is uncertain; another part was copied for an evident purpose, e.g. for classification, as were most of the texts in Ek.'s, Sh.'s, Mt.'s and Kf.'s handwriting.

. . . "Copied from (?)" always seems to be an early version, and is nearer to the original text than those called copied only. It points to one or more 'missing links'. In many cases it might well be a copy of a dictated text in the handwriting of the same person, but insufficient indications or even the absence of indications would not justify the appellation "MS." .

. . . "Copied by ... probably from her own MS." shows a shade of meaning slightly different from "MS." .

.) . . . Classification.[1)]
Close attention was given by Inayat Khan to the classification, especially of the sayings meant for publication in the "Gayan" and the "Vadan". Sometimes, however, classified sayings have not been inserted in the "Gayan", "Vadan" or "Nirtan". In such cases they can be found in Part Two of this book, as hitherto unpublished sayings.

Second column : "Different versions".

Only the words found in the archives are reproduced in this column. They are the various versions known, given in chronological order as far as this could be deduced from the available documents. There are instances, however, that a version goes back to an earlier MS. or copy, indicated under a previous item of the first column instead of being copied from the one last mentioned.

Note 1): See also Sayings I: page XVI under Classification.

Differences from the previous version are underlined and identical words are indicated by dashes. However, identical words are written out where necessary to indicate the placement of words in an altered sequence, and the published version is written out in full. The difference indicated by a line under a word may be an addition, an omission or an alteration (but if only an alteration in the sequence, it is not underlined if the meaning was not changed).

The extensive index is a word index, in which only words of minor importance have been omitted. Because of its extensiveness, moreover, it can be used as a subject index as well.

In conclusion, I wish to express my gratitude to those Sufi friends who have offered advice and suggestions and co-operated by their valuable assistance in preparing this basic work.

Munira van Voorst van Beest
April, 1981

Preface to second edition

Since the first printing of this book was sold out more than two years ago, we have prepared a new edition for inclusion in the series the *Complete Works of Pir-o-Murshid Hazrat Inayat Khan*. This has also provided an opportunity to make extensive revisions to include material which has come to light during the last eight years.

The sources of many of the sayings in "The Bowl of Sâki", not known at the time of the first printing, have now been discovered. In some cases those sayings were taken from books by Sherifa Goodenough or Zohra Williams; in all such cases, the sayings have been put in italics in this edition to indicate that, while inspired by the teachings of Pir-o-Murshid Inayat Khan, they are not his actual words. Other sayings have been found to have come from the lectures and classes given in the London Centre from 1917 to 1920. Where appropriate, these have been indicated in the "Origin" column as coming from the stencilled material of the "Old London Course".

The response to our request for help in searching for the origins of sayings has allowed us to make some headway, especially with regard to the Aphorisms. A list of already identified sources has been added to the Introduction to the Aphorisms (p. 215). We greatly appreciate the interest of readers in this project, and hope that they will continue to send us whatever they uncover.

Munira van Voorst van Beest
Sharif Graham
Staff Members of the Foundation
"Nekbakht Stichting"

34, rue de la Tuilerie
92150 Suresnes, France

October, 1989

EXPLANATION OF SIGNS AND ABBREVIATIONS.

a), b), c) etc.	indicates the presumed sequence of the stages through which the sayings went. In the case of Part One, the last item, which is the sayings published in "The Bowl of Sãki", may deviate from this rule and chronologically precede instead of follow the previous one(s).
Notebooks	= Inayat Khan's pocket notebooks.
MS. (MSS.) (manuscript(s)	= a handwritten text, taken down from Inayat Khan's dictation, or a copy of such dictated text in the handwriting of the same person.
Copied	= all handwritten texts other than MSS. Copied texts may show additions, omissions and/or corrections.
Copied from (?)	= an early version, nearer to the original text than the one called "copied" only.
Copied by ... probably from her or his own MS.	= a shade of meaning slightly different from "MS", expressed by the word 'probably'.
Classified	= placed by Inayat Khan in a definite category such as 'Sūr(a)', 'Bol(a)', 'Alankār(a)' etc.
Ed.	= edition, edited, editor.
Add.	= added, addition(al).
Corr.	= corrected, correction; a rectification of mostly grammatical errors.
Changed, Change(s)	= replacement of a word (words) by another word (words) or an idea expressed in a different way.
Altered, Alteration(s)	= slightly changed.
Cf.	= compare.
- - - - -	= quotation of the previous version. Etc. is used when a previous version of more than one line is quoted.
---------	= cancellation of a word by Inayat Khan or by one of the hereafter mentioned mureeds in their own MSS. or copies.
....	= a word or words missing.
___ ______ _	= underlined words indicate differences as compared to the previously quoted version (addition, alteration, omission). If a comparison is made with another version than the previously quoted one, this is mentioned in the first column. No comparison is made with a previous version if it shows many differences. The category of Inayat Khan's classification of a saying has been underlined, even if this same word already appears in the preceding version.

- Names -

Names of mureeds in whose handwriting the texts were found in the archives of the Nekbakht Foundation:

Mr. Mumtaz Armstrong.[1]

Miss Kitty Belfrage.[2]

Mrs. Nuria Best.

Miss Joyce Burnett.

Dr. O.C. Gruner.[1]

Begum Inayat Khan.[1] (Begum Ora Baker, Amina)

Miss Reza Jones.

Miss H. Lefèbvre.

Mrs. Rabia Martin.[1]

Miss (Mrs.?) Iris Reelfs.

Sadaruny. (It is not known who was the person signing with this name)

Names of mureeds in whose handwriting the texts were found in the archives, used in this book in an abbreviated form:

Al. Miss Angela Alt.[1]

Ek. Mrs. Ekbal Dawla van Goens - van Beyma.

Fm. Mrs. Fazal Mai Egeling.[1]

Gd. Miss Sherifa Goodenough.[1]

Gr. Miss Sophia Saintsbury Green.[1]

Kf. Mrs. Kefayat LLoyd.[1]

Km. Miss Kismet Stam.[1]

Mc. Mrs. Marya Cushing.[1]

Mf. Mr. Musheraff Khan.[1]

Mt. Mrs. Mahtab van Hogendorp.[1]

Ng. Miss Nargis Dowland.[1]

Sd. Mrs. Saida van Tuyll van Serooskerken - Willebeek le Mair.[1]

Sh. Mrs. Shadi Maheboob Khan - van Goens.[3]

Sk. Miss Sakina (Nekbakht) Furnée.[1]

Sr. Mr. Sirdar van Tuyll van Serooskerken.[1]

Sw. Miss Salima Wiseman.

Zr. Miss Zohra Williams[1] /Mrs. Kamila van Spengler - Schneider.[4]

Notes:

1. indicates that particulars about the persons mentioned can be found in the Biography of Pir-o-Murshid Inayat Khan, East-West Publications: London and The Hague, 1978.

2. a mureed to whom Ng. after 1927 dictated from sayings and words which she had received from Inayat Khan.

3. see Biography of Pir-o-Murshid Inayat Khan, under Mr. Maheboob Khan.

4. see the Complete Works of Pir-o-Murshid Hazrat Inayat Khan, Sayings, Part I, page viii.

P A R T   O N E

SAYINGS PUBLISHED IN "THE BOWL OF SÂKI".

INTRODUCTION TO PART ONE.

Part One contains the sayings published in the book "The Bowl of Sâki". In its first edition it has the following sub-title: "Thoughts for daily contemplation collected from the sayings and teachings of Pir O Murshid Inayat Khan by one of his pupils". The book was published at Southampton at the end of 1921 or perhaps at the beginning of 1922 by the Sufi Book Depot (formerly The Sufi Publishing Society). The pupil who collected the sayings most probably was Miss Sophia Saintsbury Green and the book was brought out by Miss Dowland (Nargis).
A letter by Miss Dowland to Inayat Khan, kept in the archives of the Nekbakht Foundation, gives some interesting particulars about "The Bowl of Sâki" when in its printing stage. The following lines may be quoted:

Southampton, 14.11.21

"Revered and Beloved Murshid

Miss Green has written to ask you to write something for the Magazine. I hope I am in time to ask you to please also add a few words asking all your mureeds to get a copy of "The Bowl of Sâki" and read it daily so that we may all be united in the same thought all over the world. This will also help to sell it. The cost of printing will be double the amount of the first estimate and I shall have to find nearly £ 110. So we must sell a lot or I shall find it rather difficult. I am sure it will sell in time but one has to pay ready money and wait for the return. I hope to have some copies ready by the end of the month but am afraid not in time for Geneva."

In a Quarterly Magazine for seekers after Truth: "Sufism" of December 1921, edited by Miss S. Green, the publication of "The Bowl of Sâki" is announced by the Ed., saying that it will be ready for a Christmas present, and that it is "a collection of some of the most striking and arresting sayings of Pir-o-Murshid, arranged in the form of a daily text-book". So there is a saying for each day of the year; the date is mentioned first and then follows the saying - three sayings on one page.

The following documents, found in the archives, can be considered as the sources of these sayings:
Inayat Khan's Notebook of 1914/1915, his Notebooks of 1921 and some others of his Notebooks; MSS. and copied texts in the handwriting of some British mureeds amongst whom Miss Green, Miss Dowland, Miss Goodenough, Miss Alt and Mrs. LLoyd; lectures given by Inayat Khan in England in the years 1918 - 1920, reported and revised by Dr. O.C. Gruner as published in "In an Eastern Rosegarden" 1st ed. (1920/1921) and other lectures, mainly those given in the years 1920 and 1921, also undated ones, found in the handwriting of Mrs. Nuria Best, Miss Reza Jones, Miss Joyce Burnett and other early mureeds. Sentences from these lectures were taken and turned into sayings.
As some 26 sayings have their origin in the lecture "Truth" of 13th May 1921, the information under the different items in the left column may be explained a little more extensively. This lecture was found in the handwriting of Nuria Best,

- most -

most probably copied by her from her own reporting, and also in the handwriting of Miss R. Jones, which could be copied from it, with some corrections, however, and somewhat shortened. Both versions seem to be very near to the originally spoken words. - A typewritten copy found in the archives, gives a revised version of the lecture "Truth", likely to have been made from the above mentioned versions; it is not known by whom. In many cases the revised version was used for publication in "The Bowl of Sâki".

A number of sayings were as it seems already set apart for publication in the "Gayan" at an early stage. A part of these, however, was first published in "The Bowl of Sâki" and one and a half year later again in the "Gayan", while others appeared only in "The Bowl of Sâki". Most of the sayings originally intended for the "Gayan", were found in Gd.'s handwriting and/or typed out by her or sometimes by another person on her request. There are also sayings already classified by Inayat Khan for publication in the "Gayan", but then appearing in "The Bowl of Sâki" instead. Then there are sayings published in "The Bowl of Sâki", which afterwards were published in the "Gayan" in a somewhat different version giving a different meaning to it.

As the documents with sayings published in "The Bowl of Sâki" compared to the documents with sayings for "Gayan" and "Vadan" consist of a greater number of typed copies and less MSS., on the whole there is more uncertainty about the different elaborations of these sayings.

The sayings of which no sources could as yet be traced, may still be found as sentences in the book "In an Eastern Rosegarden" and in other lectures given before September 1921. As also asked in the Preface of the book Sayings I of this same series, the assistance of those who read and study Inayat Khan's words in helping to find the origin of sayings taken from his lectures, will be most valuable for a more complete future edition of this book.

ORIGIN and elaborations:	DIFFERENT VERSIONS:
a) A sentence in the chapter "The Truth" in "A Sufi Message of Spiritual Liberty", 1914.	As water in a fountain flows as one stream, but falls in many drops, divided by time and space, so are the revelations of the one stream of Truth.
b) 1st ed. "The Bowl of Sâki" - 1st January.	As water in a fountain flows as one stream, but falls in many drops_ divided by time and space, so are the revelations of the one stream of truth.

No documents referring to the sayings under 2nd - 5th January have been found in the archives to date.

1st ed. "The Bowl of Sâki" - 2nd January.	All names and forms are the garbs and covers, under which the One Life is hidden.
1st ed. "The Bowl of Saki" - 3rd January.	Truth without a veil is always uninteresting to the human mind.
1st ed. "The Bowl of Sâki" - 4th January.	When you stand with your back to the sun, your shadow is before you; but when you turn and face the sun, then your shadow falls behind you.
1st ed. "The Bowl of Sâki" - 5th January.	No one has seen God and lived. To see God we must be non-existent.

---

a) Notebooks 1921 :	Bola. Truth cannot be spoken and what is spoken is not necessarily the Truth.
b) Copied by Ng. from (?).	The Truth cannot be spoken and the spoken word is not necessarily ___ true.
c) 1st ed. "The Bowl of Sâki" - 6th January.	The Truth cannot be spoken ; that which can be spoken is not ___ the Truth.

---

a) A sentence in the lecture 'What a Mystic wants to attain', 11th June 1921, in handwriting M.lle Lefèbvre (a reporting of the simultaneous translation in French) and annotations in English made by Sr.	Le mystique comprend que son pouvoir réside dans l'amour, c'est le pouvoir de l'amour. this desire of power - the mystic understands - must become the power of love
b) Copied by Gd. and originally meant for publication in the "Gayan".	The only power for the mystic is the power of love.
c) An old typewritten copy.	- - - - power of the - - - - - etc.
d) 1st ed. "The Bowl of Sâki" - 7th January.	The only power for the mystic is the power of love.

ORIGIN and elaborations:	DIFFERENT VERSIONS:
a) A sentence in the lecture 'Nature's Religion' (1918-1920), reported and revised by Dr. O. Gruner as published in 'In an Eastern Rose-garden', 1st ed. 1920/1921.	Did they[1)] but know their own religion, how tolerant they would become, and how free from any grudge against the religion of others!
b) 1st ed. "The Bowl of Sâki" - 8th January.	If people but knew their own religion, how tolerant they would become, and how free from any grudge against the religion of others.

Note 1): 'they' refers to the word 'people', mentioned in the previous sentence.

---

a) From a lecture 'The Freedom of the Soul', 11 Feb. 1917, published in 'In an Eastern Rose-garden', 1920/1921	The real meaning of crucifixion is to crucify this false self, and so resurrect the true self. As long as the false self is not crucified, the true self is still not realised.
b) 1st ed. "The Bowl of Sâki" - 9th January.	The real meaning of Crucifixion is to crucify the false self _ that the true self may rise. As long as the false self is not crucified_ the true self is _____ not realised.

---

a) In handwriting Miss Kitty Belfrage, dictated to her by Ng.	An ideal is beyond explanation. To analyse God is to de-throne God.
b) 1st ed. "The Bowl of Sâki" - 10th January.	An ideal is beyond explanation. To analyse God is to dethrone God.

No documents referring to the sayings under 11th - 18th January have been found in the archives to date.	
1st ed. "The Bowl of Sâki" - 11th January.	Where the flame of love rises, the knowledge of God unfolds of itself.
1st ed. "The Bowl of Sâki" - 12th January.	Peace is perfected activity ; that is perfect which is complete in all its aspects, balanced in each direction and under complete control of the will.
1st ed. "The Bowl of Sâki" - 13th January.	Do not limit God to your virtue. He is beyond your virtues, Oh! pious ones!
1st ed. "The Bowl of Sâki" - 14th January.	A man's inclination is the root of the tree of his life.

ORIGIN and elaborations:	DIFFERENT VERSIONS:
1st ed. "The Bowl of Sâki" - 15th January.	Yes, teach your principles of good, but do not think to limit God within them. The goodness of each man is peculiar to himself.
1st ed. "The Bowl of Sâki" - 16th January.	To learn to adopt the standard of God, and to cease to wish to make the world conform to one's own standard of good is the chief lesson of religion.
1st ed. "The Bowl of Sâki" - 17th January.	Thought draws the line of fate.
1st ed. "The Bowl of Sâki" - 18th January.	Mis-belief alone misleads; single-mindedness always leads to the goal.

---

a) Notebook 1914/1915 :	A king in spirit is always a king, is he crowned with jewels or he be cladded with rags.
b) 1st ed. "The Bowl of Sâki" - 19th January.	A King is ever a King, be he crowned with a jewelled crown or clad in beggar's garb.

No documents referring to the sayings under 20th - 25th January have been found in the archives to date.

1st ed. "The Bowl of Sâki" - 20th January.	To treat every human being as a shrine of God is to fulfil all religion.
1st ed. "The Bowl of Sâki" - 21st January.	The wise man should keep the balance between love and power. Should keep the love in his nature ever increasing and expanding, and at the same time strengthen the will so that the heart may not easily be broken.
1st ed. "The Bowl of Sâki" - 22nd January.	Failure comes when will surrenders to reason.
1st ed. "The Bowl of Sâki" - 23rd January.	Success comes when reason (the store of experience) surrenders to will.
1st ed. "The Bowl of Sâki" - 24th January.	There is an answer to every call; those who call on God, to them God comes.
1st ed. "The Bowl of Sâki" - 25th January.	He who thinks against his own desire, he is his own enemy.

---

a) Notebook 1914/1915 :	Brain speaks through words, heart speaks through a kind glance, and soul speaks

Cont. a)

ORIGIN and elaborations:	DIFFERENT VERSIONS:
Cont. a)	through the breath that radiates light and life and charges the whole atmosphere with magnetism.
b) 1st ed. "The Bowl of Sâki" - 26th January.	The brain speaks through words; the heart in the glance of the eyes; and the soul through a radiance that charges the whole atmosphere magnetising all.

---

a) MS. Gr. together with other sayings meant to be published in the "Gayan".	Bola. Love is the merchandise which all the world demands; if you store it in the heart every soul will become your customer.
b) Copied by Mt. and classified by Inayat Khan as 'Chal'.	Chala. - - - - - - - - - - - - - - .
c) 1st ed. "The Bowl of Sâki" - 27th January.	Love is the merchandise which all the world demands; if you store it in your heart, every soul will become your customer.

---

a) Notebook 1914/1915 :	She is a precious pearl that forms in the shell of heart and is found in the soil of the spirit, and that is sincerity.
b) 1st ed. "The Bowl of Sâki" - 28th January.	Sincerity is the jewel that forms in the shell of the heart ___ __ _____ __ ___ ___ __ ___ ______ _ .

Cf. Sayings I: "Gayan" - Bola 40.

---

a) Notebook 1914/1915 :	Saying. There is no worse poverty than self-pity.
A sentence in the lecture 'The Privilege of being human', 24th May 1921 at Southampton, in Kitty Belfrage's handwriting. She copied it from Ng.	Selfpity is the worst poverty, and it is the source of all unhappiness.
A sentence in the lecture 'The Privilege of being human', 20th June 1921 in Switzerland (Social Gatheka no.16). Fragments and sentences of this lecture were reported by Sr. and a copy in Gd.'s handwrit-	Self-pity is the worst poverty, it overwins man and he sees nothing as its own troubles and pains.

Cont. a)

ORIGIN and elaborations:	DIFFERENT VERSIONS:
Cont. a) ing, could well be a reporting.	
The third sentence under a) was found in Gd.'s handwritten copy of this lecture.	Selfpity is the worst poverty; it overwhelms man and he sees nothing but ___ ___ illness, trouble, and pain.
b) Copied by Gd. together with other sayings meant for publication in the "Gayan".	Selfpity is the worst poverty. It overwhelms mand and he sees nothing but his own ______ troubles and pains.
c) 1st ed. "The Bowl of Sâki" - 29th January.	Self-pity is the worst poverty; it overwhelms man until he sees nothing but ___ ___ illness, trouble and pain.

No documents referring to the sayings under 30th and 31st January have been found in the archives to date.	
1st ed. "The Bowl of Sâki" - 30th January.	The heart is not living until it has experienced pain.
1st ed. "The Bowl of Sâki" - 31st January.	The pleasures of life are blinding; it is love alone that clears the rust from the heart, the mirror of the soul.

No documents referring to the sayings under 1st February have been found in the archives to date.	
1st ed. "The Bowl of Sâki" - 1st February.	The pain of love is the dynamite that breaks up the heart, even if it be as hard as a rock.

---

a) From a book, 'Love, Human and Divine', by Sherifa Lucy Goodenough, published ln 1919, p. 33.	*Our virtues are made of love, and our sins are caused by its lack.*
b) 1st ed. "The Bowl of Sâki" - 2nd February	*Our virtues are made by love, and our sins are caused by the lack of it.*

ORIGIN and elaborations:	DIFFERENT VERSIONS:
No documents referring to the sayings under 3rd - 6th February have been found in the archives to date.	
1st ed. "The Bowl of Sâki" - 3rd February.	Love is the essence of all religion, mysticism and philosophy.
1st ed. "The Bowl of Sâki" - 4th February.	The fire of devotion purifies the heart of the devotee, and leads unto spiritual freedom.
Note: = duplicated under 17the June.	
1st ed. "The Bowl of Sâki" - 5th February.	Mysticism without devotion is like uncooked food, it can never be assimilated.
1st ed. "The Bowl of Sâki" - 6th February.	He who stores evil in his heart cannot see beauty.

---

a) A sentence in "A Sufi Message of Spiritual Liberty", The Personal Being, p.20, 1st ed. 1914.	The wise man, by studying Nature enters into the unity through its variety, and realises the personality of Allah by sacrificing that of his own.
b) 1st ed. "The Bowl of Sâki" - 7th February.	The wise man, by studying nature, enters into ___ unity through its variety, and realizes the Personality of God by sacrificing ___ ___ his own.

No documents referring to the sayings under 8th February have been found in the archives to date.	
1st ed. "The Bowl of Sâki" - 8th February.	Love manifests towards those whom we like as love; towards those whom we do not like as forgiveness.

---

a) A sentence in "A Sufi Message of Spiritual Liberty", Love, p.29, 1st ed. 1914.	...it is love which has brought Man from the world of unity to the world of variety, and the same force again can take him to that world of unity from that of variety.
b) 1st ed. "The Bowl of Sâki" - 9th February.	___ ___ Love ___ ___ brought man from the world of unity to that ___ of variety, and the same force ___ can take him back again to the world of unity from the world of variety.

ORIGIN and elaborations:	DIFFERENT VERSIONS:
a) From a book "A Sufi Message of Spiritual Liberty", Manifestation, p.44, 1914.	Whoever knows the mystery of vibrations, indeed knows all things.
b) 1st ed. "The Bowl of Sâki" - 10th February.	Whoever knows the mystery of vibrations _ indeed knows all things.

---

a) A sentence in "A Sufi Message of Spiritual Liberty", Interest and Indifference, p.45, 1st ed. 1914.	He who arrives at the state of indifference without experiencing interest in life is incomplete, and apt to be tempted by interest at any moment; but he who arrives at the state of indifference by going through interest, really attains the blessed state.
b) 1st ed. "The Bowl of Sâki" - 11th February.	He who arrives at the state of indifference without experiencing interest in life is incomplete_ and apt to be tempted by interest at any moment; but he who arrives at the state of indifference by going through interest_ really attains the blessed state.

---

a) A sentence in "A Sufi Message of Spiritual Liberty", Intellect and Wisdom, p.48, 1st ed. 1914.	Wisdom is greater and more difficult to attain than intellect, piety or spirituality.
b) 1st ed. "The Bowl of Sâki" - 12th February.	Wisdom is greater and more difficult to attain than intellect, piety or spirituality.

---

a) A sentence in "A Sufi Message of Spiritual Liberty", Prophets, p.33, 1st ed. 1914.	Wisdom is consciousness in its pure essence, which is not necessarily dependent upon the knowledge of names and forms.
b) 1st ed. "The Bowl of Sâki" - 13th February.	Wisdom is intelligence in its pure essence, which is not necessarily dependent upon the knowledge of names and forms.

ORIGIN and elaborations:	DIFFERENT VERSIONS:
a) A sentence in "A Sufi Message of Spiritual Liberty", Law of Action, p.50, 1st ed. 1914.	Man forms his future by his actions. His every good and bad action spreads its vibrations and becomes known throughout the universe.
b) 1st ed. "The Bowl of Sâki" - 14th February.	Man forms his future by his actions; his every good or bad action spreads its vibrations and becomes known throughout the universe.
a) A sentence in "A Sufi Message of Spiritual Liberty", Law of Action, p.51 1st ed. 1914.	The Universe is like a dome, it vibrates that which you say in it, and answers the same back to you. So also is the law of action, we reap what we sow.
b) 1st ed. "The Bowl of Sâki" - 15th February.	The Universe is like a dome; it vibrates to that which you say in it, and answers the same back to you; so also is the law of action, we reap what we sow.
No documents referring to the sayings under 16th - 18th February have been found in the archives to date.	
1st ed. "The Bowl of Sâki" - 16th February.	We are always searching for God afar off, when all the while He is nearer to us than our own soul.
1st ed. "The Bowl of Sâki" - 17th February.	Concentration and contemplation are great things; but no contemplation is greater than the life we have about us every day.
1st ed. "The Bowl of Sâki" - 18th February.	He who expects to change the world will be disappointed, he must change his view. When this is done, then tolerance will come, forgiveness will come, and there will be nothing he cannot bear.

ORIGIN and elaborations:	DIFFERENT VERSIONS:
a) A passage in an early, typewritten version of the third lesson of a Course on 'The Law of Attainment' which in a revised form became Gita Sadhana.	There are two renunciations: the renunciation by mastery and the renunciation by weakness. When you have picked an apple from the tree and thought it is sour, you don't want to eat it, it is mastery. But when you could not pick the apple and said: "it is sour, no use bothering' - then it is a weakness.
b) A sentence in an undated lecture 'The Way of Attainment' in Gd.'s handwriting.	To renounce what we cannot gain is not true renunciation, it is weakness.
c) 1st ed. "The Bowl of Sâki" - 19th February.	To renounce what we cannot gain is not true renunciation, it is weakness.

---

a) Copied by Mt. from (?).	The religion of each one is the attainment of his soul's desire.
b) 1st ed. "The Bowl of Sâki" - 20th February.	The religion of each one is the attainment of his soul's desire; when he is on the path of that attainment he is religious, when he is off that path then he is irreligious, impious.

---

a) Notebooks 1921 :	Saying. Reformer comes to prepare the ground. The Prophet comes to throw the seed, and the priest comes to take the crop.
b) Copied by Gd. from (?).	The reformer comes to plough the ground, the prophet comes to sow the seed, and then the priest ~~comes~~ to ~~take~~ reap the ~~crop~~ harvest.
c) 1st ed. "The Bowl of Sâki" - 21st February.	The reformer comes to plough the ground; the prophet comes to sow the seed; and ____ the priest comes to reap the harvest.

---

a) Notebooks 1921 :	Saying. Life is an opportunity to satisfy the hunger and thirst of our soul.
b) Copied by Gd. from (?).	______ Life is an opportunity given to - - - - - - - - - - - - - - of the soul.
c) 1st ed. "The Bowl of Sâki" - 22nd February.	Life is an opportunity given to satisfy the hunger and thirst of the soul.

Cf. Sayings I: "Gayan" - Chala 124.

ORIGIN and elaborations:	DIFFERENT VERSIONS:
1st ed. "The Bowl of Sâki" - 23rd February.	Truth alone can succeed; falsehood is a waste of time and loss of energy.

Note: For complete elaborations and different versions see Sayings I: "Gayan" - Chala 84.

1st ed. "The Bowl of Sâki" - 24th February.	Do not fear God, but consciously regard His pleasure and displeasure.

Note: For complete elaborations and different versions see Sayings I: "Gayan" - Bola 56.

1st ed. "The Bowl of Sâki" - 25th February.	He who has failed himself, has failed all; he who has conquered himself has won all.

Note: For complete elaborations and different versions see Sayings I: "Gayan" - Tala 16.

---

a) Notebooks 1921 :	Saying. As man rises above passion he begins to know what is love.
b) Copied in an unidentified handwriting, probably from a MS. Ng. In Ng.'s handwriting was added 'Saying' over it.	Saying. - - - - - - - - - - -passion, so he - etc.
c) 1st ed. "The Bowl of Sâki" - 26th February.	As man rises above passion, so he begins to know what is love.

---

a) Notebook 1914/1915 :	Simplicity with intelligence is the sign of saints.
Notebooks :	Saying. Innocence with intelligence is a true sign of spirituality.
b) MS. Gr. in which the first sentence under a) appears. A typewritten version with Bolas to be published in the "Gayan" (Gd.'s bookpreparation).	Bola. Believe in God with childlike faith; for simplicity with intelligence is the sign of the Holy Ones.
c) A later typewritten version gives b) as Bolas I, but then, probably by Gd., the sentence was divided into two sentences.	Bola. Believe in God with childlike faith. Simplicity with intelligence is the sign of the Holy Ones.

d)

ORIGIN and elaborations:	DIFFERENT VERSIONS:
d) Copied by Mt. and by Kf. as two sentences.	_____ - - - - - - - - - - - - - - . - - - - - - - - - - - - - - .
e) Copied by Ek. from (?) the second sentence under a).	_____ Innocence with intelligence is the true sign of spirituality.
f) Again copied by Ek. and classified by Inayat Khan as 'Sur', originally meant for publication in the "Gayan".	Sura. - - - - - - - - - - - - - - .
An annotation in Mc.'s handwriting: 'same as: 'Believe in God with etc.' The words 'Innocence' and 'spirituality' were put between brackets so that the version, as changed by Mc., became:	Believe in God with childlike faith, for simplicity with intelligence is the true sign of the Holy Ones.
g) 1st ed. "The Bowl of Sâki" - 27th February.	Believe in God with childlike faith; for simplicity with intelligence is the ____ sign of the Holy Ones.

Cf. Sayings I: "Gayan" - Bola 171.

1st ed. "The Bowl of Sâki" - 28th February.	Saying. He who can live up to his ideal is the king of life and who cannot live up to it is its slave.

Note: For complete elaborations and different versions see Sayings I: "Gayan" - Bola 10.

---

a) Notebooks 1921 :	Saying. Every moment in life is an invaluable opportunity given to make life worth while; who disregards this has lost his chance; who considers this has gained.
b) Copied in an unidentified handwriting, probably from MS. Ng. In Ng.'s handwriting was added 'Saying' over it.	Saying. Every moment of our life is an invaluable opportunity.
c) 1st ed. "The Bowl of Sâki" - 29th February.	Every moment of our life is an invaluable opportunity.

Cf. Sayings I: "Gayan" - Bola 132 and Chala 136.

ORIGIN and elaborations:	DIFFERENT VERSIONS:
a) Notebooks 1921 :	Saying. Nature speaks louder than the call from the minaret.
b) Copied in an unidentified handwriting, probably from MS. Ng. In Ng.'s handwriting was added 'Saying' over it.	Saying. - - - - - - - - - - - - - - .
c) 1st ed. "The Bowl of Sâki" - 1st March.	Nature speaks louder than the call from the Minaret.

---

a) Notebooks 1921 :	Saying. The priest gives the benediction of the church and the branches bending, give the blessing of God.
b) Copied in an unidentified handwriting, probably from MS. Ng. In Ng.'s handwriting was added 'Saying' over it.	Saying. The priest gives a benediction from the church. ___ The branches of the tree in bending give ___ blessing from God.
c) A typewritten copy with sayings, mostly meant for publication in the "Gayan".	Saying. - church; the -give a blessing - - - -.
d) 1st ed. "The Bowl of Sâki" - 2nd March.	The Priest gives a benediction from the Church; the branches of the tree in bending give _ blessing from God.

---

a) Notebooks 1921 :	Saying. The soul brings its light from the heaven and mind acquires its knowledge on earth, therefore when soul believes readily in a thing the mind doubts.
b) Copied in an unidentified handwriting, probably from MS. Ng., in whose handwriting was added 'Saying' over it.	Saying. - - - - - - - - - - - - - - - from ___ Heaven, ___ the mind - - - - knowledge from earth, therefore when the soul believes readily __ _ _____ the mind may still doubt.
c) 1st ed. "The Bowl of Sâki" - 3rd March.	The soul brings its light from Heaven. The mind acquires its knowledge from earth; therefore, when the soul believes readily, the mind may still doubt.

ORIGIN and elaborations:	DIFFERENT VERSIONS:
No documents referring to the sayings under 4th and 5th March have been found in the archives to date.	
1st ed. "The Bowl of Sâki" - 4th March.	Those who throw dust to the sun, the dust falls in their own eyes.
1st ed. "The Bowl of Sâki" - 5th March.	Man creates his own disharmony.

---

a) A passage in the lecture 'Truth', 13th May 1921, in Nuria Best's and in Miss R.Jones's handwriting.	The heart is the shrine of God and when the doors of the shrine are closed it is just like a light being hidden under a bushel. The pupil sees that God is love. If He is love He does not stay in the heavens. His earth body is the heart of man and when that heart is frozen and there is no love, but bitterness, coldness and prejudice and contempt, and unforgiving feelings, hatred etc. ....
b) A typewritten copy.	The heart - - - - - - - - - - - - - etc. - - - - bushel. The Bible says "God is love". If He loves He does not stay in the sky. His real abode is the heart of man and when the heart is frozen with bitterness, coldness, resentment and hatred ....
c) Copied by Mt.	The real abode of God is in the heart of man.
d) 1st ed. "The Bowl of Sâki" - 6th March. Versions b) and c).	The real abode of God is in the heart man; when it is frozen with bitterness or hatred, the doors of the shrine are closed; the light is hidden.

No documents referring to the saying under 7th March have been found in the archives to date.	
1st ed. "The Bowl of Sâki" - 7th March.	It is a false love that does not uproot man's claim of "I"; the first and last lesson of love is "I am not".

---

a) Part of a sentence in the lecture 'Truth', 13th May 1921, in Nuria Best's handwriting.	You cannot be horse and rider at the same time,
b) In Miss R.Jones's handwriting.	You cannot be a horse and a rider at the same time.

c)

ORIGIN and elaborations:	DIFFERENT VERSIONS:
c) A typewritten copy.	You cannot be the horse and the rider.
d) 1st ed. "The Bowl of Sâki" - 8th March.	You cannot be both ___ horse and ___ rider at the same time.

---

a) Part of a sentence in the lecture 'Truth', 13th May 1921, in Nuria Best's handwriting.	It is more important to find the truth about oneself than to find the truth about heaven or hell,
b) In Miss R.Jones's handwriting.	It is more important to find out the truth about one's self, than to find the truth about Heaven and or hell,
c) A typewritten copy.	It is more important to discover the truth about ____ self, than to find out the truths of Heaven and hell.
d) 1st ed. "The Bowl of Sâki" - 9th March.	It is more important to know the truth about one's self than to try to find out the truth of Heaven and Hell.

Cf. "The Bowl of Sâki" under 26th October.

---

a) A sentence in the lecture 'Truth', 13th May 1921, in Nuria Best's and Miss R.Jones's handwriting; also a typewritten copy.	Every man's pursuit is according to his state of evolution.
b) 1st ed. "The Bowl of Sâki" - 10th March.	Every man's pursuit is according to his _____ __ evolution.

---

a) Notebooks 1921 :	Bola. Man does not see beyond what he sees.
b) A typewritten copy with sayings, over which Gd. wrote "Gayan". In the margin she wrote: 'where?' (Gd.'s book-preparation).	Bola. - - - - - - - - - - - - - - what he can see.
c) Another typewritten copy with sayings under the heading 'Bola I', mostly meant for publication in the "Gayan" (Gd.'s book-preparation).	Bola. - - - - - - - - - - - - - -
d) Copied by Mt. and classified by Inayat Khan as 'Bola'.	Bola. - - - - - - - - - - - - - - .

e)

ORIGIN and elaborations:	DIFFERENT VERSIONS:
e) A sentence in the lecture 'Truth', 13th May 1921, in Nuria Best's handwriting and a typewritten version. (compared to version a)).	Man always sees what he sees, beyond it he cannot see.
f) A sentence in the same lecture as under e), in Miss R.Jones's handwriting.	Man just sees what he sees, beyond that he cannot see.
g) 1st ed. "The Bowl of Sâki" - 11th March.	Man ____ sees what he sees; beyond it he cannot see.

---

a) A sentence in the lecture 'Truth', 13th May 1921, in Nuria Best's handwriting.	The source of realizing the truth is within man, but man is the object of his realization.
b) A sentence in the same lecture as under a), in Miss R.Jones's handwriting.	- but that man himself is the - - - - - - -.
c) A typewritten copy.	The source of realization of Truth is within man. ___ ____ He himself is the - - - - - - -.
d) 1st ed. "The Bowl of Sâki" - 12th March.	The source of __________ __ truth is within man; he himself is the object of his realization.

Cf. "The Bowl of Sâki" under 24th October.

---

a) A sentence in the lecture 'Truth', 13th May 1921, in Nuria Best's handwriting.	As life unfolds itself to man, the first lesson that it teaches is humility.
b) A sentence in the same lecture as under a), in Miss R.Jones's handwriting.	- lesson that it should teach is humility.
c) A typewritten version.	- lesson he learns is humility.
d) 1st ed. "The Bowl of Sâki" - 13th March.	As life unfolds itself to man, the first lesson he learns is humility.

---

a) A sentence in the lecture 'Truth', 13th May 1921, in Nuria Best's handwriting.	God is Truth - Truth is God.

b)

ORIGIN and elaborations:	DIFFERENT VERSIONS:
b) A sentence in the same lecture as under a), in Miss R.Jones's handwriting.	God is Truth and Truth is God.
c) 1st ed. "The Bowl of Sâki" - 14th March.	God is Truth; and Truth is God.

ORIGIN and elaborations:	DIFFERENT VERSIONS:
No documents referring to the saying under 15th March have been found in the archives to date.	
1st ed. "The Bowl of Sâki" - 15th March.	Until man loses himself in the vision of God, he cannot be said to really live.

ORIGIN and elaborations:	DIFFERENT VERSIONS:
a) A sentence in the lecture 'Truth', 13th May 1921, in Nuria Best's handwriting and a typewritten version.	At every step of evolution the realization of man changes.
b) A sentence in the same lecture as under a), in Miss R.Jones's handwriting.	At every stage of man's evolution his realization changes.
c) 1st ed. "The Bowl of Sâki" - 16th March.	At every step of ______ evolution, man's realization of God changes.

ORIGIN and elaborations:	DIFFERENT VERSIONS:
1st ed. "The Bowl of Sâki" - 17th March.	Verily he is victorious who has conquered himself.

Note: For origin, complete elaborations and different versions, see Sayings I: "Gayan" - Sura 21.

ORIGIN and elaborations:	DIFFERENT VERSIONS:
a) Part of a sentence in the address to mureeds: 'Prayer', 8th May 1921, given in the first Service of the Church of All in London (Religious Gatheka I, 5, which afterwards became no.8), in Joyce Burnett's handwriting.	and morally speaking, prayer is the greatest virtue and the only way of being free from all sin.
b) The same sentence as under a) in an unidentified handwriting. Also published in the Magazine 'Sufism' of March 1922.	Prayer is a great virtue and is the only way of being free from all sin.

c)

ORIGIN and elaborations:	DIFFERENT VERSIONS:
c) 1st ed. "The Bowl of Sâki" - 18th March.	Prayer is the greatest virtue, ___ __ the only way of being free from all sin.

---

a) A sentence in the address to mureeds: 'Prayer', 8th May 1921, given in the first Service of the Church of All in London, in Joyce Burnett's handwriting.	It is the sincere devotee of God, who knows best what feeling it is to humble oneself to God.
b) A typewritten copy of the same sentence as under a) (Religious Gatheka I, 5, which afterwards was changed into no. 8).	- - - - - - - - - - - - - - of God_ who -oneself before God.
c) 1st ed. "The Bowl of Sâki" - 19th March.	It is the sincere devotee __ ___ who knows best ____ _______ __ __ how to humble himself before God.

1st ed. "The Bowl of Sâki" - 20th March.	It is wise to see all things, and yet to turn our eyes from all that should be overlooked.

Note: For complete elaborations and different versions, see Sayings I: "Gayan" - Tala 22.

---

a) Part of a sentence in the address to mureeds: 'Prayer', 8th May 1921, evening (Religious Gatheka I, 10, which afterwards became no. 9) in Joyce Burnett's handwriting, to which was added in Gd.'s handwriting:	our soul is blessed with the impression of the glory of God whenever we praise Him.
b) The same sentence as under a) in an unidentified handwriting. Also a typewritten copy.	our soul is blessed with the impression of the Glory of God whenever we praise Him.
c) 1st ed. "The Bowl of Sâki" - 21st March.	Our soul is blessed with the impression of the Glory of God whenever our lips praise Him.

Cf. "The Bowl of Sâki" under 6th November.

---

a) Part of two sentences in the lecture 'Truth',	But he forgets that there is only one Teacher and that is God Himself. We

Cont. a)

<u>ORIGIN</u> and elaborations:	<u>DIFFERENT VERSIONS</u>:
Cont. a) 13th May 1921, in Nuria Best's handwriting.	all are pupils,
b) The same sentence as under a) in Miss R. Jones's handwriting.	- and that <u>One</u> is God Himself. <u>Truly</u> <u>we</u> all are pupils,
c) A typewritten version.	<u>He</u> <u>does</u> <u>not</u> <u>know</u> that there is <u>but</u> one Teacher<u>,</u> ___ ____ __ __ God Himself. _____ __ ___ ___ ______
d) 1st ed. "The Bowl of Sâki" - 22nd March.	__ ____ ___ ____ ___ There is ___ <u>One</u> Teacher, God Himself<u>;</u> <u>we</u> <u>are</u> <u>all</u> <u>His</u> <u>pupils.</u>

Cf. "The Bowl of Sâki" under 30th October, last sentence and Sayings I: "Gayan" - Sura 35.

---

a) A sentence in the lecture 'Truth', 13th May 1921, in Nuria Best's and Miss R.Jones's handwriting.	All knowledge of the earth is as clouds covering the sun.
b) A typewritten version.	All <u>earthly</u> knowledge is as clouds <u>dimming</u> the <u>sight</u>.
c) 1st ed. "The Bowl of Sâki" - 23rd March.	All earthly knowledge is as <u>a</u> <u>cloud</u> <u>covering</u> the <u>sun</u>.

Cf. "The Bowl of Sâki" under 31st October.

---

a) Part of a sentence in the lecture 'Truth', 13th May 1921, in Nuria Best's handwriting.	The first sign of the realization of truth is tolerance to others,
b) The same sentence as under a), in Miss R. Jones's handwriting.	- -tolerance <u>towards</u> others<u>.</u>
c) A typewritten version.	- -tolerance. ______ _____
d) 1st ed. "The Bowl of Sâki" - 24th March.	The first sign of the realization of truth is tolerance.

---

a) A sentence in the lecture 'Truth', 13th May 1921, in Nuria Best's handwriting.	Man, filled with earthly knowledge, and what he calls learning, is often the knowledge only of names and forms and so has no capacity for the knowledge of truth or of God.
b) The same sentence as under a), in Miss R. Jones's handwriting.	- - - - - - - - - - - - - - - - - - - etc. and so he has no capacity for <u>true</u> <u>learning,</u> <u>and</u> <u>real</u> knowledge __ _____ __ __ ___.

c)

ORIGIN and elaborations:	DIFFERENT VERSIONS:
c) A typewritten version. (shortened form a)).	Man filled with earthly knowledge, - the knowledge of names and forms - has no capacity for the knowledge of Truth and of God.
d) Copied by Ng.	The man filled with _______ _________ _ _ the knowledge of names and forms _ _ has no capacity for the knowledge of Truth. ___ __ ___
e) 1st ed. "The Bowl of Sâki" - 25th March.	He who is filled with the knowledge of names and forms has no capacity for the knowledge of God.

Cf. "The Bowl of Sâki" under 28th October (= version d).

No documents referring to the saying under 26th March have been found in the archives to date.	
1st ed. "The Bowl of Sâki" 26th March.	Man is closer to God than the fishes are to the ocean.

1st ed. "The Bowl of Sâki" - 27th March.	We start our lives trying to be teachers; it is very hard to learn to be a pupil.

Note: For origin, elaborations and different versions see "The Bowl of Sâki" under 30th October.

Cf. "The Bowl of Sâki" under 22nd March and Sayings I: "Gayan" - Sura 35.

No documents referring to the saying under 28th March have been found in the archives to date.	
1st ed. "The Bowl of Sâki" - 28th March.	Until the heart is empty, it cannot receive the knowledge of God.

---

a) A sentence in the lecture 'Truth', 13th May 1921, in Nuria Best's and Miss R.Jones's handwriting.	according to his evolution, so man knows the truth.
b) A typewritten copy.	according to his evolution_ __ man knows the truth.
c) 1st ed. "The Bowl of Sâki" - 29th March.	According to his evolution, man knows ___ Truth.

Cf. "The Bowl of Sâki" under 27th October.

<u>ORIGIN</u> and elaborations:	<u>DIFFERENT VERSIONS</u>:
a) Part of two sentences in the address to mureeds: 'Prayer', 8th May 1921, evening (Religious Gatheka I, 10, which afterwards became no. 8), in Joyce Burnett's handwriting.	and in whatever manner you humble yourself before Him, it can never be enough. To humble yourself before His Perfection, that is to deny yourself.
b) The same sentence as under a), in an unidentified handwriting.	<u>but</u> in whatever manner you humble yourself ______ ___, it can never be enough_ <u>t</u>o humble <u>y</u>our <u>limited</u> self before ___ <u>limitless</u> Perfection<u>.</u>
c) A typewritten version. (= version a).	- - - - - - - - - - - - - - - - - - - etc. enough. To humble your <u>limited</u> self - - - - etc.
d) 1st ed. "The Bowl of Sâki" - 30th March.	We can never sufficiently humble our limited self before limitless perfection.

---

a) A sentence in the address to mureeds: 'Prayer', 8th May 1921, evening (Religious Gatheka I, 10, which afterwards became no. 9), in Joyce Burnett's handwriting.	The name of God itself - without praise - just the name, is a bliss which fills the soul with all good.
The last two words 'all good' were crossed out by Gd. and replaced by other words.	- - - etc. - - - - - with ~~all good~~ <u>light and joy and happiness as nothing else can</u>.
b) The same sentence as under a), in an unidentified handwriting.	even to utter the name of God is a blessing that can fill the soul with light and joy and happiness as nothing else can do.
c) A typewritten version (Religious Gatheka 9).	<u>E</u>ven to utter the name of God is a <u>bliss which fills</u> the soul with light and joy and happiness as nothing else can. __
d) 1st ed. "The Bowl of Sâki" - 31st March. (Version b).	<u>E</u>ven to utter the name of God is a blessing that can fill the soul with light and joy and happiness as nothing else can do.

---

a) Part of two sentences in the address to mureeds: 'Prayer', 8th May 1921, evening (Religious Gatheka I, 10, which afterwards became no. 9) in Joyce Burnett's handwriting.	to find beauty in perfection. And when, to our utmost, we praise that, the soul is filled with bliss which nothing else can give.

Cont. a)

ORIGIN and elaborations:	DIFFERENT VERSIONS:
Cont. a) 'And' was crossed out by Gd. and 'that' replaced in her handwriting by 'the beauty of God'.	___ When, to our utmost, we praise the beauty of God, our soul - - etc.
b) The same sentence in an unidentified handwriting.	when ___ we praise the beauty of God, the soul is filled with bliss ____ ____ ____ ____ ____.
c) A typewritten copy (Religious Gatheka no. 9).	When to our utmost we praise the beauty of God_ our soul is filled with bliss.
d) 1st ed. "The Bowl of Sâki" - 1st April.	When ___ one praises the beauty of God, one's soul is filled with bliss.

No documents referring to the sayings under 2nd - 6th April have been found in the archives to date.	
1st ed. "The Bowl of Sâki" - 2nd April.	Sympathy is the root of religion, and so long as the spirit of sympathy is living in your heart you have the light of religion.
1st ed. "The Bowl of Sâki" - 3rd April.	Life is a misery for the man absorbed in himself.
1st ed. "The Bowl of Sâli" - 4th April.	To give sympathy is sovereignty, to desire it from others is captivity.
1st ed. "The Bowl of Sâki" - 5th April.	God speaks to the ears of every heart, but it is not every heart that hears Him.
1st ed. "The Bowl of Sâki" - 6th April.	As one can see when the eyes are open, so one can understand when the heart is open.

---

a) Copied by Ng. from (?).	It is being dead to self that is the recognition of God.
b) 1st ed. "The Bowl of Sâki" - 7th April.	It is being dead to self that is the recognition of God.

---

a) Notebooks 1921:	Saying. As the light of the sun helps plants to grow and flourish, so the spirit of God, reflected in the soul, helps man towards perfection.

b)

ORIGIN and elaborations:	DIFFERENT VERSIONS:
b) MS. Nq. Inayat Khan add. 'Bola' over it.	Saying Bola. - - - - - - - - - - - - helps the plant to grow __ _____ _ so the Divine Spirit __ ___ _ _____ __ ___ ___ _ helps the soul towards its perfection.
c) Copied by Kf.	_____ ____ - - - - - - - - - - - - - - - - - - .
d) Typewritten under 'Bolas II', mostly meant for publication in the "Gayan" (Gd.'s bookpreparation).	Bola. - - - - - - - - - - - - - - - - - - .
e) Copied by Mt. and classified by Inayat Khan as 'Sur', meant for publication in the "Gayan".	Sura. - - - - - - - - - - - - - - - - - - .
f) 1st ed. "The Bowl of Sâki" - 8th April.	As the light of the sun helps the plant to grow, so the Divine Spirit helps the soul towards its perfection.

No documents referring to the sayings under 9th-10th April have been found in the archives to date.	
1st ed. "The Bowl of Sâki" - 9th April.	Things are worth while when we seek them; only then do we know their value.
1st ed. "The Bowl of Sâki" - 10th April.	When a man looks at the ocean, he can only see the part of it which comes within his range of vision, so it is with the Truth.

---

a) From 'Nature's Religion' reported and revised by Dr. O. Gruner, in 'In an Eastern Rosegarden', p.20, 1st ed. 1920/21.	It does not matter in what way a person offers his respects and his reverence to the deity he worships. It only matters how sincere he is in his offering.
b) 1st ed. "The Bowl of Sâki" - 11th April.	It does not matter in what way a person offers his respect and his reverence to the deity he worships, it matters only how sincere he is in his offering.

---

a) From 'The Personality of God', reported and revised by Dr.O.Gruner, in 'In an Eastern Rosegarden', p.28, 1st ed. 1920/21	Really speaking, the ideal of God is a bridge connecting the limited life with the unlimited. Whoever travels on this bridge passes safely from the limited to the Unlimited Life.
b) 1st ed. "The Bowl of	___ ____ _ The ideal of God is a bridge

Cont. b)

ORIGIN and elaborations:	DIFFERENT VERSIONS:
Cont. b) Sâki" - 12th April.	connecting the limited life with the unlimited; whoever travels over this bridge passes safely from the limited to the unlimited life.
a) Copied by Al. ated 5th February 1925, together with other sayings, meant for publication in the "Vadan".	Bola. If you don't want to understand, you will not understand.
b) Gd.'s typewritten book-preparation of "Vadan".	Bola. - - - - - - - - - - - - - - .
c) 1st ed. "The Bowl of Sâki" - 13th April.	He who wants to understand will understand.

Cf. Sayings I: "Vadan" - Bola 55.

a) From a lecture 'The Effect of Prayer', (1918-20), revised by Dr. Gruner as published in 'In an Eastern Rosegarden', 1st ed. 1920/1921.	Man is the picture or reflection of his imagination. He is as large as he thinks himself, as great as he thinks himself, as small as he thinks himself.
b) A typewritten copy with sayings found with the Gayan documents, but mostly not pub. there	Man is the picture of the reflection of his image; he is as large __ __ ____ ____ _ __ ____ __ __ ____ _____ _ or as small as he thinks himself.
c) 1st ed. "The Bowl of Sâki" - 14th April.	Man is the picture of the reflection of his imagination; he is as large or as small as he thinks himself.

a) From the lecture 'Love, Human and Divine',(1916-20), reported and revised by Dr.O.Gruner as published in 'In an Eastern Rosegarden', 1920/21.	The great teachers of humanity become streams of love.
A typewritten copy with sayings, found with the Gayan documents.	- - - - - - - - - - - - - - .
b) Ms. Km. Changed in Gd.'s handwriting.	- - - - - - - - - - - - - - . The truly great souls __ _____ become streams of love.
c) 1st ed. "The Bowl of Sâki" - 15th April (See version a)	The great Teachers of humanity become streams of love.

Cf. Sayings I: "Gayan" - Bola 69.

a) A sentence in the lecture 'Love, Human and	"God is love", - three words which open up an un-ending realm for the

Cont. a)

ORIGIN and elaborations:	DIFFERENT VERSIONS:
Cont. a) Divine', (1916 - 1920), reported and revised by Dr.Gruner as published in the book 'In an Eastern Rose-garden', 1st ed. 1920/1921.	thinker who desires to probe the depths of the secret of love.
b) A typewritten copy with sayings, found with the Gayan documents.	- - - - - - - - - - - - - - - etc. - - - - - - the secret of life.
c) 1st ed. "The Bowl of Sâki" - 16th April.	"God is love"; _ three words which open up an un-ending realm for the thinker who desires to probe the depths of the secret of life.

---

a) A sentence in the lecture 'Silent Life', 6th December 1919, reported and revised by Dr.Gruner as published in the book 'In an Eastern Rosegarden', 1st ed. 1920/1921.	It is the surface of the sea that makes waves and roaring breakers; the depth is silent.
A typewritten copy with sayings, mostly meant for publication in the "Gayan".	- - - - - - - - - - - - - .
b) 1st ed. "The Bowl of Sâki" - 17th April.	It is the surface of the sea that makes waves and roaring breakers; the depth is silent.

---

a) A sentence in the lecture 'The Will, Human and Divine', (1917-1920), reported and revised by Dr.Gruner as published in the book 'In an Eastern Rose-garden', 1st ed. 1920/1921.	Our success or failure all depends upon the harmony or disharmony of our individual will with the divine will.
b) A typewritten copy with sayings, mostly meant for publication in the "Gayan".	Our success or failure ___ depends upon the harmony or inharmony of our individual will with the Divine Will.
c) 1st ed. "The Bowl of Sâki" - 18th April.	Our success or failure depends upon the harmony or disharmony of our individual will with the Divine Will.

---

a) A sentence in the lecture 'Mind, Human and Divine', 24th October	The wave realises "I am the sea," and by falling into the sea prostrates itself to its God!

Cont. a)

ORIGIN and elaborations:	DIFFERENT VERSIONS:
Cont. a) 1919, reported and revised by Dr.Gruner as published in the book 'In an Eastern Rosegarden', 1st ed. published 1920/1921.	
b) A typewritten copy with sayings, partly meant for publication in "The Bowl of Sâki", partly for the "Gayan".	The wave realises, _I am the sea,_ and by falling into the sea prostrates itself before its God.
c) Copied by Gr., probably for her bookpreparation of "The Bowl of Sâki".	The wave realizes_ "I am the sea_" and by falling into the sea, prostrates itself to its God.
d) 1st ed. "The Bowl of Sâki" - 19th April.	The wave realizes "I am the sea," and by falling into the sea_ prostrates itself to its God.

---

a) A sentence in the lecture 'Silent Life', December 1919, reported and revised by Dr.Gruner as published in the book 'In an Eastern Rosegarden', 1st ed. 1920/1921.	The secret of happiness is hidden - hidden under the cover of spiritual knowledge.
b) Copied by Gr., probably for her bookpreparation of "The Bowl of Sâki".	The secret of happiness is hidden _ ______ under the cover of the spiritual knowledge.
c) A typewritten copy with sayings, partly meant for publication in "The Bowl of Sâki", partly for the "Gayan".	- -of ___ spiritual knowledge.
d) 1st ed. "The Bowl of Sâki" - 20th April.	The secret of happiness is hidden under the cover of spiritual knowledge.

---

a) Two sentences in the lecture 'The Will, Human and Divine', (1917-1920), reported and revised by Dr.O.Gruner as published in the book 'In an Eastern Rosegarden', 1st ed. 1920/1921.	The soul is first born into the false self; it is blind. In the true self the soul opens its eyes.
b) 1st ed. "The Bowl of Sâki" - 21st April.	The soul is first born into the false self, it is blind; in the true self the soul opens its eyes.

ORIGIN and elaborations:	DIFFERENT VERSIONS:
a) A sentence in the lecture 'The Will, Human and Divine', (1917-1920), reported and revised by Dr.O.Gruner as published in the book 'In an Eastern Rose-garden', lst ed. 1920/1921.	To learn the lesson of how to live is more important than any psychic or occult learning.
b) Copied by Gr., probably for her bookpreparation of "The Bowl of Sâki".	- - - - - - - - - - - - - .
c) 1st ed. "The Bowl of Sâki" - 22nd April.	To learn the lesson of how to live is more important than any psychic or occult learning.

ORIGIN and elaborations:	DIFFERENT VERSIONS:
a) The last sentence in the lecture 'The Symbology of Religious Ideas - The Flute of Krishna' (Gatha Symbology - Nakshi Bandi III-6), 14th May 1921, in Miss R.Jones's handwriting.	Knowledge without love is lifeless.
b) 1st ed. "The Bowl of Sâki" - 23rd April.	Knowledge without love is lifeless.

ORIGIN and elaborations:	DIFFERENT VERSIONS:
a) Part of a sentence in the lecture 'Mind, Human and Divine', 24th October 1919, reported and revised by Dr.O.Gruner as published in the book 'In an Eastern Rose-garden', lst ed. 1920/1921.	whereas the sole aim of the mystic is to keep near to the idea of unity and find out "where do we unite?".
b) A typewritten copy with sayings, partly meant for publication in "The Bowl of Sâki", partly for the "Gayan".	The ____ aim of the mystic is to keep near to the idea of unity and find out _Where do we unite_ _.
c) 1st ed. "The Bowl of Sâki" - 24th April.	The aim of the Mystic is to keep near to the idea of unity, and find out where __ we unite.

ORIGIN and elaborations:	DIFFERENT VERSIONS:
a) Notebooks :	Saying. Sleep is comfortable, but awakening is interesting.
b) 1st ed. "The Bowl of Sâki" - 25th April.	Sleep is comfortable, but awakening is interesting.

ORIGIN and elaborations:	DIFFERENT VERSIONS:
a) Notebooks 1921:	Saying. Every moment has its special message.
b) 1st ed. "The Bowl of Sâki" - 26th April.	Every moment has its special message.

---

a) Notebooks 1921 :	Saying. To make God a reality is the real object of worship.
b) 1st ed. "The Bowl of Sâki" - 27th April.	To make God a reality is the real object of worship.

---

a) A sentence in the lecture 'The Mystery of Breath', (1917-1920), reported and revised by Dr.Gruner as published in the book 'In an Eastern Rosegarden', 1st ed. 1920/1921.	Every passion, every emotion has its effect upon the mind, and every change of mind, however slight, has its effect upon man's body.
b) 1st ed. "The Bowl of Sâki" - 28th April.	Every passion, every emotion has its effect upon the mind, and every change of mind, however slight, has its effect upon man's body.

---

a) Two sentences in the lecture 'Character and Fate' (1917-1920), reported and revised by Dr.Gruner as published in the book 'In an Eastern Rosegarden', 1st ed. 1920/1921.	When souls meet one another, what truth they can exchange! It is uttered in silence, yet always surely reaches its goal!
b) 1st ed. "The Bowl of Sâki" - 29th April.	When souls meet each other, what truth they can exchange? It is uttered in silence, yet always surely reaches its goal.

---

a) A sentence in the lecture 'Character and Fate', (1917-1920), reported and revised by Dr.Gruner as published in the book 'In an Eastern Rosegarden', 1st ed. 1920/1921.	All gains, whether material, spiritual, moral or mystical - are all gains in answer to one's own character.
b) 1st ed. "The Bowl of Sâki" - 30th April.	All gains, whether material, spiritual, moral, or mystical, are ___ _____ in answer to one's own character.

ORIGIN and elaborations:	DIFFERENT VERSIONS:
a) A sentence in the lecture 'Gain and Loss', (1917-1920), reported and revised by Dr.Gruner as published in the book 'In an Eastern Rosegarden', 1st ed. 1920/1921.	You can have all good things - wealth, friends, kindness, love to give and love to take - once you have learned not to be blinded by them, learned to escape from disappointment, learned to escape from repugnance at the idea that the things are not as you would want them to be.
b) 1st ed. "The Bowl of Sâki" - 1st May.	You can have all good things - wealth, friends, kindness, love to give, and love to receive - once you have learned not to be blinded by them; learned to escape from disappointment, ______ __ ______ and from repugnance at the idea that ___ things are not as you _____ want them to be.

---

a) Notebooks :	Saying. The truth often need not be veiled for it naturally veils itself from the eyes of the (ignorant. (unintimate.
b) 1st ed. "The Bowl of Sâki" - 2nd May.	The Truth _____ need not be veiled, for it _________ veils itself from the eyes of the ignorant.

---

a) Two sentences in the lecture 'Stilling the Mind', (1917-1920), reported and revised by Dr.Gruner as published in the book 'In an Eastern Rosegarden', 1st ed. 1920/1921.	This purpose is to learn mastery, not to be the vehicle for others to use. He who does not direct his own mind lacks mastery.
b) 1st ed. "The Bowl of Sâki" - 3rd May.	No man should allow his mind to be a vehicle for others to use; he who does not direct his own mind lacks mastery.

---

a) A sentence in the lecture 'Stilling the Mind', (1917-1920), reported and revised by Dr.Gruner as published in the book 'In an Eastern Rosegarden', 1st ed. 1920/1921.	The mind's rest is equally necessary as that of the rest of the body and yet we always keep it in action.
b) 1st ed. "The Bowl of Sâki" - 4th May.	___ Rest of mind is as necessary as ____ __ ___ rest of ___ body, and yet we always keep the former in action.

ORIGIN and elaborations:	DIFFERENT VERSIONS:
a) A sentence in the lecture 'Stilling the Mind', (1917-1920), reported and revised by Dr.Gruner as published in the book 'In an Eastern Rosegarden', 1st ed. 1920/1921.	Those who have given deep thoughts to the world are those only who have controlled the activity of their minds.
b) 1st ed. "The Bowl of Sâki" - 5th May.	Those who have given deep thoughts to the world are those ____ who have controlled the activity of their minds.
a) A sentence in the lecture 'The Attainment of Power', (1917-1920), reported and revised by Dr.Gruner as published in the book 'In an Eastern Rosegarden', 1st ed. 1920/1921.	Unity in realisation is far greater than unity in variety.
b) 1st ed. "The Bowl of Sâki" - 6th May.	Unity in realization is far greater than unity in variety.
a) Two sentences in the lecture 'Stilling the Mind', (1917-1920), reported and revised by Dr.Gruner as published in the book 'In an Eastern Rosegarden', 1st ed. 1920/1921.	Your mind brings the record of the gramophone, and if you use a harsh voice, the instrument produces a harsh note; if beautiful words and things it will sing beautiful words and things. It will produce the same record that you have experienced in life.
b) 1st ed. "The Bowl of Sâki" - 7th May.	The after-life is like a gramophone; man's mind brings the records; if they are hard the instrument produces harsh notes, if beautiful, then it will sing beautiful songs. It will produce the same records that man has experienced in this life.
a) A sentence in the lecture 'The Knowledge of Past, Present and Future', (1917-1920), reported and revised by Dr.Gruner as published in the book 'In an Eastern Rosegarden', 1st ed. 1920/1921.	If we depend on our eyes for sight, and our ears for hearing, and our mouth for speech, we are still "dead"!
b) 1st ed. "The Bowl of	He who depends upon his eyes for

Cont. b)

ORIGIN and elaborations:	DIFFERENT VERSIONS:
Cont. b) Sâki" - 8th May.	sight, ___ his ears for hearing, and his mouth for speech, he is still "dead".
a) Three sentences in the lecture 'Spirits and Spiritism', (1917-1920), reported and revised by Dr.Gruner as published in the book 'In an Eastern Rosegarden', 1st ed. 1920/1921.	We cover our spirit under our body. We cover our light under a bushel. We never allow the spirit to become conscious of itself.
b) 1st ed. "The Bowl of Sâki" - 9th May.	We cover our spirit under our body, __ _____ our light under a bushel; we never allow the spirit to become conscious of itself.
a) A sentence in the lecture 'Spirits and Spiritism', (1917-1920), reported and revised by Dr.Gruner as published in the book 'In an Eastern Rosegarden', 1st ed. 1920/1921.	When we devote ourselves to the thought of Him, all illumination and revelation is ours!
b) 1st ed. "The Bowl of Sâki" - 10th May.	When we devote ourselves to the thought of God, all illumination and revelation is ours.
a) A sentence in the lecture 'Spirits and Spiritism', (1917-1920), reported and revised by Dr.Gruner as published in the book 'In an Eastern Rosegarden', 1st ed. 1920/1921.	God-communication is the best communication that true spiritualism can teach us!
b) 1st ed. "The Bowl of Sâki" - 11th May.	God-communication is the best communication that true spiritualism can teach us.
a) A sentence in the lecture 'Spirits and Spiritism', (1917-1920), reported and revised by Dr.Gruner as published in the book 'In an Eastern Rosegarden', 1st ed. 1920/1921.	The mystic will look for what Omar Khayyam calls Wine, the wine of the Christ, after drinking which no-one will ever thirst.

b)

ORIGIN and elaborations:	DIFFERENT VERSIONS:
b) 1st ed. "The Bowl of Sâki" - 12th May.	The mystic desires what Omar Khayyam calls wine; the wine of the Christ, after drinking which, no one will ever thirst.

---

a) A sentence in the lecture 'The Desire of Nations', (1917-1920), reported and revised by Dr.Gruner as published in the book 'In an Eastern Rosegarden', 1st ed. 1920/1921.	Our limited self is as a wall separating us from the self of God.
b) 1st ed. "The Bowl of Sâki" - 13th May.	Our limited self is __ a wall separating us from the Self of God.

---

a) A sentence in the lecture 'The Desire of Nations', (1917-1920), reported and revised by Dr.Gruner as published in the book 'In an Eastern Rosegarden', 1st ed. 1920/1921.	The Wisdom and Justice of God are within us, and yet they are far away under the covering of the veil of the limited self.
b) 1st ed. "The Bowl of Sâki" - 14th May.	The wisdom and justice of God are within us, and yet they are far away, hidden by the veil of the limited self.

---

a) A sentence in the lecture 'Moral Culture: The Law of Renunciation, the Relativity of Gain', March, 1920, Old London Course, Series III, nr. 6 (later published in the book 'Moral Culture', Deventer, Netherlands, 1937).	The one who is looking for a gain, is smaller than his gain, the one who has renounced a thing has risen above it.
b) 1st ed. "The Bowl of Sâki" - 15th May.	__ He who is looking for a reward, is smaller than his reward; ___ he who has renounced a thing has risen above it.

ORIGIN and elaborations:	DIFFERENT VERSIONS:
a) A sentence in the lecture 'Moral Culture: The Law of Renunciation, the Relativity of Gain', March, 1920, Old London Course, Series III, nr. 6 (later published in the book 'Moral Culture', Deventer, Netherlands, 1937).	The poverty of one who has renounced is the real riches compared with the riches of the one who holds them fast.
b) 1st ed. "The Bowl of Sâki" - 16th May.	The poverty of one who has renounced is ___ real riches compared with the riches of ___ one who holds them fast.

---

a) A sentence in the lecture 'Moral Culture: The Law of Beneficence, Our Dealings with God', July, 1919, in the handwriting of Nuria Best.	Love for God is ~~for~~ the expansion of heart, and all actions that come from the lover of God are virtues, they cannot be otherwise.
b) A stencilled copy of an edited version of a), Old London Course, Series II, nr. 10 (later published in the book 'Moral Culture', Deventer, Netherlands, 1937).	Love for God is ___ the expansion of the heart, and all - - - - - - - - - -.
c) 1st ed. "The Bowl of Sâki" - 17th May.	Love for God is the expansion of the heart, and all actions that come from the lover of God are virtues; they cannot be otherwise.

ORIGIN and elaborations:	DIFFERENT VERSIONS:
a) A sentence in the lecture 'Moral Culture: The Law of Beneficence, Our Dealings with God', July, 1919, in the handwriting of Nuria Best.	God is the ideal that raises mankind to the utmost reach of perfection.
b) A stencilled copy of an edited version of a), Old London Course, Series II, nr. 10 (later published in the book 'Moral Culture', Deventer, Netherlands, 1937).	- .
c) 1 ed. "The Bowl of Saki" - 18th May	God is the ideal that raises mankind to the utmost height of perfection.

---

a) A sentence in the lecture 'Moral Culture: The Law of Beneficence, Our Dealings with Acquaintances', February 1919, Old London Course, Series II, nr. 5 (later published in the book 'Moral Culture', Deventer, Netherlands, 1937).	He is wise who treats an acquaintance as a friend, and he is foolish who treats a friend as an acquaintance, and he is impossible who treats friends and acquaintances as strangers, you cannot help him.
b) 1 ed. "The Bowl of Saki" - 19th May	He is wise who treats an acquaintance as a friend, and he is foolish who treats a friend as an acquaintance, and he is impossible who treats friends and acquaintances as strangers; you cannot help him.

ORIGIN and elaborations:	DIFFERENT VERSIONS:
Cont.)	and he is impossible who treats friends and acquaintances as strangers; you cannot help him.
a) Part of a sentence in the lecture 'The Desire of Nations', (1917-1920), reported and revised by Dr.Gruner as published in the book 'In an Eastern Rosegarden', 1st ed. 1920/1921.	but it is the insight into life which is the real religion and which alone can help man to understand life!
b) 1st ed. "The Bowl of Sâki" - 20th May.	Insight into life ___ is the real religion, ___ which alone can help men to understand life.
a) Two sentences in the lecture 'Democracy', 26th November 1919, reported and revised by Dr.Gruner as published in the book 'In an Eastern Rosegarden', 1st ed. 1920/1921.	The realisation that the whole life must be give and take, is the realisation of the spiritual truth and fact of true democracy. Not till this spirit is formed in the individual himself can the whole world be elevated to the higher grade.
b) 1st ed. "The Bowl of Sâki" - 21st May.	The realization that the whole life must be "give and take" is the realization of the spiritual truth and fact of true democracy; not until this spirit is formed in the individual ___ can the whole world be elevated to the higher grade.
a) Three sentences in the lecture 'The Ideal Life', (1917-1920), reported and revised by Dr.Gruner as published in the book 'In an Eastern Rosegarden', 1st ed. 1920/1921.	Therefore the ideal life is in following one's own ideal. It is not in checking other people's ideals. Leave everyone to follow his own ideal.
b) 1st ed. "The Bowl of Sâki" - 22nd May.	The perfect life is ___ following one's own ideal, ___ not in checking those of others; leave everyone to follow his own ideal.
a) Two sentences in the lecture 'The Journey to the Goal', (1917-1920), reported and revised by Dr.Gruner as published	Every person's desire is according to his evolution. That which he is ready for is the desirable 1) for him.

Cont. a)

ORIGIN and elaborations:	DIFFERENT VERSIONS:
Cont. a) in the book 'In an Eastern Rosegarden', 1st ed. 1920/1921.	
b) 1st ed. "The Bowl of Sâki" - 23rd May.	Every man's desire is according to his evolution, that which he is ready for, is the desirable thing for him.

Note 1): one word omitted in the printed text.

ORIGIN and elaborations:	DIFFERENT VERSIONS:
a) Two sentences in the lecture 'The Ideal Life', (1917-1920), reported and revised by Dr.Gruner as published in the book 'In an Eastern Rosegarden', 1st ed. 1920/1921.	Discussion is for those who say "What I say is right, and what you say is wrong." A sage never says such a thing; hence there is no discussion!
b) 1st ed. "The Bowl of Sâki" - 24th May.	Discussion is for those who say, "What I say is right, and what you say is wrong." A sage never says such a thing, hence there is no discussion.

ORIGIN and elaborations:	DIFFERENT VERSIONS:
a) A sentence in the lecture 'The Journey to the Goal', (1917-1920), reported and revised by Dr.Gruner as published in the book 'In an Eastern Rosegarden', 1st ed. 1920/1921.	Forgiveness does not come by learning, it comes by understanding that a person should be allowed to travel along that path which is suited to his temperament.
b) 1st ed. "The Bowl of Sâki" - 25th May.	Tolerance does not come by learning, but __ _____ by insight; by understanding that each one should be allowed to travel along the path which is suited to his temperament.

ORIGIN and elaborations:	DIFFERENT VERSIONS:
a) A sentence in the lecture 'The Journey to the Goal', (1917-1920), reported and revised by Dr.Gruner as published in the book 'In an Eastern Rosegarden', 1st ed. 1920/1921.	As long as a person has the longing to attain to any particular motive he cannot go further.
b) 1st ed. "The Bowl of Sâki" - 26th May.	So long as a man has a longing to obtain any particular object, he cannot go further than that object.

ORIGIN and elaborations:	DIFFERENT VERSIONS:
a) Two sentences in the lecture 'The Journey to the Goal', (1917-1920), reported and revised by Dr.Gruner as published in the book 'In an Eastern Rosegarden', 1st ed. 1920/1921.	Everybody's path is for himself. Let everyone accomplish his own desires so as to be able to rise above them to the Eternal Goal.
b) 1st ed. "The Bowl of Sâki" - 27th May.	Every man's path is for himself, let him accomplish his own desires that he may thus be able to rise above them to the eternal goal.
a) A sentence in the lecture 'The Journey to the Goal', (1917-1920), reported and revised by Dr.Gruner as published in the book 'In an Eastern Rosegarden', 1st ed. 1920/1921.	The control of the self means the control of everything.
b) 1st ed. "The Bowl of Sâki" - 28th May.	The control of ___ self means the control of everything.
a) Two sentences in the lecture 'The Journey to the Goal', (1917-1920), reported and revised by Dr.Gruner as published in the book 'In an Eastern Rosegarden', 1st ed. 1920/1921.	"God is love." When love is awakened in the heart, God is awakened there.
b) 1st ed. "The Bowl of Sâki" - 29th May.	"God is love"; when love is awakened in the heart_ God is awakened there.
a) Part of two sentences in the lecture 'The Spiritual Hierarchy', (1917-1920), reported and revised by Dr.Gruner as published in the book 'In an Eastern Rosegarden', 1st ed. 1920/1921.	all the inharmony of the world is usually caused by religious differences, and the differences are caused by man's failing to understand that religion is one, truth is one, God is one. - How can there be two religions?
b) 1st ed. "The Bowl of Sâki" - 30th May.	All the disharmony of the world ___ ___ caused by religious differences_ ___ ___ ___ ___ ___ ___ is the result of man's failure to understand that religion is One, truth is One, God is One;

Cont. b)

ORIGIN and elaborations:	DIFFERENT VERSIONS:
Cont. b)	_ how can there be two religions.

---

a) From the lecture 'Moral Culture: The Law of Reciprocity, Our Dealings with Our Friends', 21 Nov. 1917, in the hwr. of Nuria Best.	The use of friendship for a selfish motive is like mixing bitter poison with the sweet rose syrup...
b) Stencilled, edited version of a), Old London Course I.2 (later pub. in bk. 'Moral Culture', 1937).	- - - - - - - - - - - -
c) 1st ed. "The Bowl of Sâki" - 31st May.	The use of friendship for a selfish motive is like mixing bitter poison with the sweet rose syrup.

---

a) Notebooks 1921 :	Saying or Philosophy. Your bodily desire takes you away from your heart's wish and the wish of your heart separates you from your soul's longing, so by every lower desire man is pulled further down from the higher goal of his soul's longing.
b) Copied by Gd. from (?). The first part of a).	Man's bodily appetites take him away from his heart's desire. His heart's desires keep him away from the abode of his soul.
c) 1st ed. "The Bowl of Sâki" - 1st June.	Man's bodily appetites take him away from his heart's desire; his heart's desires keep him away from the abode of his soul.

No documents referring to the sayings under 2nd - 3rd June have been found in the archives to date.

1st ed. "The Bowl of Sâki" - 2nd June.	Words are but the shadows of thoughts and feelings.

Cf. "The Bowl of Saki" - 14th November.

1st ed. "The Bowl of Sâki" - 3rd June.	The more elevated the soul, the broader is the outlook.

Note: See also "The Bowl of Sâki" - 9th November.

---

a) From the lecture 'Moral Culture: The Law of Reciprocity, Our Dealings	The secret of a friend should be kept as one's own secret; the fault of a friend should be hidden as one's own

Cont. a)

<u>ORIGIN</u> and elaborations:	<u>DIFFERENT</u> <u>VERSIONS</u>:
Cont. a) with Our Friends', 21 Nov. 1917, in the hwr. of Nuria Best.	fault.
b) Stencilled, edited version of a), Old London Course I.2 (later pub. in bk. 'Moral Culture', 1937).	The secret of <u>the</u> friend should be kept as one's own secret<u>.</u> The fault of <u>the</u> friend <u>one</u> should <u>hide</u> as one's own fault.
b) 1st ed. "The Bowl of Sâki" - 4th June.	The secret of <u>a</u> friend should be kept as one's own secret<u>;</u> <u>t</u>he fault of <u>a</u> friend one should hide as one's own fault.

---

a) From the lecture 'Moral Culture: The Law of Reciprocity, Our Dealings with Our Friends', 21st November, 1917, in the hwr. of Nuria Best.	Forbearance, patience tolerance are the only conditions which keep two individual hearts united.
b) Stencilled, edited version of a), Old London Course I.2 (later pub. in bk. 'Moral Culture', 1937).	Forbearance, patience<u>,</u> <u>and</u> tolerance are the only conditions which keep two individual hearts united.
c) 1st ed. "The Bowl of Sâki" - 5th June.	Forbearance, patience_ and tolerance are the only conditions which keep two individual hearts united.

---

a) A sentence in the lecture 'Mental Creation', 18th May 1919, reported and revised by Dr. O. Gruner as published in the book 'In an Eastern Rosegarden', 1st ed. 1920/1921.	We blame others for our sorrows and misfortunes, not perceiving that we ourselves are the creators of our world.
b) 1st ed. "The Bowl of Sâki" - 6th June.	We blame others for our sorrows and misfortunes, not perceiving that we ourselves are the creators of our world.

---

a) From the lecture 'Moral Culture: The Law of Beneficence, Our Dealings with Servants', Dec., 1918, in the hwr. of Nuria Best.	Nobody appears inferior to us when our heart is kindled with kindness, and our eyes are opened to the vision of God.
b) Stencilled, edited ver-	Nobody appears inferior to us when our

Cont. b)

ORIGIN and elaborations:	DIFFERENT VERSIONS:
Cont. b) sion of a), Old London Course II.3 (later published in the book "Moral Culture", 1937).	heart is kindled with kindness, and our eyes are open__ to the vision of God.
c) 1st ed. "The Bowl of Sâki" - 7th June.	Nobody appears inferior to us when our heart is kindled with kindness, and our eyes are open to the vision of God.

---

a) A sentence in the lecture 'Moral Culture: the Law of Beneficence, Our Dealings with Our Neighbours', March, 1919, in the hwr. of Nuria Best.	Selfishness keeps man blind through life...
b) Stencilled, edited version of a), Old London Course, Series II. nr. 6 (later published in the book 'Moral Culture', Deventer, Netherlands, 1937).	- - - - - - - - - - - - - .
c) 1st ed. "The Bowl of Sâki" - 8th June.	Selfishness keeps man blind through life.

---

a) A sentence in the lecture 'Moral Culture: The Law of Renunciation, The Final Victory', Old London Course, Series III, nr. 10, July 1920, (later published in the book 'Moral Culture', Deventer, Netherlands, 1937.	The final victory in the battle of life for every soul is when he has abandoned, which means when he has risen above what once he valued most.
b) 1st ed. "The Bowl of Sâki" - 9th June.	The final victory in the battle of life for every soul, is ___ __ __ _______ _ ___ ____ when he has risen above the things which once he most valued.

No documents referring to the sayings under 10th - 11th June have been found in the archives to date.

1st ed. "The Bowl of Sâki" - 10th June.	When power leads and wisdom follows, the face of wisdom is veiled and she stumbles; but when wisdom leads and power follows, they arrive Cont.)

ORIGIN and elaborations:	DIFFERENT VERSIONS:
Cont.)	safely at their destination.
1st ed. "The Bowl of Sâki" - 11th June.	Man's whole conduct in life depends upon what he holds in his thought.

---

a) A sentence in the lecture 'Moral Culture: The Law of Beneficence, Our Dealings with Our Neighbours', March, 1919, in the hwr. of Nuria Best.	In this struggle of life - if one can be considerate enough to keep his eyes open to all around him and those whom the circumstances have placed about him in life, he would see in what way he could be of help to them. Then he becomes rich, and he inherits the riches of God...
b) Stencilled, edited version of a), Old London Course, Series II, nr. 6 (later published in the book 'Moral Culture', Deventer, Netherlands, 1937.	In this struggle of life, if one can be considerate enough to keep his eyes open to all around him, ___ _____ whom ___ circumstances have placed about him in life, and would see in what way he could be of help to them. ___ He becomes rich, ___ he inherits the kingdom of God.
c) 1st ed. "The Bowl of Sâki" - 12th June.	__ ____ ________ __ ____ _ He who can be detached enough to keep his eyes open to all ______ ___ _ those whom circumstances have placed about him, __ ____ _ and _____ see in what way he can be of help to them, he it is who becomes rich; he inherits the Kingdom of God.

---

a) A sentence in the lecture 'The Desire of Nations', (1917-20) reported and revised by Dr. Gruner, as published in the book 'In an Eastern Rosegarden', 1920/21.	Real justice cannot be perceived until the veil of selfishness has been removed from the eyes.
b) 1st ed. "The Bowl of Sâki" - 13th June.	True Justice cannot be perceived until the veil of selfishness has been removed from the eyes.

---

a) A sentence in the lecture 'Mental Creation', 18th May 1919, reported and revised by Dr. O. Gruner as published in the book 'In an Eastern Rosegarden', 1920/21.	Thoughts have prepared for us that happiness or unhappiness which we experience.
b) 1st ed. "The Bowl of Sâki" - 14th June.	Our thoughts have prepared for us the happiness or unhappiness ____ we experience.

Note: See also "The Bowl of Sâki" - 11th November.

Cont. b)

ORIGIN and elaborations:	DIFFERENT VERSIONS:
Cont. b)	Cf. "The Bowl of Sâki" - 23rd August.
No documents referring to the sayings under 15th - 17th June have been found in the archives to date.	
1st ed. "The Bowl of Sâki" - 15th June.	Love is the best means of making the heart capable of reflecting the soul power; and love in the sense of pain rather than of pleasure. Every blow opens a door wherefrom the soul-power comes forth.
1st ed. "The Bowl of Sâki" - 16th June.	Every experience on the physical, astral or mental plane is just a dream before the soul.
1st ed. "The Bowl of Sâki" - 17th June.	The fire of devotion purifies the heart of the devotee, and leads unto spiritual freedom.
	Note: = "The Bowl of Sâki" - 4th February.
a) A sentence in the book 'Love, Human and Divine', by Sherifa Lucy Goodenough, Southampton, 1919, p. 15.	*When love's fire produces its flame it illuminates like a torch the devotee's path in life, and all darkness vanishes.*
b) 1st ed. "The Bowl of Sâki" - 18th June.	*When love's fire produces its flame, it illuminates like a torch the devotee's path in life, and all darkness vanishes.*
a) A sentence in the lecture 'On Vocations', 1920, copied from Nuria Best's hwr., but only available in type. Partly published in the magazine 'Sufi' of October 1920.	It is mistrust that misleads, sincerity leads straight to the goal.
b) 1st ed. "The Bowl of of Sâki" - 19th June.	It is mistrust that misleads; sincerity always leads straight to the goal.
a) A sentence in the book 'Love, Human and Divine', by Sherifa Lucy Goodenough, Southampton, 1919, p. 36.	*Love lies in service. Only that which is done, not for fame or name, nor for the appreciation or thanks of those for whom it is done, is love's service.*

b)

ORIGIN and elaborations:	DIFFERENT VERSIONS:
b) 1st ed. "The Bowl of Sâki" - 20th June.	*Love lies in service; only that which is done, not for fame or name, nor for the appreciation or thanks of those for whom it is done, is love's service.*
a) A sentence in the book 'Love, Human and Divine', by Sherifa Lucy Goodenough, Southampton, 1919, p. 41-2.	*The soul is all light, but all darkness is caused by the death of the heart. Pain makes it alive.*
b) 1st ed. "The Bowl of Sâki" - 21st June.	*The soul is all light, ___ ___ darkness is caused by the deadness of the heart, pain makes it alive.*
No documents referring to the sayings under 22nd June have been found in the archives to date.	
1st ed. "The Bowl of Sâki" - 22nd June.	The quality of forgiveness that burns up all things except beauty, is the quality of love.
a) Two sentences in the lecture 'On Spheres', 1920, copied from Nuria Best's hwr., but only available in type. Partly published in the magazine 'Sufi' of October 1920.	Each individual composes the music of his own life - if he injures another, he leaves his musical tract. When his sphere is disturbed, he is disturbed himself, and there is a discord in the melody of his life.
b) 1st ed. "The Bowl of Sâki" - 23rd June.	Each individual composes the music of his own life; if he injures another _ he breaks the harmony, ___ ___ ___ __ ___ _ __ __ ___ ___ _ and there is _ discord in the melody of his life.
a) A sentence in the lecture 'On Vocations', 1920, copied from Nuria Best's hwr., but only available in type. Partly published in the magazine 'Sufi' of October 1920.	He who with sincerity seeks his real purpose in life is himself sought by that purpose.
b) 1st ed. "The Bowl of Sâki" - 24th June.	He who with sincerity seeks his real purpose in life, is himself sought by that purpose.
a) Sentences in the lecture 'Constancy', 1920, in Nuria Best's hand-	A mystic calls life motion. It is constant motion in every aspect (.. ...etc.).(....) Our whole life is in

Cont. a)

ORIGIN and elaborations:	DIFFERENT VERSIONS:
Cont. a) writing. Between brackets is indicated by compiler that only parts of the sentences in this version have been given.	constant change (.....etc.) We live in the life of change, but we seek that which is constant. It is this search after constancy which has brought man back to God. If it was not for this desire man would not have discovered the God Ideal.
b) In the old Magazine 'Sufi' of October 1920 some parts of the lecture 'Constancy' were published; among these the following two sentences:	Through motion and change life becomes intelligible. We live a life of change; but it is constancy that we seek, and it is this innate desire that leads man to God.
c) 1st ed. "The Bowl of Sâki" - 25th June.	Through motion and change, life becomes intelligible; we live a life of change, but it is constancy ____ we seek; ___ it is this innate desire of the soul that leads man to God.

---

a) Two sentences in the lecture 'On Vocations', 1920, known to have been copied from Nuria Best's handwriting but only available in type. This lecture was partly published in the old Magazine 'Sufi' of October 1920.	Every being has a definite vocation, and his vocation is the light which illuminates his life. The man who disregards his vocation is a lamp unlit.
b) 1st ed. "The Bowl of Sâki" - 26th June.	Every being has a definite vocation, and his vocation is the light that illumines his life. The man who disregards his vocation is as a lamp unlit.

---

a) Two sentences in the lecture 'Constancy', 1920, in Nuria Best's handwriting.	The heart is like a being which is asleep and receiving a sharp blow it awakens. Also the heart is like a stone and the fire hidden within it can only be brought to life when it is struck by a hard material.
b) In the old Magazine 'Sufi' of October 1920 some parts of the lecture 'Constancy' were published; among these the following two sentences:	The heart is a being that sleeps sound until it is awakened to life by a blow. The heart is a rock and the hidden fire within it flashes out when it is struck by another rock.
c) 1st ed. "The Bowl of Sâki" - 27th June.	The heart __ __ _____ ____ sleeps _____ until it is awakened to life by a blow. It is as a rock, and the

Cont. c)

ORIGIN and elaborations:	DIFFERENT VERSIONS:
Cont. c)	hidden fire ___ ___ flashes out when __ __ struck by another rock.

---

a) Two sentences in the lecture 'Constancy', 1920, in Nuria Best's handwriting.	The method of attainment is to endeavour always to make others happy. Real happiness is entering the gate.
b) In the old Magazine 'Sufi' of October 1920 some parts of the lecture 'Constancy' were published; among these the following two sentences:	The awakened heart says, "I must give, I must not demand. It is I who must love another, and must make another happy." Thus it enters a gate that leads to a constant happiness.
c) 1st ed. "The Bowl of Sâki" - 28th June.	The awakened heart says, "I must give, I must not demand." __ __ _ ___ ___ ___ ______ ___ ___ ___ ______ ____ __ Thus it enters a gate that leads to a constant happiness.

---

a) Three sentences in the lecture 'On Spheres', 1920, known to have been copied from Nuria Best's handwriting but only available in type. This lecture was partly published in the old Magazine 'Sufi' of October 1920.	The worlds are held together by the heat of the sun. Each of us are atoms held in position by that eternal sun we call God. Within us is that same central power - we call it the light of God, or the love of God - and by it we too hold up the human beings within our sphere; or lacking it, we let them fall.
b) 1st ed. "The Bowl of Sâki" - 29th June.	The worlds are held together by the heat of the sun; each of us are atoms held in position by that Eternal Sun we call God; within us is the same central power we call __ the light __ ___, or the love of God; ___ by it we __ hold __ together the human beings within our sphere, or, lacking it, we let them fall.

---

a) Some sentences in the lecture 'Constancy', 1920, in Nuria Best's handwriting. It is uncertain if these sentences are the origin of b). A passage in the reporting may be missing.	Therefore the attitude of man seeking these things outwardly must change and become inward. Somewhere we must find them, because they are innate qualities of life and are the only salvation and goal of life. By self-realisation and self-control and self-observation we realise this.
b) In the old Magazine 'Sufi' of October 1920	As a man dives within, he finds that his real self is not subject to motion.

Cont. b)

ORIGIN and elaborations:	DIFFERENT VERSIONS:
Cont. b) some parts of the lecture 'Constancy' were published; among these the following sentence:	
c) 1st ed. "The Bowl of Sâki" - 30th June.	When a man dives within, he finds that his real self is above the perpetual motion of the universe.

---

a) Part of a sentence in the lecture 'Belief', 1920, as published in the Magazine 'Sufi' of October 1920.	man's pride and satisfaction in what he knows limits the scope of his vision.
b) Copied by Ng.	Man's - - - - - - - - - - - - - - etc.
c) 1st ed. "The Bowl of Sâki" - 1st July.	Man's pride and satisfaction in what he knows limits the scope of his vision.

---

a) A sentence in the lecture 'Sufism', 1920, of which the first part became a Gatheka (Old Series I no.4), as published in the Magazine 'Sufi' of October 1920.	He must first create peace in himself, if he desires to see peace in the world; for lacking the peace within, no effort of his can bring any result.
b) 1st ed. "The Bowl of Sâki" - 2nd July.	Man must first create peace in himself_ if he desires to see peace in the world, for lacking ___ peace within, no effort of his can bring any result.

---

a) Two sentences in the lecture 'Sufism', 1920, of which the first part became a Gatheka (Old Series I no.4), as published in the Magazine 'Sufi', October 1920.	Now it is the knowledge of the self, of the ego, that gives knowledge of humanity; and in the understanding of the human being lies that understanding of nature, which reveals the law of the whole creation. The knowledge of the self is therefore the essential.
b) 1st ed. "The Bowl of Sâki" - 3rd July.	The knowledge of ___ self is ________ the essential knowledge, it gives knowledge of humanity; ___ in the understanding of the human being lies that understanding of nature_ which reveals the law of ___ _____ creation.

---

a) A verse in 'The Man and the Wise Man', 1918, in Mt.'s handwriting and	While man blames another for causing him harm, The wise man first takes himself

Cont. a)

ORIGIN and elaborations:	DIFFERENT VERSIONS:
Cont. a) published in the Magazine 'Sufi' of January 1919.	to task.
b) Published in the book 'La Voie de la Révélation', Geneva, Switzerland, 1921. 1)	Tandis que l'homme blâme le prochain du mal qu'il lui cause, Le sage s'en prend d'abord à lui-même.
c) 1st ed. "The Bowl of Sâki" - 4th July.	While Man blames another for causing him harm, the Wise Man first takes himself to task. 2)

Note 1): The same book in English was published in 1922 as 'The Way of Illumination'.
2): The words 'Man' and 'Wise Man' were printed in italics.

---

a) A sentence in the lecture 'Sufism', 1920, of which the first part became a Gatheka (Old Series I no.4), as published in the Magazine 'Sufi' of October 1920.	Whatever their faith, the wise have always been able to meet each other beyond those boundaries of external forms and conventions, which are natural and necessary to human life, but which none the less separate humanity.
b) 1st ed. "The Bowl of Sâki" - 5th July.	Whatever their faith, the wise have always been able to meet each other beyond those boundaries of external forms and conventions which are natural and necessary to human life, but which none the less separate humanity.

---

a) Notebooks 1921 :	Saying. It is the Message that proves the Messenger, not the claim.
b) Copied by Gd. from (?) in February 1921.	Saying. - - - - - - message that must prove the messenger, - - - - - - - .
c) Copied by Km.	Saying. - messenger, and not - - -.
d) Copied by Ek. and classified by Inayat Khan as 'Bol', originally meant for publication in the "Gayan".	Bola. - - - - - - - - - - - - - - .
e) 1st ed. "The Bowl of Sâki" - 6th July. (Version a)).	It is the message 3) proves the messenger, not the claim.

Note 3): 'That' probably omitted by mistake.

ORIGIN and elaborations:	DIFFERENT VERSIONS:
a) Two sentences in the lecture 'Sufism', 1920, of which the first part became a Gatheka (Old Series I no.4), as published in the Magazine 'Sufi' of October 1920.	Every soul has a definite task, and the fulfilment of this individual purpose can alone lead him aright. Illumination comes to him through the medium of his own talent.
b) 1st ed. "The Bowl of Sâki" - 7th July.	Every soul has a definite task, and the fulfilment of each individual purpose can alone lead man aright; illumination comes to him through the medium of his own talent.

---

a) A verse in 'The Man and the Wise Man', 1918, in Mt.'s handwriting and published in the Magazine 'Sufi' of January 1919.	While man judges another from his own moral standard, The wise man looks also at the point of view of another.
b) Published in the book 'La Voie de la Révélation, Geneva, Switzerland, 1921. 1)	Tandis que l'homme juge autrui d'après son propre point de vue _____, Le sage regarde aussi du point de vue d'autrui.
c) 1st ed. "The Bowl of Sâki" - 8th July.	While Man judges another from his own moral standpoint, the Wise Man looks also at the point of view of another. 2)

Notes 1) and 2): see notes with the saying under "The Bowl of Sâki" - 4th July.

---

a) A verse in 'The Man and the Wise Man', 1918, in Mt.'s handwriting and published in the Magazine 'Sufi' of January 1919.	While man rejoices over his rise and sorrows over his fall, The wise man takes both as the natural consequences of life.
b) Published in the book 'La Voie de la Révélation', Geneva, Switzerland, 1921. 3)	Tandis que l'homme se réjouit de son élévation et s'attriste de son abaissement_ Le sage les accepte toutes deux comme la conséquence naturelle de la vie.
c) 1st ed. "The Bowl of Sâki" - 9th July.	While Man rejoices over his rise and sorrows over his fall, the Wise Man takes both as the natural consequences of life. 4)

Notes 3) and 4): see notes with the saying under "The Bowl of Sâki" - 4th July.

ORIGIN and elaborations:	DIFFERENT VERSIONS:
a) A sentence in the lecture 'Communion with God', 1919, as found in Kemila van Spengler's handwriting (probably copied from an early MS.), and as published in the Magazine 'Sufi' of June 1919.	It is the lover of God whose heart is filled with devotion who can commune with God, not the one who makes an effort with his intellect in analysing God.
b) 1st ed. "The Bowl of Sâki" - 10th July.	It is the lover of God whose heart is filled with devotion, who can commune with God; not he who makes an effort with his intellect to analyse God.

---

a) A sentence in the lecture 'Inayat Khan's Visit to Scotland', 1918/1919, as published in the Magazine 'Sufi', June 1919.	I do not bemoan the past, and I do not worry about the future, but try to make the best of to-day.
b) 1st ed. "The Bowl of Sâki" - 11th July.	Do not bemoan the past; do not worry about the future, but try to make the best of to-day.

---

a) Part of a sentence in the lecture 'On Spheres', 1920, known to have been copied from Nuria Best's handwriting but only available in type. This lecture was partly published in the old Magazine 'Sufi' of October 1920.	If he can quicken the feeling of another to joy, or to gratitude - by that much he adds to his own life;
b) 1st ed. "The Bowl of Sâki" - 12th July.	He who can quicken the feeling of another to joy or to gratitude, by that much he adds to his own life.

---

a) A sentence in a lecture 'The Message', 1921, found with Gd.'s bookpreparation of 'The Unity of Religious Ideals'.	Praise cannot exist without blame, it has no existence without its opposite.
b) 1st ed. "The Bowl of Sâki" - 13th July.	Praise cannot exist without blame, it has no existence without its opposite.

Cf. Sayings I: "Gayan" - Bola 80.

ORIGIN and elaborations:	DIFFERENT VERSIONS:
a) A sentence in the chapter 'The Purpose of Life', from the book 'Pearls from the Ocean Unseen', by Mary Zohra Williams, p.11, London, 1919.	*Riches and power may vanish because they are outside of us, but only that which is within can we call our own.*
b) 1st ed. "The Bowl of Sâki" - 14th July.	*Riches and power may vanish because they are outside ourselves; __ only that which is within can we call our own.*

---

a) A sentence in the chapter 'The Purpose of Life', from the book 'Pearls from the Ocean Unseen', by Mary Zohra Williams, p.11, London, 1919.	*When the world is evolving from imperfection towards perfection, it needs all love and sympathy; great tenderness, and watchfulness is required of each one of us.*
b) 1st ed. "The Bowl of Sâki" - 15th July.	*___ The world is evolving from imperfection towards perfection, it needs all love and sympathy; great tenderness_ and watchfulness is required from each one of us.*

---

a) A sentence in the chapter 'The Purpose of Life', from the book 'Pearls from the Ocean Unseen', by Mary Zohra Williams, p.11, London, 1919.	*The heart of every man, both good and bad, is the abode of God, and care should be taken never to wound anybody by word or act.*
b) 1st ed. "The Bowl of Sâki" - 16th July.	*The heart of every man, both good and bad, is the abode of God, and care should be taken never to wound anyone by word or act.*

Note: Cf. Part Two, no. 415 (p.169).

---

a) A sentence in the chapter 'Blessed are the Poor in Spirit', from the book 'Pearls from the Ocean Unseen', by Mary Zohra Williams, p.13, London, 1919.	*We should be careful to take away from ourselves any thorns that prick us in the personality of others.*
b) 1st ed. "The Bowl of Sâki" - 17th July.	*We should be careful to take away from ourselves any thorns that prick*

Cont. b)

ORIGIN and elaborations:	DIFFERENT VERSIONS:
Cont. b)	*us in the personality of others.*
a) A sentence in the chapter 'Cause' from the book 'Pearls from the Ocean Unseen', by Mary Zohra Williams, p.21, London, 1919.	*There is a light within every soul. It only needs the clouds which overshadow it to be broken for it to beam forth.*
b) 1st ed. "The Bowl of Sâki" - 18th July.	*There is a light within every soul; it only needs the clouds that overshadow it to be broken for it to beam forth.*
a) A sentence in the chapter 'Blessed Are They That Mourn', from the book 'Pearls from the Ocean Unseen', by Mary Zohra Williams, p.14, London, 1919.	*The soul's true happiness lies in experiencing the inner joy, and it will never be fully satisfied with outer seeming pleasures. Its connection is with God, and nothing short of perfection will ever satisfy it.*
b) 1st ed. "The Bowl of Sâki" - 19th July.	*The soul's true happiness lies in experiencing the inner joy, and it will never be fully satisfied with outer, seeming pleasures; its connection is with God, and nothing short of perfection will ever satisfy it.*
a) A sentence in the chapter 'Blessed Are They That Mourn', from the book 'Pearls from the Ocean Unseen', by Mary Zohra Williams, p.15, London, 1919.	*Every blow we get in life pierces through the heart, and awakens our feelings to sympathize with others, and every swing of comfort lulls us to sleep, and we become unaware of all.*
b) 1st ed. "The Bowl of Sâki" - 20th July.	*Every blow __ ___ in life pierces _______ the heart_ and awakens our feelings to sympathise with others; and every swing of comfort lulls us to sleep, and we become unaware of all.*
a) A sentence in the chapter 'The Effect	*A study of life is the greatest of all religions, and there is no greater and*

Cont. a)

ORIGIN and elaborations:	DIFFERENT VERSIONS:
Cont. a) of Deeds', from the book 'Pearls from the Ocean Unseen', by Mary Zohra Williams, p.37, London, 1919.	*more interesting study.*
b) 1st ed. "The Bowl of Sâki" - 21st July.	*A study of life is the greatest of all religions, and there is no greater or more interesting study.*
a) A sentence in the chapter 'The Prayerful Attitude', from the book 'Pearls from the Ocean Unseen', by Mary Zohra Williams, p.28, London, 1919.	*We can learn virtue even from the greatest sinner, if we consider him as a teacher.*
b) 1st ed. "The Bowl of Sâki" - 22nd July.	*We can learn virtue even from the greatest sinner_ if we consider him as a teacher.*
a) A sentence in the chapter 'Repent Ye, for the Kingdom of God Is at Hand', from the book 'Pearls from the Ocean Unseen', by Mary Zohra Williams, p. 18, London, 1919.	*Warmth melts, while cold freezes. Drops of water fallen on a warm place and on a cold place are affected differently. The drop in the warm sphere spreads and becomes larger, covers a larger space, whereas a drop in the cold place freezes, becomes limited. Repentance has the effect of a drop spread in the warm sphere. It causes the heart to expand and become universal, while the hardening of the heart brings limitation.*
b) 1st ed. "The Bowl of Sâki" - 23rd July.	*Warmth melts, while cold freezes. A drop of ice ____ __ _ ____ _____ __ __ _ ____ _____ __ ______ ________ _ ___ ____ in a warm place spreads and ______ _____ _ covers a larger space, whereas a drop of water in a cold place freezes_ and becomes limited. Repentance has the effect of spreading a drop in a warm sphere, __ causing the heart to expand and become universal_ while the hardening of the heart brings limitation.*
a) A sentence in the chapter 'Balance', from the book 'Pearls from the Ocean Unseen', by Mary Zohra Williams,	*There should be a balance in all our actions; to be either extreme or lukewarm is equally bad.*

Cont. a)

ORIGIN and elaborations:	DIFFERENT VERSIONS:
Cont. a) p.39, London, 1919.	
b) 1st ed. "The Bowl of Sâki" - 24th July.	*There should be a balance in all our actions, to be either extreme or lukewarm is equally bad.*

---

a) A sentence in the chapter 'The Alchemy of Happiness', from the book 'Pearls from the Ocean Unseen', by Mary Zohra Williams, p.44, London, 1919.	*Our spirit is the real part of us; the body is but its garment. There is absolute peace in the abode from whence the spirit came, and the true happiness of the soul lies in that peace. As man would not find peace at the tailor's because his coat came from there, so the spirit cannot get true happiness from the earth just because the body belongs to the earth.*
b) 1st ed. "The Bowl of Sâki" - 25th July.	*Our spirit is the real part of us: the body ___ but its garment. ___ A man would not find peace at the tailor's, because his coat comes from there: ___ neither can the spirit obtain true happiness from the earth just because his body belongs to ___ earth.*

---

a) Notebooks 1921 :	Saying. Every purpose has a birth and death, therefore God is beyond purpose.
b) 1st ed. "The Bowl of Sâki" - 26th July.	Every purpose has a birth and death; therefore God is beyond purpose.

No documents referring to the saying under 27th July have been found in the archives to date.	
1st ed. "The Bowl of Sâki" - 27th July.	Belief and disbelief have divided mankind into so many sects, blinding his eyes to the vision of the Oneness of all life.

---

a) Notebooks 1921 :	Sangata. Phy. The spirit in loving form disillusions itself, for spirit can only love spirit and ....
	Saying. Spirit can only love spirit, in loving form it disillusions itself.

b)

ORIGIN and elaborations:	DIFFERENT VERSIONS:
b) MS. Sd. Second version a).	Saying. - it ~~desillusions~~ deludes itself.
c) 1st ed. "The Bowl of Sâki" - 28th July.	Spirit can only love spirit; in loving form it deludes itself.
a) Two sentences in a lecture 'The Message', 1921, found only in type with Gd.'s book-preparation of 'The Unity of Religious Ideals'.	It is one thing to love and another thing to understand. The one who loves the Messenger is a devotee, but the one who knows the Messenger is his friend.
b) 1st ed. "The Bowl of Sâki" - 29th July.	__ To love is one thing, to understand is another ___ ; he who loves __ ______ is a devotee, but he who understands __ ______ is a friend.
1st ed. "The Bowl of Sâki" - 30th July.	Among a million believers in God there is scarcely one who makes God a reality.

Note: For complete elaborations and different versions see Sayings I: "Gayan" - Chala 14.

ORIGIN and elaborations:	DIFFERENT VERSIONS:
a) Notebooks 1921 :	Saying. The soul feels suffocated when the doors of the heart are closed.
b) 1st ed. "The Bowl of Sâki" - 31st July.	The soul feels suffocated when the doors of the heart are closed.
a) Notebooks 1921 :	Saying. Understanding makes the troubles / tragedies of life lighter to bear.
b) 1st ed. "The Bowl of Sâki" - 1st August.	Understanding makes the trouble of life lighter to bear.
a) A sentence in the lecture 'Sufism', 1920, as published in the Magazine 'Sufi' of October 1920.	The same herb planted in various atmospheric conditions, will vary in form accordingly, but retain its characteristics.
b) 1st ed. "The Bowl of Sâki" - 2nd August.	The same herb planted in various atmospheric conditions_ will vary in form accordingly, but will retain its characteristics.

ORIGIN and elaborations:	DIFFERENT VERSIONS:
No documents referring to the saying under 3rd August have been found in the archives to date.	
1st ed. "The Bowl of Sâki" - 3rd August.	Think, before envying the position of your fellowman, with what difficulty he has arrived at it.

---

a) Notebooks 1921 :	Saying. Tala. Life is what it is, you cannot change it, but you can change yourself.
b) 1st ed. "The Bowl of Sâki" - 4th August.	Life is what it is, you cannot change it; but you can always change yourself.

Note: See for complete elaborations and different versions Sayings I: "Gayan" - Bola 244.

---

a) Notebooks 1921 :	Saying. Life is one continual series of experiences, one leading to the other, till the soul arrives at its final destination.
b) MS. Gr. and a typewritten copy of sayings with corr. and add. by Inayat Khan, meant for publication in the "Gayan".	Saying. Life is a continual - - - - etc. - - - - - - - - - - arrives at its _____ destination.
c) 1st ed. "The Bowl of Sâki" - 5th August.	Life is a continual series of experiences, one leading to the other_ until the soul arrives at its destination.

---

a) Notebooks 1921 :	Saying. The external life is but a shadow of the inner reality.
b) 1st ed. "The Bowl of Sâki" - 6th August.	___ External life is ___ the shadow of the inner reality.

Note: For complete elaborations and different versions see Sayings I: "Gayan" - Bola 46.

---

a) Notebooks 1921 :	Saying. At the cost of one failure the wise learns a lesson for the whole life.
b) MS. Gr. and a typewritten copy of sayings with corr.	Saying. - - - - - - - - - - - - - - - - - - - learns his lesson - - - - - - - - .

Cont. b)

ORIGIN and elaborations:	DIFFERENT VERSIONS:
Cont. b) and add. by Inayat Khan, meant for publication in the "Gayan".	
c) 1st ed. "The Bowl of Sâki" - 7th August.	At the cost of one failure, the wise learn the lesson for the whole life.

---

a) Notebooks 1921 :	Saying. The more you evolve spiritually, the further you pass from the understanding of every man.
b) MS. Gr. to which Inayat Khan added the remark: 'Sangita I Nasihat (also a saying)'	Saying. Sangita I Nasihat (also a saying). - - - - - - - - - - - spiritually the - - - - - - - - - - - - - - - - - - etc.
c) A typewritten copy of sayings with corr. and add. by Inayat Khan, meant for publication in the "Gayan". Inayat Khan added: 'Saying, Sangita II (as well)' over it.	Saying. Sangita II (as well). - - - - - - - - - - - - - - .
d) Copied by Gr.	Saying. - - - - - - - - - - - - - - - - - -, the more you - - - - - - - - - - - - - etc.
e) 1st ed. "The Bowl of Sâki" - 8th August.	The more you evolve spiritually, the further you pass from the understanding of every man.

---

a) Notebooks 1921 :	Saying. One word can be more precious than all the treasures of the earth.
b) 1st ed. "The Bowl of Sâki" - 9th August.	One word can be more precious than all the treasures of the earth.

Note: For complete elaborations and different versions see Sayings I: "Gayan" - Bola 33.

---

a) Notebooks 1921 :	Saying. Narrowness is primitiveness, it is the breadth of heart that proves evolution.
b) MS. Gr. and a typewritten copy of sayings with corr. and add. by Inayat Khan, meant for publication in the "Gayan".	Saying. - - - - - - - - primitiveness; it is - .

c)

ORIGIN and elaborations:	DIFFERENT VERSIONS:
c) 1st ed. "The Bowl of Sâki" - 10th August.	Narrowness is primitiveness; it is the breadth of heart that proves evolution.

ORIGIN and elaborations:	DIFFERENT VERSIONS:
a) Notebooks 1921 :	Saying. A way to heaven is simpler to find than to find the way on the earth.
b) MS. Gr. Inayat Khan added '(heathen saying)' over it.	Saying. Heathen Saying. It is simpler to find a way to Heaven than to find a way on ___ earth.
c) A typewritten copy of sayings mostly meant for publication in the "Gayan".	Tala. ________ ______ - - - - - - - - - - - - - .
d) 1st ed. "The Bowl of Sâki" - 11th August.	It is simpler to find a way to Heaven than to find a way on earth.

ORIGIN and elaborations:	DIFFERENT VERSIONS:
a) Notebooks 1921 :	Saying. In nature it is the hand of man that designs God's proposed plan. In nature it is God Who by the hand of man designs and carries out His intended plans.
b) 1st ed. "The Bowl of Sâki" - 12th August. Second version a).	It is God who, by the hand of man, designs and carries out His intended plans in nature.

Note: For complete elaborations and different versions see Sayings I: "Gayan" - Bola 202.

ORIGIN and elaborations:	DIFFERENT VERSIONS:
a) Notebooks 1921 :	Saying. The admirer of nature is the true worshipper of God. 1)

Note: For complete elaborations and different versions see Sayings I: "Gayan" - Bola 259.

ORIGIN and elaborations:	DIFFERENT VERSIONS:
b) 1st ed. "The Bowl of Sâki" - 13th August.	The lover of nature is the true worshipper of God.

ORIGIN and elaborations:	DIFFERENT VERSIONS:
a) Notebooks 1921 :	Saying. In the country you can see God's Glory and in the city you can glorify His name. 2)

Note 2): For complete elaborations and different versions see Sayings I: "Gayan" - Chala 40.

ORIGIN and elaborations:	DIFFERENT VERSIONS:
b) 1st ed. "The Bowl of Sâki" - 14th August.	In the country you ___ see the glory of God; ___ in the city you ___ glorify His name.

ORIGIN and elaborations:	DIFFERENT VERSIONS:
a) MS. Gr. See for complete elaborations Sayings I: "Gayan" - Bola 157.	Tala. The pain of life is a price paid for the quickening of the heart.
b) 1st ed. "The Bowl of Sâki" - 15th August.	The pain of life is the price paid for the quickening of the heart.

Cf. Sayings II: Part Two, no. 293.

---

a) Notebook 1914/1915 :	The words that enlighten are more precious than jewels. 1)

Note 1): See for complete elaborations and different versions: Sayings I: "Gayan" - Chala 66.

b) 1st ed. "The Bowl of Sâki" - 16th August.	___ Words that enlighten the soul are more precious than jewels.

---

a) MS. Gr. Inayat Khan added 'Saying' over it.	Saying. Love is the current coin of all people of all periods.
b) Two typewritten copies of sayings originally meant for publication in the "Gayan": one copy under the heading 'Sayings', the other under the heading 'Bola'. (Gd.'s bookpreparation).	- - - - - - - - - - - - - .
c) 1st ed. "The Bowl of Sâki" - 17th August.	Love is the current coin of all peoples in all periods.

---

a) See for complete elaborations and different versions: Sayings I: "Gayan" - Bola 93.	
b) 1st ed. "The Bowl of Sâki" - 18th August.	Do not take the example of another as an excuse for your own wrong-doing.

---

a) See for complete elaborations and different versions: Sayings I: "Gayan" - Bola 153.	
b) 1st ed. "The Bowl of Sâki" - 19th August.	Overlook the greatest fault of another, but do not partake of it yourself in the smallest degree.

ORIGIN and elaborations:	DIFFERENT VERSIONS:
a) MS. Gr.	Saying. Cleverness and complexity are not necessarily wisdom.
b) 1st ed. "The Bowl of Sâki" - 20th August.	Cleverness and complexity are not necessarily wisdom.

---

a) Notebook 1914/1915 :	Saying. The whole world's treasure is too small a price for a word that lightens the soul. 1)

Note 1): See for complete elaborations and different versions: Sayings I: "Gayan" - Chala 68.

b) 1st ed. "The Bowl of Sâki" - 21st August.	The whole world's treasure is too small a price to pay for a word that kindles the soul.

---

a) See for complete elaborations Sayings I: "Gayan" - Tala 53.	
b) 1st ed. "The Bowl of Sâki" - 22nd August.	He is living whose sympathy is awake; and he is dead whose heart is asleep.

---

a) A sentence in the lecture 'Mental Creation', 18th May 1919, reported and revised by Dr.Gruner as published in the book 'In an Eastern Rose-garden', 1st ed. 1920/1921.	Thoughts have prepared for us that happiness or unhappiness which we experience.
b) 1st ed. "The Bowl of Sâki" - 23rd August.	By our thoughts we have prepared for ourselves the happiness or unhappiness ____ we experience.

Note: Cf. "The Bowl of Sâki" - 14th June and 11th November.

---

a) See for complete elaborations and different versions: Sayings I: "Gayan" - Alapa 17.	
b) A typewritten copy of sayings originally meant for publication in the "Gayan", under the heading 'Bola I'. (Gd.'s bookpreparation).	Put your trust in God for support and see His hidden Hand working through all sources.

 c)

ORIGIN and elaborations:	DIFFERENT VERSIONS:
c) 1st ed. "The Bowl of Sâki" - 24th August.	Put your trust in God for support and see His hidden hand working through all sources.
a) Two sentences in the lecture 'The Effect of Prayer', (1917-1920), reported and revised by Dr.O.Gruner as published in the book 'In an Eastern Rosegarden', 1st ed. 1920/1921.	Faith is the A, B, C of the revelation of God. This faith is begun by prayer.
b) 1st ed. "The Bowl of Sâki" - 25th August.	Faith is the A B C of the realization of God. This faith begins by prayer.
a) Notebooks 1921 :	Saying. Passion is the smoke and emotion is glow from love's fire and consideration is the flame that illuminates the path. 1)

Note 1): See for complete elaborations and different versions: Sayings I: "Gayan" - Tala 39.

b) 1st ed. "The Bowl of Sâki" - 26th August.	Passion is the smoke and emotion is the glow of love's fire. Unselfishness is the flame that illumines the path.
a) See for complete elaborations and different versions: Sayings I: "Gayan" - Chala 25.	
b) 1st ed. "The Bowl of Sâki" - 27th August.	The Soul of Christ is the Light of the Universe.
a) See for complete elaborations: Sayings I: "Gayan" - Bola 87.	
b) 1st ed. "The Bowl of Sâki" - 28th August.	Death is a tax the soul has to pay for having had a name and a form.
a) Notebooks 1921 :	Saying. A pure life and clear conscience are as wings attached to the soul. 2)

Note 2): See for complete elaborations and different versions: Sayings I: "Gayan" - Bola 148.

b)

ORIGIN and elaborations:	DIFFERENT VERSIONS:
b) 1st ed. "The Bowl of Sâki" - 29th August.	A pure life and a clean conscience are as two wings attached to the soul.
a) MS. Gr.	Tala. The giver is greater than the gift; the receiver is smaller than the reward.
b) A typewritten copy of sayings originally meant for publication in the "Gayan", under the heading 'Tala' (Gd.'s bookpreparation).	- - - - - - - - - - - - - - - - gift, the -.
c) 1st ed. "The Bowl of Sâki" - 30th August.	The giver is greater than the gift. ___ ___ ___ ___ ___ ___
a) See for elaborations: Sayings I: "Gayan" - Tala 40.	
b) 1st ed. "The Bowl of Sâki" - 31st August.	He who has spent has used; he who has collected has lost; but he who has given has saved his treasure for ever.
a) See for complete elaborations and different versions: Sayings I: "Gayan" - Chala 134.	
b) 1st ed. "The Bowl of Sâki" - 1st September.	Joy and sorrow both are for each other. If it were not for joy, sorrow could not be, and if it were not for sorrow, joy could not be experienced.
a) See for complete elaborations and different versions: Sayings I: "Gayan" - Bola 135.	
b) 1st ed. "The Bowl of Sâki" - 2nd September.	Self-pity is the cause of all life's grievances.
a) MS. Gr. Inayat Khan add. 'Sangitha I Thasawuf' 1) over it, and wrote in the margin: 'also a saying'.	Sangitha I Thasawuf. How can the Unlimited Being be limited, since all that seems limited is, in its depth beyond all limitations?

b)

ORIGIN and elaborations:	DIFFERENT VERSIONS:
b) A typewritten copy of sayings originally meant for publication in the "Gayan", under the heading 'Tala' (Gd.'s bookpreparation).	- - - - - - - - - - etc. - - - - - - - - is_ in its depth - - etc.
c) Sangita I - 39:	Tassawuf. How can the Unlimited Being be limited, since all that seems limited is in its depth beyond all limitations?
d) 1st ed. "The Bowl of Sâki" - 3rd September.	How can the unlimited Being be limited? _____ All that seems limited is in its depth beyond all limitations.

Note 1): A phonetic transcription of such words from the original languages, may cause differences in the spelling.

---

a) See for elaborations: Sayings I: "Gayan" - Bola 27.	
b) 1st ed. "The Bowl of Sâki" - 4th September.	Pleasure blocks, but pain clears the way of inspiration.

---

a) See for elaborations and a different version: Sayings I: "Gayan" - Bola 154.	
b) 1st ed. "The Bowl of Sâki" - 5th September.	There is no source of happiness other than that in the heart of man.

---

a) See for elaborations: Sayings I: "Gayan" - Tala 18.	
b) 1st ed. "The Bowl of Sâki" - 6th September.	Happy is he who does good to others; miserable is he who expects good from others.

---

a) See for complete elaborations and different versions: Sayings I: "Gayan" - Bola 183.	
b) 1st ed. "The Bowl of Sâki" - 7th September.	One virtue is more powerful than a thousand vices.

ORIGIN and elaborations:	DIFFERENT VERSIONS:
a) See for complete elaborations and different versions: Sayings I: "Gayan" - Bola 221.	
b) 1st ed. "The Bowl of Sâki" - 8th September.	The soul is either raised or cast down by the power of its own thought, speech and action.

---

a) See for complete elaborations and different versions: Sayings I: "Gayan" - Bola 126.	
b) 1st ed. "The Bowl of Sâki" - 9th September.	Love is the divine mother's arms; when those arms are spread, every soul falls into them.

---

a) Cf. this sentence in the lecture 'The Power of the Word', pub. in 'Sufism', Dec., 1921.	There is a saying among the Hindus that the tree that bears much fruit bows low.
b) 1st ed. "The Bowl of Sâki" - 10th September.	It is the fruit that makes the tree bow_ low.

---

a) The first sentence in the lecture 'The Training of the Ego' (= Gatha Moral Culture Series II no. 9), 14th May 1921, in Miss R.Jones's handwriting.	In order to learn forgiveness man must learn tolerance first.
b) 1st ed. "The Bowl of Sâki" - 11th September.	In order to learn forgiveness, man must first learn tolerance.

---

a) A sentence in the lecture 'The Training of the Ego' (= Gatha Moral Culture, Series II no.9), 14th May 1921, in Miss R.Jones's handwriting.	The first step towards forgiveness is to forget.
b) 1st ed. "The Bowl of Sâki" - 12th September.	The first step towards forgiveness is to forget.

---

a) Part of a sentence in the lecture 'The Training of	and the only thing he can do to live in the midst of all kinds of

Cont. a)

ORIGIN and elaborations:	DIFFERENT VERSIONS:
Cont. a) the Ego' (= Gatha Moral Culture, Series II no. 9), 14th May 1921, in Miss R.Jones's handwriting.	inharmonies is to strengthen his will power so as to bear all things, and yet keeping the fineness of character and the nobleness of manner together with an ever-living heart.
b) Copied by Gr., probably from Inayat Khan's handwriting, and written by her in one of Sr.'s notebooks (1921). b) Was not compared with a).	'The only way to live in the midst of all inharmonious influences is to strengthen the will-power and endure all things; yet keeping the fineness of character and nobility of manner together with an ever-living heart. I.K.'
c) 1st ed. "The Bowl of Sâki" - 13th September.	_ The only way to live in the midst of ___ inharmonious influences is to strengthen the will power and endure all things, yet keeping ___ fineness of character and nobility of manner together with an ever living heart full of love.

---

a) A sentence in the lecture 'About Discipleship', 18th May 1921, in Kf.'s handwriting. This lecture has become Sangatha III-30.	Devotion to the Teacher is not for the sake of the Teacher, it is for God.
b) 1st ed. "The Bowl of Sâki" - 14th September.	Devotion to a spiritual teacher is not for the sake of the teacher, it is for God.

---

a) Two sentences in the lecture 'The Training of the Ego' (= Gatha Moral Culture, Series II no. 9), 14th May 1921, in Miss R.Jones's handwriting.	To become cold with the coldness of the world is a weakness, and to become broken by the hardness of the world is feebleness. But to be in the world, and yet to keep above the world is like walking on the water.
b) 1st ed. "The Bowl of Sâki" - 15th September.	To become cold from the coldness of the world is _ weakness, ___ to become broken by the hardness of the world is feebleness, but to live in the world_ and yet to keep above it is like walking on the water.

---

a) A sentence in the lecture 'About Discipleship', 18th May 1921, in Kf.'s handwriting. This lecture has become Sangatha III-30.	God alone deserves all love and the freedom of Love is in giving it to God.

b)

ORIGIN and elaborations:	DIFFERENT VERSIONS:
b) 1st ed. "The Bowl of Sâki" - 16th September.	God alone deserves all love, and the freedom of love is in giving it to God.
a) Part of a sentence in the lecture 'About Discipleship', 18th May 1921, in Kf.'s handwriting. This lecture has become Sangatha III-30.	... for life 1) has the power to open the door of Eternal Life.
b) 1st ed. "The Bowl of Sâki" - 17th September.	___ Love has the power to open the door of eternal life.
	Note 1): 'life' may have been wrongly understood for 'love'.
a) A sentence in the lecture 'About Discipleship', 18th May 1921, in Kf.'s handwriting. This lecture has become Sangatha III-30.	Love has its limitations when it is directed to limited beings, but love that is directed to God has no limitations.
b) 1st ed. "The Bowl of Sâki" - 18th September.	Love has its limitations when it is directed towards limited beings, but love ___ __ directed to God has no limitations.
a) Two sentences from Inayat Khan's answers to questions about the symbolism of the refusal of the wise virgins to give their oil to the foolish, May 1921, reported by Kf.	The Teacher however great can never give his knowledge to the pupil. The pupil must create his own knowledge.
These answers were also written down by Ng. in her notebook, probably after the lecture, and Gd. copied them in a somewhat different sequence.	The Teacher, however great, can - etc.
b) 1st ed. "The Bowl of Sâki" - 19th September.	The teacher, however great, can never give his knowledge to the pupil; the pupil must create his own knowledge.
a) A sentence from Inayat	One thing is true that Murshid cannot

Cont. a)

ORIGIN and elaborations:	DIFFERENT VERSIONS:
Cont. a) Khan's answers to questions, May 1921, reported by Kf.	give the knowledge, but he can kindle the light if the oil is there.
These answers were also written down by Ng. in her notebook, probably after the lecture, and Gd. copied them in a somewhat different sequence.	One thing is true, ____ Murshid cannot give ___ knowledge_ but - - - - etc.
b) 1st ed. "The Bowl of Sâki" - 20th September.	One thing is true, although the teacher cannot give the knowledge, ___ he can kindle the light if the oil is in the lamp.

---

a) A sentence from Inayat Khan's answers to questions about asceticism, May 1921, reported by Kf.	Will power is the keynote of Mastery, and asceticism is the development of will power.
These answers were also written down by Ng. in her notebook, probably after the lecture, and Gd. copied them in a somewhat different sequence.	- - - - - - - - - - - - - - of mastery, - - - - - - - - - - - - - - - - - - etc.
b) 1st ed. "The Bowl of Sâki" - 21st September.	Will-power is the keynote of mastery, and asceticism is the development of will-power.

No documents referring to the saying under 22nd September have been found in the archives to date.	
1st ed. "The Bowl of Sâki" - 22nd September.	Real generosity is an unfailing sign of spirituality.

---

a) Notebooks 1921 :	Saying. Generosity is born of two sources, vanity and love, one false and the other true.
b) Copied from (?) in an unidentified handwriting. This copy also contains other sayings meant originally for publication in the "Gayan" with some corr. and add. by Inayat Khan.	Saying. - - - - - - - - - - - - - - sources: The vanity and love: one false, and the other true.

c)

ORIGIN and elaborations:	DIFFERENT VERSIONS:
c) 1st ed. "The Bowl of Sâki" - 23rd September.	There are two kinds of generosity, the real and the shadow; the former is prompted by love, the latter by vanity.

No documents referring to the saying under 24th September have been found in the archives to date.	
1st ed. "The Bowl of Sâki" - 24th September.	It is better to pay than receive from the vain, for such favours demand ten times their cost.

---

a) A sentence in the chapter 'Repent ye, for the Kingdom of Heaven...', from the book 'Pearls from the Ocean Unseen' by Mary Zohra Williams, p.17, 1st ed. 1919.	*The Kingdom of Heaven is in the hearts of those who realize God:*
b) 1st ed. "The Bowl of Sâki" - 25th September.	*The Kingdom of Heaven is in the hearts of those who realize God.*

---

a) A sentence in the chapter 'The Purpose of Life', from the book 'Pearls from the Ocean Unseen' by Mary Zohra Williams, p.11, 1st ed. 1919.	*To relieve the hunger of others we must forget our own hunger.*
b) 1st ed. "The Bowl of Sâki" - 26th September.	*In order to relieve the hunger of others, we must forget our own hunger.*

---

a) A sentence in the chapter 'Cause', from the book 'Pearls from the Ocean Unseen', by Mary Zohra Williams, p.20, 1st ed. 1919.	*It is when man has lost the idea of duality and feels himself at one with all creation, that his eyes are opened and he sees the cause of everything.*
b) 1st ed. "The Bowl of Sâki" - 27th September.	*It is when man has lost the idea of separateness and feels himself at one with all creation_ that his eyes are opened and he sees the cause of all things.*

---

a) A typewritten document	To fall beneath one's Ideal is to

Cont. a)

ORIGIN and elaborations:	DIFFERENT VERSIONS:
Cont. a) containing the text of the book 'Sex', intended for publication at the end of 1920, but of which the 1st ed. appeared only in 1938, with the title 'Rassa Shastra'. This document was found among the papers of Mrs. Elizabeth Bailey of Kents Town, who acted as hostess from time to time when Pir-o-Murshid Inayat Khan visited Brighton (England). A sentence at the beginning of the lecture 'On Some Ideals', 1914-1918.	lose one's tract of life;...
b) Sherifa Goodenough's typescript for the book.	- - - - - - - - - one's ideal is to loose one's - - - - - .
c) 1st ed. "The Bowl of Sâki" - 28th September.	To fall beneath one's ideal is to lose one's share of life.
d) Book, 'Rassa Shastra: The Science of Life's Creative Forces', Deventer, Netherlands, 1st. ed. 1938.	To fall beneath one's ideal is to lose one's track of life.

---

a) A typewritten document containing the text of the book 'Sex' intended to be published at the end of 1920, but of which the 1st ed. appeared only in 1938, with the title 'Rassa Shastra'. This document was found among the papers of Mrs. Elizabeth Bailey of Kents Town, who acted as hostess from time to time when Pir-o Murshid Inayat Khan visited Brighton (England). A sentence toward the beginning of the lecture 'On Some Ideals', 1914-1918.	And the wise of all ages have taught that it is the knowledge of the Divine Being that is life and the only reality.
b) Sherifa Goodenough's typescript for the book and the book 'Rassa Shastra: The Science of Life's Creative Forces', Deventer, Netherlands, 1938.	And the wise of all ages have taught that it is the knowledge of the divine being that is life and the only reality.

ORIGIN and elaborations:	DIFFERENT VERSIONS:
c) 1st ed. "The Bowl of Sâki" - 29th September.	___ The wise of all ages have taught that it is ___ knowledge of the Divine Being that is life, and the only reality.
a) A typewritten document containing the text of the book 'Sex' intended to be published at the end of 1920, but which appeared, as 'Rassa Shastra', only in 1938. This document was found among the papers of Mrs. Elizabeth Bailey of Kents Town, who acted as hostess from time to time when Pir-o-Murshid Inayat Khan visited Brighton (England). A sentence near the middle of the lecture 'Courtship', 1914-1918.	When the stream of love flows in its full strength, it purifies all that stands in its path, as the Ganges, in the teachings of the Ancients, purifies all those who plunge into its sacred waters.
b) Sherifa Goodenough's typescript for the book.	- in its course, as the Ganges _ in the tractings of the ancients_ purifies -.
c) 1st ed. "The Bowl of Sâki" - 30th September.	When the stream of love flows in its full strength, it purifies all that stands in its way, as the Ganges - according to the teaching of the ancients - purifies all those who plunge into its sacred waters.
d) Book 'Rassa Shastra: The Science of Life's Creative Forces', Deventer, Netherlands, 1st ed. 1938.	When the stream of love flows in its full strength_ it purifies all that stands in its course, as the Ganges, ________ in the teachings of the ancients, purifies all _____ who plunge into its sacred waters.

---

a) A sentence in the lecture 'The Way of Attainment', undated, found in Sherifa Goodenough's handwriting.	Each soul's attainment is according to its evolution.
b) 1st ed. "The Bowl of Sâki" - 1st October.	Each soul's attainment is according to its evolution.

No documents referring to the saying under 2nd October have been found in the archives to date.

ORIGIN and elaborations:	DIFFERENT VERSIONS:
1st ed. "The Bowl of Sâki" - 2nd October.	It always means that you must sacrifice something very dear to you when His call comes.

ORIGIN and elaborations:	DIFFERENT VERSIONS:
a) Found with Gd.'s book-preparation of 'The Unity of Religious Ideals', in an unidentified handwriting.	Renunciation is always for a purpose, it is to kindle the soul, that nothing can hold the soul back from God, but when the soul is kindled the life of Renunciation is not a necessity.
b) 1st ed. "The Bowl of Sâki" - 3rd October.	Renunciation is always for a purpose; it is to kindle the soul_ that nothing may hold it back from God, but when it is kindled, the life of renunciation is not necessary.

ORIGIN and elaborations:	DIFFERENT VERSIONS:
a) Found with Gd.'s book-preparation of 'The Unity of Religious Ideals', typewritten as part of a passage about the Messengers.	There are those who are lighted candles, they can light other candles. These are they who can inspire others. But the other candles must be of wax; if they are of steel, they cannot be lighted.
b) Copied in an unidentified handwriting.	There are those who are like a lighted candle, they can light other candles, these - - - - - - - - - - - - - others, but - - - - - - etc.
c) 1st ed. "The Bowl of Sâki" - 4th October.	There are those who are like a lighted candle, they can light other candles; ____ ___ ____ ___ ___ ______ ______ - but the other candles must be of wax, if they are of steel_ they cannot be lighted.

ORIGIN and elaborations:	DIFFERENT VERSIONS:
a) A sentence in the lecture 'Cupid and Psyche', 5th May 1921, found in an unidentified handwriting.	Therefore, it is no exaggeration to say that there is no greater Scripture than nature, for nature is life itself.
b) 1st ed. "The Bowl of Sâki" - 5th October.	________ _ _ _ _ __________ __ ___ ____ There is no greater Scripture than nature, for nature is life itself.

ORIGIN and elaborations:	DIFFERENT VERSIONS:
a) Part of a sentence in the lecture 'Cupid and Psyche', 5th May 1921, found in an unidentified handwriting.	because wisdom can only be learnt gradually and every soul is not ready to receive or to understand the complexity of the purpose of life.

b)

ORIGIN and elaborations:	DIFFERENT VERSIONS:
b) 1st ed. "The Bowl of Sâki" - 6th October.	_____ Wisdom can only be learnt gradually, and every soul is not ready to receive or to understand the complexity of the purpose of life.

ORIGIN and elaborations:	DIFFERENT VERSIONS:
a) Part of a sentence in the lecture 'Cupid and Psyche', 5th May 1921, found in an unidentified handwriting.	It is a very high stage in the path of love when man really learns to love another with a love that asks no return,
b) 1st ed. "The Bowl of Sâki" - 7th October.	It is a very high stage on the path of love when a man really learns to love another with a love that asks no return.

ORIGIN and elaborations:	DIFFERENT VERSIONS:
a) A sentence in the lecture 'Cupid and Psyche', 5th May 1921, found in an unidentified handwriting.	Love alone is a fountain from which all virtues fall as drops of sparkling water.
b) 1st ed. "The Bowl of Sâki" - 8th October.	Love alone is the fountain from which all virtues fall as drops of sparkling water.

ORIGIN and elaborations:	DIFFERENT VERSIONS:
a) A sentence in the lecture 'Cupid and Psyche', 5th May 1921, found in an unidentified handwriting.	The purpose of one's whole life is to make God a reality.
b) 1st ed. "The Bowl of Sâki" - 9th October.	The whole purpose of _____ _____ life is to make God a reality.

ORIGIN and elaborations:	DIFFERENT VERSIONS:
a) Part of a sentence in the lecture 'Cupid and Psyche', 5th May 1921, found in an unidentified handwriting.	but if you will seek for good in everything, you will always find it, for God is in all things, and still more He is in all beings.
b) 1st ed. "The Bowl of Sâki" - 10th October.	___ If you ___ seek ___ the good in every soul, you will always find it, for God is in all things. ___ Still more, He is in all beings. 1)

Note 1): The words 'things' and 'beings' were printed in italics.

ORIGIN and elaborations:	DIFFERENT VERSIONS:
a) Two sentences in the	Knowledge of God is beyond man.

Cont. a)

ORIGIN and elaborations:	DIFFERENT VERSIONS:
Cont. a) lecture 'Unity and Uniformity', 6th May 1921, in an unidentified handwriting.	But the secret of God is hidden in the knowledge of unity.
b) 1st ed. "The Bowl of Sâki" - 11th October.	The knowledge of God is beyond man's reason. ___ The secret of God is hidden in the knowledge of unity.

---

a) A sentence in the lecture 'Cupid and Psyche', 5th May 1921, in an unidentified handwriting.	Seek Him in all souls, good and bad, wise and foolish, attractive or unattractive, for in the depth of each there is God.
b) 1st ed. "The Bowl of Sâki" - 12th October.	Seek Him in all souls, good or bad, wise and foolish, attractive and unattractive; ___ in the depths of each there is God.

---

a) A sentence in the lecture 'Unity and Uniformity', 6th May 1921, in an unidentified handwriting.	When there is an inharmony in one's individual self, how can one spread harmonious vibrations and atmosphere?
b) 1st ed. "The Bowl of Sâki" - 13th October.	When in ourselves there is inharmony, how can we spread harmony. 1)

Note 1): This same shortened version was published in the Magazine 'Sufism' of December 1923 in a report of the lecture 'Unity and Uniformity'.

---

a) Part of a sentence in the lecture 'Unity and Uniformity', 6th May 1921, in an unidentified handwriting.	it is the innermost being of man that is the real Being of God.
b) 1st ed. "The Bowl of Sâki" - 14th October.	__ __ The innermost being of man ____ is the real being of God.

---

a) A sentence in the lecture 'Unity and Uniformity', 6th May 1921, in an unidentified handwriting.	Love itself is the healing power and remedy to all pain.
b) 1st ed. "The Bowl of Sâki" - 15th October.	Love itself is the healing power and the remedy for all pain.

ORIGIN and elaborations:	DIFFERENT VERSIONS:
a) A sentence in the lecture 'Unity and Uniformity', 6th May 1921, in an unidentified handwriting.	You will realise that your heart goes forward to everyone, that you are ready to tolerate and forgive everyone and see brotherhood and God in all; till the vision of life becomes one single vision of the Unity and Sublimity of God.
b) 1st ed. "The Bowl of Sâki" - 16th October.	By loving, forgiving and serving, it is possible for your whole life to become one single vision of the Sublime Beauty of God. 1)

Note 1): This same shortened version was published in the Magazine 'Sufism' of December 1923 in a report of the lecture 'Unity and Uniformity.

No documents referring to the saying under 17th October have been found in the archives to date.	
1st ed. "The Bowl of Sâki" - 17th October.	Mysticism to the mystic is both science and religion.

---

a) Copied by Sk. from (?).	Saying. The principles of mysticism rise from the heart of man; they are learned by intuition and proved by reason.
b) 1st ed. "The Bowl of Sâki" - 18th October.	The principles of mysticism rise from the heart of man; they are learnt by intuition and proved by reason.

---

a) A sentence in the lecture 'The Dance of the Soul', 11th May 1921, as published in the Magazine 'Sufism' of September 1921.	Your work in life must be your religion, whatever your occupation may be.
b) 1st ed. "The Bowl of Sâki" - 19th October.	Your work in life must be your religion, whatever your occupation may be.

---

a) Part of two sentences in the lecture 'The Dance of the Soul', 11th May 1921, as pub-	the true joy of every soul is the realization of the divine spirit. The absence of realization keeps the soul in despair.

Cont. a)

ORIGIN and elaborations:	DIFFERENT VERSIONS:
Cont. a) lished in the Magazine 'Sufism' of September 1921.	
b) 1st ed. "The Bowl of Sâki" - 20th October.	The true joy of every soul is in the realization of the divine spirit, and the absence of realization keeps the soul in despair.
a) Part of a sentence in the lecture, 'The Dance of the Soul', 11th May 1921, as published in 'Sufism' Sept., 1921.	...and the desire for service, for the sake of the God in whom we can all unite beyond the narrow barriers of race and creed.
b) 1st ed. "The Bowl of Sâki" - 21st October.	Beyond the narrow barriers of race and creed we can all unite, because we all belong to One God.
a) From a lecture, "The Power of the Word", 'Sufism', Dec., 1921.	..., for all forms of worship or belief should draw man closer to God,...
b) 1st ed. "The Bowl of Sâki" - 22nd October.	_ __ All forms of worship or prayer must draw man closer to God.
a) From a lecture, "The Power of the Word", 'Sufism', Dec., 1921.	When man is separated from God in thought his belief is no use to him, his worship is but little use to him,...
b) 1st ed. "The Bowl of Sâki" - 23rd October.	When man is separated from God in his thought, his belief is of no use __ ___, his worship is __ of little use __ ___ .
a) Part of a sentence in the lecture 'Truth', 13 May 1921, in the hwr. of Nuria Best and of Miss R. Jones.	...the source of realizing the truth is within man, but man is the object of his realization.
b) 1st ed. "The Bowl of Sâki" - 24th October.	The source of the realization of truth is within man, ___ he himself is the object of his realization.

Note: For complete elaborations and different versions see "The Bowl of Saki" under 12 March.

a) Same origin as the one cited for 24 Oct. a).	...the real self denial meant, is the losing of oneself in God.

b)

ORIGIN and elaborations:	DIFFERENT VERSIONS:
b) A typewritten version.	___ True self-denial _____ _ is ___ losing oneself in God.
c) 1st ed. "The Bowl of Sâki" - 25th October.	True self-denial is losing one's self in God.

ORIGIN and elaborations:	DIFFERENT VERSIONS:
a) Part of a sentence in the lecture 'Truth', 13th May 1921, in Nuria Best's and in Miss R. Jones's handwriting.	It is more important to find the truth about oneself than to find the truth about heaven or hell,
b) 1st ed. "The Bowl of Sâki" - 26th October.	It is more important to find out the truth about one's self than to find out the truth of Heaven and Hell.

Note: For complete elaborations and different versions, see "The Bowl of Sâki" under 9th March.

ORIGIN and elaborations:	DIFFERENT VERSIONS:
a) Part of two sentences in the lecture 'Truth', 13th May 1921, in Nuria Best's and in Miss R. Jones's handwriting.	according to his evolution, so man knows the truth. And the more a man knows, the more he finds there is to learn.
b) See for complete elaborations and versions of the second sentence: Sayings I: "Gayan" - Bola 73.	
c) 1st ed. "The Bowl of Sâki" - 27th October.	According to his evolution, __ man knows the Truth; and the more he knows, the more he finds there is to know.

Note: For complete elaborations and different versions of the first sentence, see "The Bowl of of Sâki" under 29th March.

ORIGIN and elaborations:	DIFFERENT VERSIONS:
a) A sentence in the lecture 'Truth', 13th May 1921, in Nuria Best's and in Miss R.Jones's handwriting.	Man, filled with earthly knowledge, and what he calls learning, is often the knowledge only of names and forms and so has no capacity for the knowledge of truth or of God.
b) 1st ed. "The Bowl of Sâki" - 28th October.	The man filled with the knowledge of names and forms has no capacity for the knowledge of Truth.

Note: For complete elaborations and different versions, see "The Bowl of Sâki" under 25th March.

ORIGIN and elaborations:	DIFFERENT VERSIONS:
a) A sentence in the lecture 'Truth', 13th May 1921, in Nuria Best's handwriting.	But where man makes a mistake is that, when a man cultivates the heart he wishes to sow the seed himself instead of leaving the sowing to God.
b) The same sentence as under a), in Miss R. Jones's handwriting.	But where man makes a mistake is ____, when he cultivates the heart, he wishes - - - - - etc.
c) An early typewritten copy.	, but where man makes a mistake is that when he cultivates the heart, he wants to sow the seed himself, instead of leaving the sowing of the seed to God.
d) 1st ed. "The Bowl of Sâki" - 29th October.	Man mistakes when he begins to cultivate the heart by wanting to sow the seed himself instead of leaving the sowing to God.

---

a) Part of four sentences in the lecture 'Truth', 13th May 1921, in Nuria Best's and in Miss R. Jones's handwriting. As in the latter's version this passage was somewhat shortened, Nuria Best's more complete version is taken here as being the most original one.	Friends, we often start our lives as teachers, then it is hard to become a pupil. but there are many whose only difficulty in life is that they are teachers already. What one has to learn is pupilship. But he forgets that there is only one Teacher and that is God Himself.
b) An old typewritten version.	what one has to learn is pupilship. Friends, we _____ start our lives as teachers, and it is very hard for us to learn to become pupils. ___ There are many whose only difficulty in life is that they are teachers already. He does not know that there is but one Teacher, ___ ____ __ God Himself.
c) 1st ed. "The Bowl of Sâki" - 30th October.	Friends, we start our lives as teachers, and it is very hard for us to learn to become pupils. There are many whose only difficulty in life is that they are teachers already. What we have to learn is pupilship. __ ____ ___ ____ ____ There is but one Teacher, God Himself.

Cf. "The Bowl of Sâki" under 22nd and 27th March.
Cf. Sayings I: "Gayan" - Sura 35.

---

a) Two sentences in the lecture 'Truth', 13th	All knowledge of the earth is as clouds covering the sun. It is the

Cont. a)

ORIGIN and elaborations:	DIFFERENT VERSIONS:
Cont. a) May 1921, in Nuria Best's handwriting.	breaking of these clouds and it is the clearness of the sky, or in other words, it may be called the purity of the heart, which gives the capacity for the knowledge of God.
b) The same sentences as under a) in Miss R. Jones's handwriting.	All knowledge - - - - - etc. - - - - - breaking of these clouds of darkness, and it is the clearness of the sky_ or ___ ___ _ it may be - etc.
c) An early typewritten version.	All earthly knowledge is as clouds dimming the sight, and it is the breaking of these clouds, in other words, the purity of the heart, that gives the capacity for the knowledge of God to rise.
d) 1st ed. "The Bowl of Sâki" - 31st October.	___ Earthly knowledge is as clouds dimming the sight, and it is the breaking of these clouds, in other words, ___ purity of ___ heart, that gives the capacity for the knowledge of God to rise.

Cf. "The Bowl of Sâki" under 23rd March.

---

a) Part of a sentence in the lecture 'Truth', 13th May 1921, in Nuria Best's and in Miss R. Jones's handwriting.	and unless man is moved to that selflessness, he does not know justice, right, or truth, but his self stands above ~~all~~ or between himself and God.
b) An early typewritten version has only the last part of the sentence.	Self stands as a wall between man and God.
c) 1st ed. "The Bowl of Sâki" - 1st November.	Self stands as a wall between man and God.

---

a) A sentence in the lecture 'Truth', 13th May 1921, in Nuria Best's handwriting.	It is patient pursuit which will bring the water from the depth of the ground ~~that even~~ for one must meet with the ~~mode~~ mould 1) in digging, until one reaches the water of Love.
b) As under a), in Miss R.Jones's handwriting.	- ground, -mould 1) in digging, before ___ ___ the water of Life and Love can be found.

Note 1) 'mould' may have been wrongly understood for 'mud'.

c) An early typewritten version.	It is a patient pursuit to bring ___ water from the depth of

Cont. c)

ORIGIN and elaborations:	DIFFERENT VERSIONS:
Cont. c)	the ground, for one has to deal with much mud in digging_ before one reaches the water of life. No love is true love which has not deep roots.
d) 1st ed. "The Bowl of Sâki" - 2nd November.	It is a patient pursuit to bring water from the depth of the ground; ___ one has to deal with much mud in digging before one reaches the water of life. __ ____ __ ____ ____ _____ ___ ___ ____ _____ -

---

a) Parts of several sentences in the lecture 'Truth', 13th May 1921, in Nuria Best's and in Miss R.Jones's handwriting. See also "The Bowl of Sâki", under 1st November: a).	the process of this attainment is a sincere research into Truth and Life and an understanding of what I am and what the other man is. This, together with the contemplation of God, a selfless consciousness and a continual pursuit to receive the knowledge of God. The first and last lesson in love is "I am not, and Thou art" and unless man is moved to that selflessness, he does not know justice, right or truth,
b) A revised typewritten version, most probably made from a).	In man's search for Truth, the first lesson and the last is love. There must be no I am, and Thou art not, no separateness, until man has arrived at that selfless consciousness, he does not know Love, Life or Truth.
c) 1st ed. "The Bowl of Sâki" - 3rd November.	In man's search for Truth, the first lesson and the last is Love. There must be no separation. No "I am, and Thou art not." Until man has arrived at that selfless consciousness, he cannot know ____ _ Life and Truth.

---

a) Part of a sentence in Inayat Khan's address to mureeds at the first Service of the Church of All, London, 8th May, 1921, in Joyce Burnett's handwriting.	and it is by the power of prayer that man opens the doors of the heart in which God the Merciful, abides.
b) 1st ed. "The Bowl of Sâki" - 4th November.	___ __ __ By the power of prayer ____ man opens the door of the heart, in which God, the ever-forgiving, the all-merciful, abides.

Note: The version under a) is to be found in the address to mureeds: 'Prayer', which originally

Cont.)

ORIGIN and elaborations:	DIFFERENT VERSIONS:
Cont.)	became Religious Gatheka I no.5.

---

a) A sentence in Inayat Khan's address to mureeds 'Prayer', given at the first Service of the Church of All, London, 8th May 1921, in Joyce Burnett's handwriting.	To be really sorry for one's error is really like opening the doors of Heaven.
b) The same sentence as under a) in a typewritten version. (Religious Gatheka I, no. 5).	- - - - - - - - - - - - - - - - -errors is ___ like opening the gates of heaven.
c) 1st ed. "The Bowl of Sâki" - 5th November.	To be really sorry for one's errors is like opening the doors of Heaven.

1st ed. "The Bowl of Sâki" - 6th November.	Our soul is blessed with the impression of the Glory of God whenever we praise Him.

Note: For Origin, elaborations and different versions see "The Bowl of Sâki" under 21st March.

---

a) Part of two sentences in Inayat Khan's address to mureeds at the first Service of the Church of All, London, 8th May 1921, on 'Prayer', in Joyce Burnett's handwriting.	and his progress can only be made through life, as a little child learns to walk. He falls a thousand times before he can stand, and so many times falls again when he begins to walk, and so we human beings, however wise and great, we are not more than the child before God.
b) The same sentences as under a), in an unidentified handwriting.	- - - - - - - - - - - etc. - - - - - - - - - - - - life_ as the little child learns to walk, falling _ thousand - - - - - - - - stand_ and after that falling again and again until at last he begins to walk, ___ so we are no more ___ ___ ___ ___ ___ than little children before ___ _ God,
c) A typewritten copy of the address on 'Prayer' - Religious Gatheka I no. 5.	and his progress through life can only be made as a little child learns to walk. The child falls a thousand times before he can stand, and so many times he falls again ___ ___ ___ ___ ___ when he begins to walk. We human beings are not more than the child before God.
d) 1st ed. "The Bowl of Sâki" - 7th November.	As a ___ child learning to walk_ ___ ___ falls a thousand times

Cont. d)

ORIGIN and elaborations:	DIFFERENT VERSIONS:
Cont. d) First part a) omitted.	before he can stand, and after that __ falls again and again until at last he can walk, so are we as little children before God.

---

a) A sentence in the address on 'Prayer', 8th May 1921, evening, in an unidentified handwriting, which could be a reporting.	Self denial is not renouncing of things, it is denying the self and the first lesson of self denial is humility.
b) A reporting of the same address by Joyce Burnett.	Self denying is not renouncing - Its first lesson is humility.
Add. in Gd.'s handwriting. (Cf. version a)).	- - - - - - - - - - - renouncing __ things, it is denying the self. Its - - - - - - - - - - - - - .
c) 1st ed. "The Bowl of Sâki" - 8th November.	Self-denial is not renouncing things, it is denying the self, and the first lesson of self-denial is humility.

1st ed. "The Bowl of Sâki" - 9th November.	The more elevated the soul, the broader the outlook.

Note: See "The Bowl of Sâki" under 3rd June.

---

a) Part of a sentence in the lecture 'Stilling the Mind', 1917-1920, reported and revised by Dr.Gruner as published in the book 'In an Eastern Rosegarden', 1st ed. 1920/1921.	Mastery lies not merely in stilling the mind, but in directing it towards whatever point you desire,
b) 1st ed. "The Bowl of Sâki" - 10th November.	Mastery lies not merely in stilling the mind, but in directing it towards whatever point you desire.

1st ed. "The Bowl of Sâki" - 11th November.	Our thoughts have prepared for us the happiness or unhappiness we experience.

Note: See "The Bowl of Sâki" under 14th June and cf. the saying under 23rd August.

No documents referring to the sayings under 12th - 15th November have been found in the archives to date.

<u>ORIGIN</u> and elaborations:	<u>DIFFERENT VERSIONS</u>:
1st ed. "The Bowl of Sâki" - 12th November.	When the mind and body are restless, nothing in life can be accomplished. Success is the result of control.
1st ed. "The Bowl of Sâki" - 13th November.	When speech is controlled, the eyes speak; the glance says what words can never say.
1st ed. "The Bowl of Sâki" - 14th November.	Words are but the shells of thoughts and feelings. 1)

Note 1): Cf. "The Bowl of Sâki" under 2nd June.

1st ed. "The Bowl of Sâki" - 15th November.	Wisdom is not in words, it is in understanding.

---

a) Part of a sentence in a lecture about 'The Message', 1921, as partly published in the pamphlet 'The Message', January 1922, and as in Gd.'s bookpreparation of 'The Unity of Religious Ideals'.	the Message is like a spring of water, it rises and falls, and makes its way by itself.
b) 1st ed. "The Bowl of Sâki" - 16th November.	<u>The</u> message <u>of God</u> is like a spring of water<u>:</u> it rises and falls, and makes its way by itself.

---

a) Part of a sentence in a lecture about 'The Message', 1921, as published in the pamphlet 'The Message', January 1922.	If the eyes and ears are open the leaves of the tree become as the pages of the Bible,
b) A typewritten copy of this sentence, found with Gd.'s bookpreparation of 'The Unity of Religious Ideals'.	- - - - - - - - - - - - - - -open<u>,</u> the leaves of the <u>trees</u> become - - etc.
c) 1st ed. "The Bowl of Sâki" - 17th November.	If the eyes and ears are open, the leaves of the trees become as ___ pages of the Bible<u>.</u>

---

a) A sentence in a lecture about 'The Message', 1921, as published in the pamphlet 'The Message', January 1922.	For the Soul of All is one Soul, and Truth is one Truth under whatever guise it may be hidden.
b) A typewritten copy of this sentence, found with	<u>because</u> the <u>s</u>oul of <u>a</u>ll is one <u>s</u>oul_ and Truth is one Truth under

Cont. b)

ORIGIN and elaborations:	DIFFERENT VERSIONS:
Cont. b) Gd.'s bookpreparation of 'The Unity of Religious Ideals'.	whatever religion it is hidden.
c) 1st ed. "The Bowl of Sâki" - 18th November.	___ The soul of all is one soul, and the Truth is One Truth, under whatever religion it is hidden.

No documents referring to the sayings under 19th and 20th November have been found in the archives to date.	
1st ed. "The Bowl of Sâki" - 19th November.	Narrowness is not necessarily devotion, but often appears so.
1st ed. "The Bowl of Sâki" - 20th November.	It is the soul's light which is natural intelligence.

---

a) A sentence in the lecture 'The Message', 13th January 1921, in Joyce Burnett's handwriting.	The wave is the sea itself, and yet when the sea rises in the form of a wave, it is the wave, and when you look at the whole it is the sea.
b) The same sentence as published in the pamphlet 'The Message' in January 1922.	- - - - - - - - - - - itself, ___ yet - - - - - - - - - - - - - - - - - - -of a wave_ it - - - - - - - - - - - - - you look at it as a part of the whole it is the sea.
c) 1st ed. "The Bowl of Sâki" - 21st November.	The wave is the sea itself; yet, when it rises in the form of a wave, it is the wave; and when you look at __ __ _ ____ __ the whole of it, it is the sea.

---

a) A sentence in a lecture 'The Message', 1921, in Joyce Burnett's handwriting. The same version was published in the pamphlet 'The Message', January 1922. It was also found in a passage with Gd.'s bookpreparation of 'The Unity of Religious Ideals'.	It is not the solid wood that can become a flute, it is the empty reed.
b) 1st ed. "The Bowl of Sâki" - 22nd November.	It is not the solid wood that can become a flute, it is the empty reed.

ORIGIN and elaborations:	DIFFERENT VERSIONS:
1st ed. "The Bowl of Sâki" - 23rd November.	Reason is learned from the everchanging world; but true knowledge comes from the essence of life.

Note: For complete elaborations and different versions, see Sayings I: "Gayan" - Bola 229.

---

a) Part of a sentence in the lecture 'Prayer', 8th May 1921, evening, in Joyce Burnett's handwriting.	And in reality, God is within you and as He is within you, you are the instrument of God and through you God experiences the external world,
b) As under a), in an unidentified handwriting.	___ In reality_ God is within you, and - - - - - - - - - - - - - - - etc.
c) 1st ed. "The Bowl of Sâki" - 24th November.	__ _______ God is within you. ___ __ __ __ _____ ___ _ You are His instrument; and through you He expresses Himself to the external world.

---

a) Part of a sentence in the lecture 'Prayer', 8th May 1921, evening, in Joyce Burnett's and in an unidentified handwriting.	it is according to the extent of your consciousness of prayer, that your prayer reaches God.
b) 1st ed. "The Bowl of Sâki" - 25th November.	It is according to the extent of our consciousness of prayer_ that our prayer reaches God.

---

a) A sentence in the lecture 'Truth', 13th May 1921, in Nuria Best's handwriting.	So the heart that should be empty to receive the knowledge, is occupied by the knowledge that one has acquired.
b) As under a), in Miss R.Jones's handwriting.	so the heart that should be open and ready to receive the knowledge_ is occupied by the learning ___ one has acquired.
c) 1st ed. "The Bowl of Sâki" - 26th November.	__ The heart ____ must be empty in order to receive the knowledge of God. ___ ___ ___ ___ ___ ___ ___ ___

No documents referring to the sayings under 27th - 30th November have been found in the archives to date.

ORIGIN and elaborations:	DIFFERENT VERSIONS:
1st ed. "The Bowl of Sâki" - 27th November.	As long as in love there is "You" and "Me", love is not fully kindled.
1st ed. "The Bowl of Sâki" - 28th November.	Once you have given up your limited self willingly to the Unlimited, you will rejoice so much in that consciousness that you will not care to be small again.
1st ed. "The Bowl of Sâki" - 29th November.	The deeper your prayers echo in your own consciousness, the more audible they are to God.
1st ed. "The Bowl of Sâki" - 30th November.	It is the depth of thought that is powerful, and sincerity of feeling which creates atmosphere.

No documents referring to the sayings under 1st, 2nd and 3rd December have been found in the archives to date.

1st ed. "The Bowl of Sâki" - 1st December.	The higher you rise, the wider becomes the margin of your view.
1st ed. "The Bowl of Sâki" - 2nd December.	Justice can never be developed while we judge others. The only way is by constantly judging ourselves.

Cf. Sangathas II-40: Saluk, first sentence: 'Justice is developed by judging one's own actions, not those of others'.

1st ed. "The Bowl of Sâki" - 3rd December.	Joy and sorrow are the light and shade of life. Without light and shade no picture is clear.

---

a) MS. Sr., dated 1921, and a typewritten copy with sayings, mostly meant for publication in the "Gayan" (Gd.'s bookpreparation).	Saying. The wise submits to conditions when he is helpless, bowing to the will of God; but the evil that is avoidable he roots out without sparing one single moment or effort.
b) 1st ed. "The Bowl of Sâki" - 4th December.	The wise <u>man</u> submits to conditions when he <u>is</u> helpless, bowing to the will of God<u>.</u> <u>B</u>ut the evil that is avoidable h<u>e</u> roots out without sparing one single moment or effort.

---

a) Notebooks 1921 :	Saying. Enviable is he who loveth and asketh for no return.

b)

ORIGIN and elaborations:	DIFFERENT VERSIONS:
b) For complete elaborations and different versions, see Sayings I: "Gayan" - Sura 18.	
c) 1st ed. "The Bowl of Sâki" - 5th December.	Enviable is he who loveth and asketh ___ no return.

---

a) Notebooks 1921 :	Saying. To deny the changeableness of life is as fancying a motionless sea, which can only exist in one's imagination.
b) MS. Sr.	Saying. - is like fancying - - - - - - - etc.
c) A typewritten copy of sayings, mostly meant for publication in the "Gayan" (Gd.'s book-preparation).	Saying. To deny the ~~changeableness~~ changeability of life - - - - - - - - - - etc.
d) 1st ed. "The Bowl of Sâki" - 6th December.	To deny the changeableness of life is like fancying a motionless sea, which can only exist in one's imagination.

---

a) Notebooks 1921 :	Saying. Learn) Live) a true life and you will know the truth.
b) For complete elaborations and different versions, see Sayings I: "Gayan" - Bola 130.	
c) 1st ed. "The Bowl of Sâki" - 7th December.	Learn to live a true life and you will know the Truth.

1st ed. "The Bowl of Sâki" - 8th December.	Wisdom is attained in solitude.

Note: For complete elaborations see Sayings I: "Gayan" - Bola 248.

---

a) Notebooks 1921 :	Saying. The seeming death is the real birth of the soul.
b) For complete elaborations and different versions, see Sayings I: "Gayan" - Chala 96.	

c)

ORIGIN and elaborations:	DIFFERENT VERSIONS:
c) 1st ed. "The Bowl of Sâki" - 9th December.	The seeming death of the body is the real birth of the soul.

---

a) Copied by Gd. from (?). Inayat Khan add. 'Saying' over it.	Saying. As the rose blooms amidst thorns, so the great souls shine out through all oppositions.
b) A typewritten copy of sayings, mostly meant for publication in the "Gayan" (Gd.'s book-preparation).	Saying. - - - - - - - - - - - - - .
c) 1st ed. "The Bowl of Sâki" - 10th December.	As the rose blooms amidst thorns, so ___ great souls shine out through all opposition.

---

a) Notebooks 1921 :	Saying. When the artist loses himself in his art, it is then that his art comes to life.
b) Copied by Gd. from (?).	Saying. - - - - - - - - - - - - - - - - - - - art_ __ __ then ____ the art comes - - - .
c) A typewritten copy with sayings, mostly meant for publication in the "Gayan" (Gd.'s book-preparation).	Saying. - art, then - - - - - - - - - - - - etc.
d) 1st ed. "The Bowl of Sâki" - 11th December.	When the artist loses himself in his art, then the art comes to life.

Cf. Sayings I: "Gayan" - Chala 31.

---

a) Notebooks 1921 :	Saying. Do not do anything with fear, and fear not whatever you do. Fear not whatever you do. Do not do what you are afraid of doing.
b) MS. Sr., dated 1921. First version a).	______ Do not do anything with fear_ and fear not whatever you do.
c) Copied by Gd. Inayat Khan add. 'Saying' over it.	Saying. - - - - - - - - - - - - - - fear, and fear not, whatever you do.
d) 1st ed. "The Bowl of Sâki" - 12th December.	Do not __ anything with fear; and fear not_ whatever you do.

ORIGIN and elaborations:	DIFFERENT VERSIONS:
a) Notebooks 1921 :	Saying. Love develops into the harmony and in the harmony is born beauty.
b) See for complete elaborations: Sayings I, "Gayan" - Bola 200.	
c) 1st ed. "The Bowl of Sâki" - 13th December.	Love develops into ___ harmony, and of ___ harmony is born beauty.

---

a) Notebooks 1921 :	Saying. Who keeps no secrets has no depth in his heart. Saying. The heart that cannot keep secret is like a vessel upside down.
b) For complete elaborations and different versions, see Sayings I - "Gayan" - Bola 247.	
c) 1st ed. "The Bowl of Sâki" - 14th December.	He who keeps no secrets has no depth in his heart.

1st ed. "The Bowl of Sâki" - 15th December.	Behind us all is One Spirit and One Life; how then can we be happy if our neighbour is not also happy.

Note: For complete elaborations and different versions, see Sayings I: "Gayan" - Bola 123.

---

a) Some sentences in the lecture 'What the Mystic wants to attain', 11th June 1921, in M.elle Lefèbvre's handwriting (a reporting of the simultaneous translation in French) and annotations in English, made by Sr.	Miracle of Christ, walking on the water. in Sanscrit life is pictured as a sea always making waves, you can never stop it. Everyone is trying to stop the waves = intoxication = bewilderment
b) Copied by Gd. together with other sentences from lectures, mostly meant for publication in the "Gayan".	The sea of life is continually in motion, no-one can stop its unending waves. The Master walks over the waves, while the wise swims in the water, but the ignorant is drowned in his effort to cross.
c) 1st ed. "The Bowl of Sâki" - 16th December.	The sea of life is in constant motion, no one can stop its ever-moving

Cont. c)

ORIGIN and elaborations:	DIFFERENT VERSIONS:
Cont. c)	waves. The Master walks over the waves. _____ The wise man swims in the water, but the ignorant man is drowned in his effort to cross.

Cf. Gatha Symbology (Nakshi Bandi) III-3: 'Christ walking on the water', 4th May 1921.

ORIGIN and elaborations:	DIFFERENT VERSIONS:
a) A sentence in the lecture 'The Privilege of being human', 20th June 1921 (Social Gatheka no. 17) of which fragments were reported by Sr. This lecture was also found in Gd.'s handwriting and may well be a reporting.	But man's greatest privilege in life is to become a suitable instrument of God.
b) Copied by Gd. together with other sentences from lectures, mostly meant for publication in the "Gayan".	Man's greatest privilege __ ____ is to become - - - - - - - - etc.
c) 1st ed. "The Bowl of Sâki" - 17th December.	___ Man's greatest privilege is to become a suitable instrument of God.

ORIGIN and elaborations:	DIFFERENT VERSIONS:
a) A sentence in the lecture 'The Privilege of being human', 20th June 1921 (Social Gatheka no. 16) of which fragments were reported by Sr. and a copy was found in Gd.'s handwriting, probably a reporting.	The trees in the forest await that blessing
b) Copied by Gd. together with other sentences from lectures, mostly meant for publication in the "Gayan".	The trees of the forest silently await God's blessing.
c) 1st ed. "The Bowl of Sâki" - 18th December.	The trees of the forest silently await God's blessing.

ORIGIN and elaborations:	DIFFERENT VERSIONS:
a) MS. Sr., dated 1921.	The plain truth is too simple for the seeker after complexity who looks for things that he cannot understand.
b) Copied by Gd. together with other sentences from lectures, mostly	Saying. -complexity, who

Cont. b)

ORIGIN and elaborations:	DIFFERENT VERSIONS:
Cont. b) meant for publication in the "Gayan".	- etc.
c) Copied by Ng.	____ - - who is looking for things ____ he - etc.
d) 1st ed. "The Bowl of Sâki" - 19th December.	The plain truth is too simple for the seeker after complexity, who is looking for things he cannot understand.

---

a) A sentence in a lecture of 1921 of which Sr. made annotations.	Often man impresses himself with a failure, he says my life was a failure and he denies always something that is different from failure, the success.
b) Copied by Gd. together with other sentences from lectures, mostly meant for publication in the "Gayan".	Saying. An unsuccessful man often keeps away success by the impression of his former failure.
c) 1st ed. "The Bowl of Sâki" - 20th December.	An unsuccessful man often keeps success away by the impression of his former failures.

---

a) A sentence in the lecture 'The Privilege of being human', 20th June 1921 (Social Gatheka no. 16) of which fragments were reported by Sr.	Man himself is the tree of desire and the root of that tree is in his heart.
A copy in Gd.'s handwriting, probably a reporting.	it is man himself who is the tree of his desire and the root of the tree is in the heart of man.
b) Copied by Gd. together with other sentences from lectures, mostly meant for publication in the "Gayan".	Saying. __ Man himself ___ is the tree of desire and the root of that tree is __ his heart. __ ___
c) 1st ed. "The Bowl of Sâki" - 21st December.	Man himself is the tree of desire, and the root of that tree is in his own heart.

1st ed. "The Bowl of Sâki" - 22nd December.	With goodwill and trust in God, self-confidence, and a hopeful attitude towards life, a man can always win his battle, however difficult.

Note)

ORIGIN and elaborations:	DIFFERENT VERSIONS:

Note: For complete elaborations and different versions, see Sayings I: "Gayan" - Chala 168.

---

a) Three sentences in the lecture 'The Journey to the Goal', 1917-1920, reported and revised by Dr.Gruner as published in the book 'In an Eastern Rosegarden', 1st ed. 1920/1921.	These four are diverse paths! And each considers his own the best and wisest. Let each choose the way that belongs to his own temperament
b) 1st ed. "The Bowl of Sâki" - 23rd December.	There ____ are many paths, and each man considers his own the best and wisest. Let each one choose that ___ which belongs to his own temperament.

---

a) A sentence in the lecture 'The Journey to the Goal', 1917-1920, reported and revised by Dr.Gruner as published in the book 'In an Eastern Rosegarden', 1st ed. 1920/1921.	Failure means that there has been lack of self-control - whether it be a failure in affairs or in health.
b) 1st ed. "The Bowl of Sâki" - 24th December.	Failure, either in health or affairs, means there has been lack of self-control.

---

a) Two sentences in the lecture 'The Journey to the Goal', 1917-1920, reported and revised by Dr.Gruner as published in the book 'In an Eastern Rosegarden', 1st ed. 1920/1921.	Love is the water of the Ganges. It is in itself a purification.
b) 1st ed. "The Bowl of Sâki" - 25th December.	Love is as the water of the Ganges; it is in itself a purification.

---

a) Two sentences in the lecture 'The Presence of God', 1917-1920, reported and revised by Dr.Gruner as published in the book 'In an Eastern Rosegarden', 1st ed. 1920/1921.	Life is unlimited and it wants a scope to expand and rise. Without that scope, life is unhappy.

b)

ORIGIN and elaborations:	DIFFERENT VERSIONS:
b) 1st ed. "The Bowl of Sāki" - 26th December.	Love is unlimited, but it needs _ scope to expand and rise; without that scope_ life is unhappy.
a) Part of a sentence in the lecture 'The Presence of God', 1917-1920, reported and revised by Dr.Gruner as published in the book 'In an Eastern Rosegarden', 1st ed. 1920/1921.	and every wave, as it rises upward, seems to be stretching its hands upward as if to say "take me up, take me up, higher and higher".
b) 1st ed. "The Bowl of Sāki" - 27th December.	__ Every wave of the sea, as it rises ______, seems to be stretching its hands upwards, as if to say _take me up_ ____ __ __ _ higher and higher_.
a) From a lecture, "The Will, Human and Divine", 24 Oct. 1919, published in 'In an Eastern Rosegarden", 1920/1921.	True pleasure lies in the sharing of joy with another.
b. 1st ed. "The Bowl of Sāki" - 28th December.	True pleasure lies in the sharing of joy with another.
a) Two sentences in the lecture 'Gain and Loss', 1917-1920, reported and revised by Dr.Gruner as published in the book 'In an Eastern Rosegarden', 1st ed. 1920/1921.	The gain or loss which is momentary is not real. If we knew the realities we should never grieve over the loss of any things which experience shows to be only of transient character.
b) 1st ed. "The Bowl of Sāki" - 29th December.	A gain or loss which is momentary is not real; if we knew ___ realities we should never grieve over the loss of anything_ which experience shows to be only transitory.
a) A sentence in the lecture 'The Spiritual Hierarchy, 1917-1920, reported and revised by Dr.Gruner as published in the book 'In an Eastern. Rosegarden', 1st ed. 1920/1921.	The soul is as great as the circle of its influence.

b)

ORIGIN and elaborations:	DIFFERENT VERSIONS:
b) 1st ed. "The Bowl of Sâki" - 30th December.	A soul is as great as the circle of its influence.

Cf. the lecture 'On Spheres', 1920, parts of which were published in the Magazine 'Sufi' of October 1920.

ORIGIN and elaborations:	DIFFERENT VERSIONS:
a) A sentence in the lecture 'The Presence of God', 1917-1920, reported and revised by Dr.Gruner as published in the book 'In an Eastern Rosegarden', 1st ed. 1920/1921.	Happiness only lies in thinking or doing that which one considers beautiful.
b) 1st ed. "The Bowl of Sâki" - 31st December.	Happiness ____ lies in thinking or doing that which one considers beautiful.

P A R T   T W O

HITHERTO UNPUBLISHED SAYINGS.

INTRODUCTION TO PART TWO.

This part consists of hitherto unpublished[1)] sayings and other words of Inayat Khan, found in the manuscripts mentioned hereafter and grouped together in the following way:

sayings 1 - 35[a],	from Inayat Khan's Notebooks, with elaborations in the handwriting of one or several mureeds and classified by Inayat Khan;
sayings 36 - 50,	from MSS. or copied texts, with elaborations in the handwriting of one or several mureeds and classified by Inayat Khan;
sayings 51 - 120,	from Inayat Khan's Notebooks, with elaborations in the handwriting of one or several mureeds but not classified by Inayat Khan;
sayings 121 - 440,	from Inayat Khan's Notebooks and his notes on loose papers; no elaborations, no classification;
sayings 441 - 517,	from MSS. or copied texts, with elaborations in the handwriting of one or several mureeds but not classified by Inayat Khan.

Note 1): An exception was made for the sayings nrs. 508, 509 and 510, which were added to the Bolas (after Bola 61) in later editions of the "Nirtan". They are not found in the original "Nirtan" published by Kismet Stam, nor in the edition published by the Sufi Movement. (See Sayings I: Preface, pages XII/XIII) Another exception was made for some sayings published in old Sufi Magazines and pamphlets which are no longer available, and for one saying quoted by Ng. in her book 'The Way of Return'. These publications are mentioned with the saying in the left column.

A number of sayings are to be found in published lectures as e.g. in the book 'In an Eastern Rose-garden'. In such cases the sentences, when published, had not yet been turned into a saying and therefore are considered to be 'hitherto unpublished' as sayings.

ORIGIN and elaborations:	DIFFERENT VERSIONS:
1. a) Notebooks :	Saying. The artist does not imitate nature, he improves upon it.
b) MS. Gd.	Saying. - - - - - - - - - not only imitate nature_ but he - - - - - - - -.
c) Copied by Km.	Saying. - nature, but he - - - - - - - -.
d) Copied by Ek. and classified by Inayat Khan as 'Bol', meant for publication in the "Gayan".	Bola. - - - - - - - - - - - - - - .
Alteration, probably in Mc.'s handwriting.	The artist ____ not only imitates nature, but he improves upon it.

ORIGIN and elaborations:	DIFFERENT VERSIONS:
2. a) Notebooks, probably of 1922 :	Bola. Once blessed is always blessed and once cursed is cursed for ever.
b) MS. Sk. (in shorthand and longhand), dated Summer 1922. Copied by Km.	Bola. - - - - - - - - - - - - - - .
c) Copied by Sh. and classified by Inayat Khan as 'Bol', meant to be published in the "Gayan".	Bola. - - - - - - - - - - - - - - .

ORIGIN and elaborations:	DIFFERENT VERSIONS:
3. a) Notebooks :	Saying. What you cannot afford to do you must not do.
b) MS. Fm. Inayat Khan crossed out 'Bola' and wrote 'Saying' beside it, also altering the first part of the sentence.	Bola. - - - - - - - - - - - - - - do, you - - - - - - -. ~~Bola~~ Saying. What you are not able to do, you - - - - - - -.
c) Copied by Km.	Saying. - - - - - - - - - - - - - - .
d) Copied by Sh. and classified by Inayat Khan as 'Chal', meant for publication in the "Gayan".	Chala. - - - - - - - - - - - - - - .
Mc. changed the sequence of the two parts of the sentence.	You must not do what you are not able to do.

ORIGIN and elaborations:	DIFFERENT VERSIONS:
4. a) Notebooks :	Dust atoms. We are the fairies of the earth,

Cont. a)

ORIGIN and elaborations:	DIFFERENT VERSIONS:
Cont. a)	in the air we always fly, We shine in the bright day light, when the stars are hidden in the sky. We are the atoms of the dust, in the search of light we rise. We partake light from the sun, and give out as do the wise.
b) Copied by Gd. from (?). Not in the form of a poem as under a).	Alankara. (Notes) - fly_ and shine - - - - - - - - - -day light_ when - - - - - - - - - - - - - - - - - -. We are ___ specks of ___ dust_ in ___ search of light we rise, we partake light from the sun_ and give - - - - - - - - - - - - - - .
c) Copied by Km. as under b), only a comma added after 'dust'.	Alankara. (Notes) - - - - - - - - - - - - - - - - - etc. - - - - - - - - - - - - - - of dust, in - - - - - - - - - - - - - - - - - etc.
d) Copied by Sh. and classified by Inayat Khan as 'Alankar', meant for publication in the "Gayan".	Alankara. ___ - - - - - - - - - - - - - - - - - etc. - - - - - - - - - - - - - - of dust_ in - - - - - - - - - - - - - - - - - etc.
Some alterations in Mc.'s handwriting.	We are the fairies of the earth; in the air we always fly; and we shine in the bright day light, when the stars are hidden in the sky; we are specks of dust floating in space __ rise_ and __ partake of light from the sun and we give ___ as do the wise.
Underneath this altered text Inayat Khan wrote the following lines, again in the form of a poem and without punctuation marks.	We are specks of dust ~~in-search-of-the-light~~ toward the sun we rise ~~and-we-partake-of-light-from-the-sun~~ And give out as do the wise We partake and reflect light as always have done the wise.

5.

a) Notebooks 1921 :	Saying. Do not resist evil. A good person can never succeed in competing with the wicked, for the destructive power of evil destroys quicker than the constructive power of good can build.
b) MS. Ng.	Saying. - - - - - - - - - - - - - - succeed when competing with the wicked; for - - - - - - - - - - - - - - -evil works quicker - - - - - - - - - - - - - - - of good. ___ ___ Cont. b)

ORIGIN and elaborations:	DIFFERENT VERSIONS:
Cont. b)	(__ Resist not evil 1))
	Note 1): an illegible abbreviation in Ng.'s handwriting after 'evil'.
c) Copied by Km. without the sentence between brackets.	Saying. - - - - - - - - - - - - - - .
d) Copied by Ek. and classified by Inayat Khan as 'Tal', meant for publication in the "Gayan".	Tala. - - - - - - - - - - - - - - .
One alteration in Mc.'s handwriting.	- - - - - - - - - - - - -evil works more quickly than the constructive - - - - - - - - - - .

6.

a) Notebooks :	Bola. Friend is a friend first and last.
b) MS. Fm. Copied by Km.	Bola. - - - - - - - - - - - - - - .
c) Copied by Gd.	____ - - - - - - - - - - - - - - .
d) Copied by Sh. and classified by Inayat Khan as 'Bol', meant for publication in the "Gayan".	Bola. - - - - - - - - - - - - - - .
Then crossed out, most probably by Mc.	

7.

a) Notebooks 1921 :	Saying. Friendship is more secure when friends keep distance.
b) MSS. Mf. and Zr. Copied by Km.	Saying. Friendship is ____ secure ____ ______ ____ at a distance.
c) Copied by Ek. and classified by Inayat Khan as 'Bol', meant for publication in the "Gayan".	Bola. - - - - - - - - - - - - - - .

8.

a) Notebooks 1921 :	Saying. As difficult it is to keep friendship, so easy it is to break it.
b) Copied by Km. from (?).	Saying. __ It is difficult to make a real friendship, and it is easy to break it.
c) Copied by Ek. and classified by Inayat Khan as 'Tal', meant for publication in the "Gayan".	Tala. - - - - - - - - - - - - - - .

d)

ORIGIN and elaborations:	DIFFERENT VERSIONS:
d) A typewritten copy together with other sayings (Gd.'s book-preparation for the Gayan, with corr. by Inayat Khan and some notes by Gd. (The heading "Gayan" is written by Gd.). Inayat Khan wrote in the margin: 'two sayings'.	It is easy to tie a knot of attachment, but it is difficult when you wish to unravel it.1) It is difficult to create a real friendship_ and it is easy to break it.

Note 1): see Sayings I: "Gayan" - Tala 29.

9.

a) Notebooks 1921 :	Saying. Heathen- You cannot love the God of reality, you can only love the God you make.
b) MS. Sr. Copied by Km.	Heathen Saying. - you have made.
c) Copied by Ek. and classified by Inayat Khan as 'Bol', meant for publication in the "Gayan".	Bola. - - - - - - - - - - - - - - .

10.

a) Notebooks :	Grass blades, why do you stand shoulder to shoulder? In defence against the invasion of the sweeping wind.
b) MS. Sd.	Tana. Grassblades, why do you stand side by side? Answer: in defence against the invasion by the sweeping wind.
c) Copied by Gd.	Tana. Blades of grass, - - - - - - - - - Answer. In defence against ___ invasion - - - - - - - - - - - .
d) Copied by Sh. and classified by Inayat Khan as 'Tan or Verna', meant for publication in the "Gayan". Version as under b).	Tana. - - - - - - - - - - - - - - .
Mc. crossed out two words.	Grassblades, - - - - - - - - - - side? ______ _ in defence against ___ invasion by the sweeping wind.

11.

a) Notebook 1914/1915 :	A welcome visitor in the house 1) gives more joy (comfort) than a beautiful furniture.

ORIGIN and elaborations:	DIFFERENT VERSIONS:
	Note 1): the four preceding words are not very clearly legible in the notebook.
b) MS. Gr. Copied by Km.	Saying. A welcome guest in the house gives more comfort than _ beautiful furniture.
c) Copied by Ek. and classified by Inayat Khan as 'Chal', meant for publication in the "Gayan".	Chala. - - - - - - - - - - - - - - .
d) A typewritten copy which seems to be Gd.'s book-preparation of the "Gayan".	Bola. - - - - - - - - - - - - - - .

12.

a) Notebooks :	Saying. It is the hungry who really enjoy food.
b) MS. Fm.	Bola. It is the hungry, who _____ enjoy food.
Inayat Khan crossed out 'Bola' and wrote 'Saying' instead, and altered the sentence a little.	~~Bola.~~ Saying. __ __ The hungry_ ___ can enjoy food.
c) Copied by Km.	Bola. - - - - - - - - - - - - - - .
d) Copied by Sh. and classified by Inayat Khan as 'Bol', meant for publication in the "Gayan".	Bola. - - - - - - - - - - - - - - .
Two words were added in Mc.'s handwriting.	The hungry can alone fully enjoy food.

13.

a) Notebooks :	Alankara. My kindness, thy beautiful countenance seldom changeth into the face of a witch.
b) Copied by Ng. from (?).	Alankara. My kindness; - - - - - - - - - - - - - - - - - - -changeth __to the face of a horrible witch.
c) Copied by Ek. and classified by Inayat Khan as 'Alankar', meant for publication in the "Gayan".	Alankara. - - - - - - - - - - - - - - .

ORIGIN and elaborations:	DIFFERENT VERSIONS:
14.	
Notebooks :	My kindness, often on thy return thy beautiful countenance changeth into the face of a witch.

ORIGIN and elaborations:	DIFFERENT VERSIONS:
15.	
a) Notebooks 1921 :	Saying. Bola. All that covers man's eyes from reality is forbidden.
b) MS. Sr. Copied by Kf.	_____ ____ - - - - - - - - - - - - - - .
c) MS. Gd. Inayat Khan wrote 'Bola' over it.	Bola. - - - - - - - - - - - - - - .
d) Copied by Mt. and classified by Inayat Khan as 'Sur', meant for publication in the "Gayan".	Sura. - - - - - - - - - - - - - - .
In Mc.'s handwriting was written underneath	All that covers reality from man's eyes is forbidden.
e) A typewritten copy with sayings meant for publication in the "Gayan" (Gd.'s bookpreparation): first version under d).	Bola. - - - - - - - - - - - - - - .

ORIGIN and elaborations:	DIFFERENT VERSIONS:
16.	
a) Notebooks 1922 :	It is better that a mistake is found out before it is made than after.
b) MS. Sk. dated Summer 1922, in shorthand and her transcription of it.	Saying. A mistake rather be realised before than after it is made.
c) In Sk.'s handwriting (version a), with a reference to the version in shorthand as under b).	Saying. It is better that a mistake is found out before it is made than after.
d) The two sentences were copied by Sk.	Saying. A mistake rather be realised before than after it is made. It is better that a mistake is found out before it is made than after.
Sk. crossed out the word 'rather' in the first sentence, and inserted it after 'realised'.	A mistake ~~rather~~ be realised rather before than after it is made.
Mc. crossed out the first sentence and wrote 'duplicated' in the margin.	
e) Second version d) copied by Km.	Saying. - is made, than after.

f)

ORIGIN and elaborations:	DIFFERENT VERSIONS:
f) Copied by Sh. and classified by Inayat Khan as 'Chal', meant for publication in the "Gayan".	Chala. - - - - - - - - - - - - - -
Alterations in Mc.'s handwriting.	It is better to find out a mistake before it is made, than afterwards.

---

17. a) Notebooks 1922 :	Saying. The slightest mistake in time would turn into a greatest folly as a small hole in a garment soon becomes a large hole.
b) Copied by Ek. from (?).	Saying. The slightest mistake would - - - - - - - - - - - - - - - -folly in time as a small hole in the garment would turn in time into a large one.
c) Copied by Km.	Saying. - time, as - - - - - - - - - - - - - - - - etc.
Altered by Inayat Khan.	- -garment would ____ in time become _ large ___.
d) Copied by Sh. and classified by Inayat Khan as 'Chal', meant for publication in the "Gayan"-	Chala. - - - - - - - - - - - - - - - - .
Changed in Mc.'s handwriting.	The slightest mistake if not corrected will in time turn into the greatest folly just as a small tear in a garment enlarges if not mended.

---

18. a) Notebooks 1921 :	Tana. Cruel orchids, how could you eat your admirer? Beauty always lives on its lover's life.
b) Copied by Ng. from (?). Underneath her copy is written in Sk.'s handwriting: 'different in Gayan'. Copied by Km.	Tana. How could you _____ orchid _ feed upon your admirer? "Beauty ______ lives on its lover's life."
c) Copied by Ek. and classified by Inayat Khan as 'Tan or Verna', meant for publication in the "Gayan".	Tana. - - - - - - - - - - - - - - - - .
Mc. put 'Orchid' between	How could you, Orchid, feed - etc.

Cont. c)

ORIGIN and elaborations:	DIFFERENT VERSIONS:
Cont. c) commas.	

19.

a) Notebooks :	Saying. You will attract ~~the-world~~ people by smiling and will frighten them away by ~~weeping~~ sighing.
b) Copied by Ng. from (?).	Tala. - smiling, but will - - - - - - etc.
c) Copied by Ek. and classified by Inayat Khan as 'Tal', meant for publication in the "Gayan".	Tala. - - - - - - - - - - - - - - .

20.

a) Notebooks :	A good person without good manner is like an uncut diamond.
b) Copied by Ng. from (?). Copied by Km.	Saying. - - - - - - - - without a good - etc.
c) Copied by Ek. and classified by Inayat Khan as 'Chal', meant for publication in the "Gayan".	Chala. - - - - - - - - - - - - - - .
Two alterations in Mc.'s handwriting.	- - - - - - - - without _ good manners is like - - - - - - - .

21.

a) Notebooks :	Saying. The greatest problem of the world will be solved from the day, when woman will no longer be man's own property and man will not be counted among woman's belongings.
b) MS. Ng. Copied by Km.	Saying. - solved on the day_ when the woman will not ______ be man's own property, and - - - - - - - etc.
c) Copied by Ek. and classified by Inayat Khan as 'Chal', meant for publication in the "Gayan".	Chala. - - - - - - - - - - - - - - .
Changed in Mc.'s handwriting.	- -be solved __ ___ ___ when a woman will not be considered a man's ___ property, and when a man - etc.

22.

a) Notebooks 1922 :	Saying. The good reputation begins as a bud

Cont. a)

ORIGIN and elaborations:	DIFFERENT VERSIONS:
Cont. a)	and blooms as a rose.
b) Copied by Gd. from (?), and copied by Km.	Saying. ___ Good - - - - - - - - - - - - etc.
c) Copied by Sh. and classified by Inayat Khan as 'Chal', meant for publication in the "Vadan".	Chala. - - - - - - - - - - - - - - .
Mc. added 'A' to it.	A good - - - - - - - - - - - - - - etc.

23.

a) Notebooks :	Tala. What is said is said, what is done is done.
b) MS. Zr.	Tala. - - - - - - - - - - - - - - .
	Tala. What has been has been, what will be will be.
c) Copied by Ng. as one Tala.	Tala. What is said is said, what is done is done, what has been has been, and what will be will be.
d) Copied by Ek. and classified by Inayat Khan as 'Tal'. Probably meant for publication in the "Gayan".	Tala. - - - - - - - - - - - - - - .

24.

a) Notebooks :	The sea : What does thou bring that maketh me so intoxicated? The sea : What givest me thou that maketh me so intoxicated. Wind (smilingly) : Wine.
b) Copied by Ek. from (?) and classified by Inayat Khan as 'Tan or Verna', meant for publication in the "Vadan" or "Gayan".	Tana. The sea : What givest thou me that maketh me so intoxicated? The wind, (smiling__) _ Wine.
Mc. altered the punctuation marks.	- The wind_ _smiling_ _"Wine"_.

25.

a) Notebooks 1922 :	Saying. When selfinterest causes you to do a deed of beneficence, its virtue vanishes.
b) Copied by Ek. from (?), and copied by Km.	_______ - - - - - - - - - - - - - - .
c) Copied by Ek. and classified by Inayat Khan	Sura. - - - - - - - - - - - - - - .

Cont. c)

ORIGIN and elaborations:	DIFFERENT VERSIONS:
Cont. c) as 'Sur', meant for publication in the "Gayan".	

26.

a) Notebooks :	Saying. Sins of the youth pursue man to his grave.
b) Copied by Ek. from (?).	Saying. The sins of the youth often pursue man to his grave.
c) Copied by Km. and a typewritten copy with sayings (Gd.'s book-preparation of the "Gayan".)	Saying. The sins of his youth - - - - etc.
d) Copied by Ek. and classified by Inayat Khan as 'Sur', meant for publication in the "Gayan".	Sura. The sins of the youths often pursue man to his grave.
Mc. crossed out one word.	- - - - -of ___ youths - - - etc.

27.

a) Notebooks 1922 :	Saying. Stupidity is caused by inharmony in one's being and life.
b) Copied by Ek. from (?).	Saying. - being or in one's life.
c) Copied by Km.	Saying. - - - - - - - - - - - - - - .
Inayat Khan crossed out the last four words.	Stupidity is caused by inharmony in one's being __ __ ____ ____.
d) Copied by Ek. and classified by Inayat Khan as 'Chal', meant for publication in the "Gayan".	Chala. - - - - - - - - - - - - - - .
In Mc.'s handwriting the saying was crossed out and replaced. Then she wrote in the margin: 'Omit'.	Stupidity is nothing but the result of the lack of inharmony in one's being.

28.

a) Notebooks 1921 :	Saying. To guard anything jealously one must certainly value it.
b) Copied by Gd. from (?). Inayat Khan added 'Saying' to it. Copied by Km.	Saying. - - - - - - - - - - - - - - .
c) Copied by Ek. and clas-	Bola.

Cont. c)

ORIGIN and elaborations:	DIFFERENT VERSIONS:
Cont. c) sified by Inayat Khan as 'Bol', meant for publication in the "Gayan".	- - - - - - - - - - - - - - .

29.

a) Notebooks 1922 :	Saying. Abstain from tyranny if you possess any power.
b) Copied by Gd. from (?).	Saying. - - - - - - - - - - - - - - .
c) Copied by Km.	Saying. Refrain from - - - - - - - - - etc.
d) A typewritten copy with sayings (Gd.'s book-preparation of the "Gayan").	Saying. - - - - - - - - - - - - - - .
e) Copied by Sh. and classified by Inayat Khan as 'Bol', meant for publication in the "Gayan".	Bola. - - - - - - - - - - - - - - .

30.

a) Notebook 19th April - 12th May 1923 :	Saying. A verse without a twist in it is like food without flavour.
b) Copied by Ng. from (?). (together with other sayings meant for publication in the "Gayan"). Copied by Km.	Saying. - - - - - - - - - - twist __ __ is like an unflavoured dish.
c) Copied by Ek. and classified by Inayat Khan as 'Chal', meant for publication in the "Gayan".	Chala. - - - - - - - - - - - - - - .
One word changed in Mc.'s handwriting.	- - - - - - - - - - - - - - - - - is like an unseasoned dish.

31.

a) Notebooks :	Tana. Waterlily, what are you? I am the soul of the water lake.
b) Copied by Ng. from (?). Underneath her copy is written in Sk.'s handwriting: 'different in Gayan'. Copied by Km.	Tana. Waterlily! What relation are you to this Lake? "I am its soul __ ___ ____ _".
c) Copied by Ek. and classified by Inayat Khan as 'Tan or Verna', meant for publication in the "Gayan".	Tana. Water-lily! - - - - - - - - - - etc.

Cf. Sayings I: "Gayan" - Tana 4.

ORIGIN and elaborations:	DIFFERENT VERSIONS:
32.	
a) Notebooks 1922 :	Saying. What passeth beyond words that the eyes can express.
b) MSS. Mf. and Zr.	Saying. - - - - - - - - - - - - - - - - - - - eyes ___ express.
In MS. Mf. Gd. crossed out one word.	What passeth ______ words - - etc.
c) Copied by Km.	Saying. - - - - - - - - - - - - - - .
d) Copied by Ek. and classified by Inayat Khan as 'Chal', meant for publication in the "Gayan".	Chala. - - - - - - - - - - - - - - .
Add. in Mc.'s handwriting.	What passes beyond words, that - etc.

Cf. Sayings II : Part Two no. 112.

ORIGIN and elaborations:	DIFFERENT VERSIONS:
33.	
a) Notebooks :	Saying. When the foolish offend it is a fault, but when the wise hurt another by their clever ways it is a sin.
b) Copied by Gd. from (?).	Saying. - - - - - - - - - -offends it is his fault_ but when the wise hurts another by his clever - - - - etc.
c) Copied by Km.	Saying. - - - - - - - - - - - - - - - - - - fault, but - - - - - - - - - - etc.
d) Copied by Ek. and classified by Inayat Khan as 'Bol', meant for publication in the "Gayan".	Bola. When the foolish offends, it is - etc.

ORIGIN and elaborations:	DIFFERENT VERSIONS:
34.	
a) Notebooks 1922 :	Saying. Tradition is that which time alone can make.
b) Copied by Ek. and copied by Km. A typewritten copy (Gd.'s bookpreparation of the "Gayan".)	Saying. - - - - - - - - - - - - - - .
c) Copied again by Ek. and classified by Inayat Khan as 'Sur', and also as 'Chal', meant for publication in the "Gayan".	Chala. - - - - - - - - - - - - - - . Sura. - - - - - - - - - - - - - - .
Mc. cancelled the saying under 'Chal' and wrote	

Cont. c)

ORIGIN and elaborations:	DIFFERENT VERSIONS:
Cont. c) 'duplicated' over it. Inayat Khan changed the whole saying, where it was found as 'Sur'.	Sura. Tradition has its own value and no learning wealth or power can make it except time.

35.

a) Notebooks :	Saying. The world will smile on your success and will laugh at your failure.
b) Copied by Ng. from (?).	Tala. - - - - - - - - - - - - - - .
c) Copied by Ek. and classified by Inayat Khan as 'Tal', together with other sayings, meant for publication in the "Gayan".	Tala. - - - - - - - - - - - - - - .

35A.

a) Notebooks 1921 :	Saying. It is wicked to pick holes in people. It is clever to see through the subtle ways.

Note: For complete elaborations and versions see Sayings I: "Gayan" - Tala 22.

36.

a) MS. Gd.	Saying. The profit that one makes by putting an honourable person in a helpless situation is as taking poison in the form of sweet.
b) Copied by Gd. and a typewritten copy with unclassified sayings, likely to be Gd.'s bookpreparation of the "Gayan" at an early stage.	______ The profit made by putting an honourable person in ~~a difficulty~~ straits is ~~like~~ ______ a poison ~~which there~~ in the form of a sweet.
c) Copied by Km.	Saying. - - - - - - - - - - - - - .
The first three words were crossed out and changed by Inayat Khan.	An advantage taken by putting - etc.
d) Copied by Ek. and classified by Inayat Khan as 'Sur', meant for publication in the "Gayan".	Sura. An advantage taken by putting an honourable person in straits is a poison in the form of a sweet.
Mc.'s suggestions.	- person into straits is like giving a poison - - - - - - .

ORIGIN and elaborations:	DIFFERENT VERSIONS:
37.	
a) Copied by Ek. from (?), and copied by Km.	Saying. There is no difficulty which cannot be surmounted.
b) Copied again by Ek. and classified by Inayat Khan as 'Bol', meant for publication in the "Gayan".	Bola. - - - - - - - - - - - - - .
The whole saying was crossed out by Mc., who wrote over it instead:	Every difficult problem has its solution.

ORIGIN and elaborations:	DIFFERENT VERSIONS:
38.	
a) MS. Mf.	Saying. Gifts of gab 1) is a sign of illuminated soul.
The first three words were crossed out by Gd., who replaced them by the word 'eloquence'.	Eloquence is a - - - - - - - - - etc.
b) MS. Zr.	Saying. Gift of gab is a sign of an illuminated soul.
c) Copied by Km. (the altered version under a)).	Eloquence is the sign of the illuminated soul.
d) Copied by Ek. and classified by Inayat Khan as 'Bol', meant for publication in the "Gayan".	Bola. - - - - - - - - - - - - - .

Note 1): The 'gift of the gab' is an existing colloquial expression for 'much talking' (Oxford Dict.).

ORIGIN and elaborations:	DIFFERENT VERSIONS:
39.	
a) MS. Zr.	Saying. To defend ourselves from our folly is as hoarding our fault in the safe of our heart, but admitting our error is like throwing it out.
b) Copied by Ng.	Saying. - - - - - - - - - - - - - .
c) Copied by Ek. and classified by Inayat Khan as 'Chal', meant for publication in the "Gayan".	Chala. -our faults in the safe of our own heart, - - - - - - etc.
In Mc.'s handwriting one word and a comma were altered.	- - - - - - - - - - - - - - - - - - -folly is like hoarding - - - - - - - - - - - - - - - -heart; but - - - - - - etc.

ORIGIN and elaborations:	DIFFERENT VERSIONS:
40.	
a) MS. Gr., over which	Tala.

Cont. a)

ORIGIN and elaborations:	DIFFERENT VERSIONS:
Cont. a) Inayat Khan added 'Tala'.	Avoid him who says he knoweth, and knoweth not; for he is a fool. Teach him who knoweth not, and admits that he knoweth not; for he is innocent. Honour him who knoweth, and says he knoweth not, for he is a Saint. Follow him who knoweth, and speaketh what you know not; for he is the ~~Messenger~~ Prophet.
b) Copied by Mt. and classified by Inayat Khan as 'Tal', meant for publication in the "Gayan".	Tala. Avoid him who saith he knoweth, and knoweth not, for he is a fool. Teach him who knoweth not, and confesseth that he knoweth not, for he is innocent. Honour him who knoweth_ and saith he knoweth not, for he is a saint. Follow him who knoweth, and speaketh what ye know not, for he is the prophet.
c) A typewritten copy of sayings under the heading 'Tala' II. (Gd.'s book-preparation for the "Gayan").	Tala. - - - - - - - - - - - - - .

41.

a) MS. Gr.	Bola. As life is full of thorns try to make of yourself a rose.
b) Copied by Kf.	__ Life is full of thorns, try and make __ yourself a rose.
c) Copied by Mt. and classified by Inayat Khan as 'Tal'. The saying was found in an envelope marked 'Tal' in Gujerati script; a number of sayings in that same envelope have 'Sur' written over them in Gujerati. The envelope marked 'Sur', in which originally these may have been put, was found empty.	Tala. - - - - - - - - - - - - - - - -try to make of yourself - - - -.
Inayat Khan altered one word.	- - - - - - - - - - - - - - - -try and make - - - - - - - - - - .
One word added in an unidentified handwriting.	- - - - - - - - - - -thorns, but try - - - - - - - - - - - - - - .
d) A typewritten copy together with other sayings meant for publication in the "Gayan", under the heading 'Bola'	Bola. As life is full of thorns try to make of yourself a rose.

Cont. d)

ORIGIN and elaborations:	DIFFERENT VERSIONS:
Cont. d) I. (Gd.'s book-preparation) = version as under a). 'As' was crossed out, probably by Gd.	__ Life - - - - - - - - - - - - etc.

42.

a) MSS. Mf. and Zr.	Saying. Love guides its own way.
b) Copied by Km.	Saying. Love <u>finds</u> its own way.
c) Copied by Ek. and classified by Inayat Khan as 'Bol', meant for publication in the "Gayan". The saying was crossed out by Mc., and in her handwriting was written over it instead: 'Rocks will open and make way for the lover.' 1)	<u>Bola</u>. - - - - - - - - - - - - - .

Note 1): See 'Sayings I' : " Gayan" - Bola 41.

43.

a) MS. Fm.	Bola. What man makes is the personality of God, not His reality.
b) Copied by Sh. and classified by Inayat Khan as 'Chal'.	<u>Chala</u>. - - - - - - - - - - - - - - . 2)

Note 2): See for further elaborations and versions: Sayings I: "Gayan" - Bola 11.

44.

a) MSS. Mf. and Zr. Mf. writes 'crule'.	Saying. The kindest person can also be most cruel.
b) Copied by Km.	Saying. The kindest person can <u>be also the</u> most cruel.
c) Copied by Ek. and classified by Inayat Khan as 'Bol', meant for publication in the "Gayan".	<u>Bola</u>. - - - - - - - - - - - - - .

45.

a) Copied by Gd. from (?), together with other sayings meant for publication in the "Gayan".	Saying. All is beautiful in its place, the hair is beautiful on the head, not on the feet.
b) Copied by Km.	Saying. - - - - - - - - - - - -

Cont: b)

ORIGIN and elaborations:	DIFFERENT VERSIONS:
Cont. b) Altered by Inayat Khan.	- not on the sole of the foot.
c) Copied by Sh. and classified by Inayat Khan as 'Chal', meant for publication in the "Gayan".	Chala. - - - - - - - - - - - - - - - place; the - - - - - - - - - - - - - - - - - etc.
46.	
a) MS. Gd.	Bola. Be thankful for your privileges rather than proud of them.
b) Copied by Ek. and classified by Inayat Khan as 'Bol', meant for publication in the "Gayan".	Bola. - - - - - - - - - - - - - - .
47.	
a) Copied by Gd. from (?). Copied by Km.	To be serious and yet pleasant spoken is the sign of the wise.
Inayat Khan added 'Saying' over Gd.'s copy.	Saying. - - - - - - - - - - - - - - .
b) Copied by Ek. and classified by Inayat Khan as 'Bol', meant for publication in the "Gayan".	Bola. - - - - - - - - - - - - - - .
Mc. changed one word, then combined this saying with another one.	- -is the way of the wise.

Note: For complete elaborations and different versions see Sayings I: "Gayan" - Bola 150.

ORIGIN and elaborations:	DIFFERENT VERSIONS:
48.	
a) MS. Fm.	Saying. Everything leads to something.
Inayat Khan replaced 'Saying' by 'Alankara' first, then by 'Tana' instead.	~~Alankara~~ Tana. - - - - - - - - - - - - - - .
b) Copied by Gd. and by Km.	Tana. - - - - - - - - - - - - - - .
c) Copied by Sh. and classified by Inayat Khan as 'Chal', meant for publication in the "Gayan".	Chala. - - - - - - - - - - - - - - .
49.	
a) MS. Fm.	Bola. The tongue of flame was the sword of the prophets.
b) Copied by Km.	Bola. - - - - - - - - - - - -

Cont: b)

ORIGIN and elaborations:	DIFFERENT VERSIONS:
Cont. b) Inayat Khan altered word.	- - - - - - - - flame is the - - etc.
c) Copied by Sh. and classified by Inayat Khan as 'Bol', meant for publication in the "Gayan". Mc. crossed out the whole sayings and underneath was written in her handwriting: 'It is the tongue of flame that speaks truth, not the tongue of flesh.' 1)	Bola. - - - - - - - - - - - - - - .

Note 1): See Sayings I: "Gayan" - Bola 249.

50.

a) MS. Fm. Copied by Km.	Tala. The mocking world will mock. The working souls will work.
b) Copied by Sh. and classified by Inayat Khan as 'Tal', meant for publication in the "Gayan".	Tala. - - - - - - - - - - - - - - .

51.

a) Notebook 1921 :	Saying. It is not the action in itself, it is the condition that makes it sin or virtue. It is not the action in itself that is sin or virtue, it is the condition which makes it either one or the other.
b) MS. Gd., together with other sayings meant for publication in the "Gayan". See the second version under a).	Saying. It is not the action __ itself that is a sin or a virtue, but it is the condition that makes it ______ ___ __ ___ ______ so.

Cf. Sayings I, "Gayan" - Bola 24 and "Nirtan" - Bola 33.

52.

a) Notebooks :	Bola. Do not take advantage of anyone's weakness.
b) MS. Sk., dated Summer 1922.	Bola. - - - - - - - - - - - - - - .

ORIGIN and elaboration:	DIFFERENT VERSIONS:
53.	
a) Notebooks 1921 :	Phy. Every aspect of life wants sacrifices, while the immortal life wants your activity sacrificed, the mortal life wants your peace.
b) A typewritten copy, together with other sayings originally meant for publication in the "Gayan" (Gd.'s bookprep-aration).	Philosophy. Every aspect of life demands sacri-fices, while the immortal life demands the sacrifice of your activity_ the mortal life demands the sacrifice of your peace.
54.	
a) Notebooks 1921 :	Message. Do not think that Christ was crucified because the people at that time were unevolved. No, it is most difficult to live among people after rising above their standard of goodness. If Christ appeared to-day he would even now be put to the cross; for Christ cannot be without the cross. Christ and cross both stand together.
b) A sentence in the lec-ture 'The Message, part-ly published in January 1922 in the pamphlet 'The Message'.	__ ___ _____ ____ Was Christ cru-cified because the people of His time were unevolved? No! but because it is always difficult to live amidst the people above whose standard of good-ness one has risen. If Christ appeared to-day with the claim of Christhood, even to-day He would be crucified. ____ Christ cannot be without the Cross, nor can the Cross be without Christ. Christ and Cross both stand together.
55.	
a) Notebooks 1921 :	Message. The claim of Rissālat in man's life-time is a burden which is heavier than the earth and heaven. It is only possible that his name be identified with the Spirit of Guidance, when he has passed away from the limitations of the life on earth.
b) A typewritten copy, to-gether with other sayings meant for pub-lication in the "Vadan" (Gd.'s bookpreparation of the "Vadan"). Also found with Gd.'s bookpreparation of 'The Unity of Religious Ideals', Chapter 'The Messenger'.	~~Boula~~. Chala. The claim of Risālat in man's life-time is a great burden, _____ __ heavier than ___ earth and larger than Heaven. It is the fulfilment of the Message which must identify his name with the Spirit of Guidance. _ ____ __ ___ ______ ____ ____ ___ __________ __ ___ ____ __ _____

c)

ORIGIN and elaboration:	DIFFERENT VERSIONS:
c) Copied by Gd.	MS. Message. - - - - - - - - - - - - - .

56.

a) Notebooks :	Saying or Philosophy. Your bodily desire takes you away from your heart's wish and the wish of your heart separates you from your soul's longing, so by every lower desire man is pulled further down from the higher goal of his soul's longing.
b) The first part of this saying was published in "The Bowl of Sâki", 1921, under 1st June.	

Note: See for complete elaborations and different versions Sayings II : Part One under 1st June.

57.

a) Notebooks :	Saying. Let the devil sleep rather than be awake.

Note: See for further elaborations and different versions Sayings I : "Gayan" - Bola 22.

58.

a) Notebooks 1921 :	Saying. It is difficult to keep wise, while it is easy to become foolish.
b) MS. Gd., together with other sayings meant for publication in the "Gayan".	It is difficult to be wise, and it is still more difficult to act wisely. It is easy to be foolish, and it is easier still to act foolishly.

59.

a) Notebooks :	Saying. Disappointment is the discovering of the error of having built hope on the false object.
b) MS. Ng., together with other sayings meant for publication in the "Gayan".	Saying. By disappointment one discovers the fact that one had built a hope on a false object.

60.

a) Notebooks 1921 :	Peace and war both mean fight.
b) MS. Sk., dated Summer 1922.	- - - - - - - - - - - - - .

Cf. Sayings I : "Gayan" - Tala 31.

ORIGIN and elaboration:	DIFFERENT VERSIONS:
61.	
a) Notebooks 1921 :	Saying. A life long effort is not sufficient to develop a kind nature.
b) Copied by Gd. from (?), together with other sayings meant for publication in the "Gayan". Inayat Khan wrote in the margin: 'also Sangita III Suluk'.	Saying. - develop kindness in nature.
62.	
a) Notebooks 1921 :	Ego. An ego whose vanity is fed by seeing someone love him, admire him, and go in agonies in his love, and him to see for himself and for others to see how lovable he is which grows even to such an extent that his joy becomes the torture of another.
b) MS. Gd., together with other sayings meant for publication in the "Gayan".	Philosophy. There are egos whose vanity is fed by being loved and admired who grew in time so tyrannous that even the agony of a loving heart becomes their joy and amusement.
63.	
a) Notebooks :	The essence of milk is butter. The essence of flowers is honey. The essence of grapes is wine, and the essence of life is wisdom.
b) MS. Ng.	Tala. - - - - - - - - - - - - - -butter; the - - - - - - - - - - - - - honey; the - - - - - - - - - - - - -wine and the - - - - - - - - - - - - - - - .
64.	
a) Notebooks 1921 :	P.S. Expression) / Extension) of love spreads your influence, retention of love deepens your (spirit (spiritpower
b) MS. Gd.	Ph. The outlet of the love impulse spreads out man's influence, and the control of the love impulse deepens man's personality.
65.	
a) Notebooks :	Do not accuse another of his fault,

ORIGIN and elaboration :	DIFFERENT VERSIONS:
Cont. a)	for it will only strengthen its root.
b) MS. Mf.	Do not accuse your friend of his fault, let him see it for himself, if not, your accusation will make him more firm in his fault.

Note: See for complete origins, elaborations and different versions: Sayings I, "Gayan" - Bola 39.

66.

a) Notebooks 1921 :	Saying. It is the force of pursuit that opens the way.
b) MS. in an unidentified handwriting, together with other sayings meant for publication in the "Gayan".	Saying. - - - - - - - - - - - - - - .

67.

a) Notebooks :	Saying. Do not chum even in fun with a monkey, for if you pat her, she will scratch you in return, if you kiss her, she will bite you in reciprocity.
b) MS. Sd. Copied by Km., meant for publication in the "Gayan".	Saying. - if you pat it, it will - - - - - - - - - - - - - - -if you kiss it, it will - - - - - - - - - - - - etc.

68.

a) Notebooks 1921 :	Bola. In reality God is man's own perfection.
b) Copied by Gd., probably from her own MS.	Bola. (Pagan) God in reality is man's own perfection.
Inayat Khan crossed out the word 'Pagan' and replaced it by 'heathen saying', adding: 'also Sangita III'. In the margin Inayat Khan wrote: 'Sangita III - Tasauf'.	Bola. Heathen Saying. - - - - - - - - - - - - - - .

68A.

a) Notebooks :	God has one thing against him and that is his name. 1)

Note 1): See for complete elaborations and different versions: Sayings I, "Vadan" - Bola 32.

ORIGIN and elaborations:	DIFFERENT VERSIONS:
69.	
a) Notebooks 1921 :	God makes the world and we make the moral.

See for elaborations and different versions:
Sayings I : "Gayan" - Alapa 8.

70.	
a) Notebooks 1923 :	God through His limitations judges you and forgives you out of His perfection.

See for elaborations and different versions:
Sayings I : "Vadan" - Bola 27.

71.	
a) Notebooks 1922 :	Even in goodness there must be no rivalry. Goodness must be done out of charity, not out of rivalry.
b) MS. Sk., dated Summer 1922.	- - - - - - - - - - - - - .

72.	
a) Notebooks :	Sura. Verily he alone is happy who occupies himself through life in giving happiness to others.
b) A stencilled copy of sayings for the "Vadan" (Gd.'s bookpreparation).	Sura. - - - - - - - - - - - - - -who <u>is</u> <u>occupied</u> _______ _______ _____ in giving happiness __ ______.

73.	
a) Notebooks :	By diving deep into the heart of Islam what they found was the pearl of Sufism; for Sufism, as water under the earth, can be found in the depth of every religion.
b) MS. Sk.	- - - - - - - - - - - - - .
c) Published in the pamphlet 'The Sufi Movement', first half 1924.	- - - - - - - - - - - - - - - - - etc. - - - - - - -for Sufism, <u>like</u> water - - - - - - - - - - - - - - - - - etc.

74.	
a) Notebooks 1921 :	Saying. Motto. The heart that receiveth the light from above is liberated.
b) MS. Gd.	<u>Sufi</u> Motto. The heart <u>receptive</u> <u>to</u> the <u>divine</u> light ____ ____ is liberated.
c) Copied by Gd.	Sufi Motto. <u>For</u> <u>Sufi</u> <u>Order.</u> - - - - - - - - - - - - - .

Cf.)

ORIGIN and elaboration:	DIFFERENT VERSIONS:

Cf. Sayings I: "Gayan" - Suras 14, 15, 16.
Cf. Gatha Symbology, Series I no. 6: 'The Symbol of the Sufi Order'.

75.

a) Notebooks 1921 :	Saying. The heart speaks louder than the spoken words.
b) MS. in an unidentified handwriting over which Inayat Khan wrote 'Sayings', together with other sayings which originally may have been meant for publication in the "Gayan".	Saying. - - - - - - - - - - - - - - .

76.

a) Notebooks 1922 :	One who fights his nature against his ideal is the saint. One who dominates his ideal under his realization of truth is the master. One who makes an ideal is a prophet. One who gives ideal to others is the Messenger.

Note: The first two sentences of this saying were published in the "Gayan" - Tala 51. See there, in Sayings I, for elaborations and different versions of these verses. The last two sentenc were not published, but they form part of one saying.

77.

a) Notebooks 1921 :	P.S. Every impulse is a power, every time when the will withdraws any wave of impulse, the withdrawal of the impulse charges it with a new strength and life, so that in time the will of a Master-man makes him the Master of the sea which is constantly moving in the heart of man.
b) MS. Gd., together with other sayings meant for publication in the "Gayan". It is also Sangita I - 121. No differences between a) and b) have been underlined, as the version under b) was shortened and considerably changed.	Every impulse is a power in itself and every time when the will withdraws an impulse the will is charged with a new strength and life, which makes the selfmastered man master of all.

ORIGIN and elaborations:	DIFFERENT VERSIONS:
78.	
a) Notebooks 1921 :	P.S. Every impulse, when breaks out uncontrolled, results into an accident, the reaction of which is serious.
b) Copied by Gd. from (?), together with other sayings meant for publication in the "Gayan".	Ph. Every impulse_ that breaks out uncontrolled_ results in__ an accident_ and reacts seriously.
79.	
a) Notebooks 1921 :	Saying. If you wish to be happy, avoid all inharmony in life.
b) MS. in an unidentified handwriting, together with other sayings, meant for publication in the "Gayan".	Saying. - - - - - - - - - - - - - - .
80.	
a) Notebooks :	Life is a symphony and the action of every person in this life is the playing of his particular part in the music.
b) MS. Gd., together with other sayings meant for publication in the "Vadan".	Chala. - - - - - - - - - - - - - - .
Changed in Gd.'s handwriting and written by her in the margin: 'not sent yet'.	Life is a music, and - - - - - etc. - - - - - - - - - - - - - - - part in the symphony.
c) Copied by Gd. together with other 'Chalas' to be published in the "Vadan".	Chala. - - - - - - - - - - - - - - .
81.	
a) Notebooks 1921 :	Saying. When the lips close, the heart speaks.
b) MS. in an unidentified handwriting, with other sayings meant for publication in the "Gayan".	Saying. - - - - - - - - - - - - - - .
82.	
a) Notebooks :	Bola. Love's best expression is indifference.

Note: For elaborations and different versions see Sayings I, "Gayan" - Bola 108.

ORIGIN and elaboration:	DIFFERENT VERSIONS:
83.	
a) Notebooks :	A man cannot understand woman's point of view and a woman cannot have man's outlook on life.
b) MS. Ng., together with other sayings meant for publication in the "Vadan" and "Nirtan".	A woman cannot see from a man's point of view; a man cannot have a woman's outlook on life.
In Gd.'s handwriting 'Tala' was written over it.	Tala. - - - - - - - - - - - - - - .
84.	
a) Notebooks 1921 :	P.S. When a person, keeping his light high, directs another person to darkness, he fails, for his own light shows the man the right way.
b) MS. Gd., together with other sayings meant for publication in the "Gayan".	Ph. - - - - - - - - - - - - - - - - - - high_ directs another person in the path of darkness_ he ____ must be disappointed, for his own light will show_ the person he directs the right way.
Also part of Sangita I - 121.	
85.	
a) Notebooks 1921 :	Saying. You cannot guide man on a wrong path with a lantern in your hand, even if you did so, he will not take the wrong road, for your lantern will show him the right road, if you did not.
b) MS. Gd. with other sayings, meant for publication in the "Gayan".	Saying (Alternative). You cannot -hand. Even if you did so_ he - - - - - - - etc. - - - - -the right one. __ __ __ __
86.	
a) Notebooks 1921 :	Saying. Man's atmosphere explains the condition of his soul.
b) MS. in an unidentified handwriting, together with other sayings with some add. and a corr. by Inayat Khan, found with the "Gayan' documents.	Saying. Men's atmosphere - - - - - - - etc.

ORIGIN and elaboration:	DIFFERENT VERSIONS:
87.	
a) Notebooks 1921 :	Psychology. Man's heart is like a piece of ground, you may sow anything in it and rear it, when the fruit comes to, then man knows whether it was a sweet fruit or a poison.
b) MS. Gd., together with other sayings mostly meant for publication in the "Gayan". Also Sangatha I-22 and part of Sangita I - 121.	____________ - and rear it. When the fruit comes __ _ then we shall realize whether it was a sweet fruit or a poisonous.
88.	
a) Notebooks 1921 :	Characters. There are several sides to human nature and the idealist sees one - and the best one - which often he exaggerates to himself and sometimes he makes a mountain out of a mole hill.
b) MS. Gd., together with other sayings, mostly meant for publication in the "Gayan". It is part of Sangita I-121 and the beginning of Sangita II.	Ph. - sees one, ___ the best one, which he often exaggerates __ _______ and _________ __ makes - - - - - - - - - - - - - .
89.	
a) Notebooks 1921 :	Psychology. There are many sides to human nature and it depends which side of an individual's nature we touch, whether the right one which must answer our purpose or the wrong one.
b) MS. Gd., together with other sayings, mostly meant for publication in the "Gayan". In her handwriting this saying was added to the previous one. Also in Sangita I-121 the two sentences appear as one single paragraph.	Ph. There are several sides to human nature and the idealist sees one, the best one, which he often exaggerates and makes a mountain out of a mole-hill. There are many sides to human nature and it depends which side of an individual's nature we touch_ whether the right one which must answer our purpose or the wrong one which may destroy it.
90.	
a) Notebooks 1921 :	P.S. When the deeper side of man's nature

Cont. a)

ORIGIN and elaborations:	DIFFERENT VERSIONS:
Cont. a)	is touched, what is hidden in him manifests on the surface.
b) MS. Gd., together with other sayings, mostly meant for publication in the "Gayan".	Ph. - - - - - - - - - - - - - - .
Sangita I-121.	

91.	
a) Notebooks 1922 :	Saying. To find a Master aside even if one could meet a true man through life, it would be the greatest privilege.
b) MS. Mf. Copied by Km., together with other sayings meant for publication in the "Gayan".	Saying. To see a saint apart ___ if you meet with a true man in life_ it must be considered your life's greatest privilege.
MS. Zr.	Saying. - - - - - - - - -apart, if - - - - - - - - - - - - - - - - - - -life, it - - - - considered ___ life's - - - - - - - - - -.

92.	
a) Notebooks 1921 :	The Message. The Message is the answer to the cry of the individual and collective souls.
b) A sentence in an undated lecture 'Religion', given by Inayat Khan before the second half of 1921. Gd. dictated this same lecture in 1921, probably in autumn, at Geneva to Sk., who took it down in longhand as 'Gatheka, Series I No. 6'.	The divine Message is the answer to the cry of souls, individually and collectively. 1)
c) Published in January 1922 in a pamphlet called 'The Message', which contains parts of two lectures on this subject.	, the ______ Message is the answer to the cry of individual and collective souls.

Note 1): This lecture has become 'Religious Gatheka No.3' and in Sr.'s handwriting exists the following annotation: 'There are older papers in which this Gatheka is not one of the Religious Gathekas, but one of the Gathekas. It appears as Gatheka Series I No.6.' After 1927 Headquarters changed the original sequence of a part of the Religious Gathekas.

ORIGIN and elaborations:	DIFFERENT VERSIONS:
93.	
a) Notebooks 1921 :	Poem. The Message is rising to fulness. The workers must answer the call. Good tidings to those who are wakeful, And blessing and peace be on all. God's Blessings and peace be on all.
b) MS. Zr., first part a).	- - - - - - - - - - - - - - - - - - etc. And blessing and peace be to all.
94.	
a) Notebooks 1921 :	Message. The Messenger has five aspects to his being: 1. The Divine 2. The Ideal 3. The Prophet 4. The Message-bearer, and 5. The Message. All four aspects pertaining to the personality of the Messenger have been terminated for the future, leaving the fifth, the Message.
b) MS. Sr., dated 1921. (Notes taken down from Inayat Khan's words during the lecture). Differences as to the version under a) have not been underlined.	Five different aspects of the divine Message and the Message itself. 1. divine 2. ideal 3. the prophet 4. the Message from God 5. the message itself.
c) Dictated by Ng. to Miss K. Belfrage. 1. - 4.: see version under a).	Message. 1. - - - - - 2. - - - - - 3. - - - - - 4. - - - - - 5. the Teacher.
d) Published in 'The Unity of Religious Ideals' - The Messenger (compilation).	The Messenger has five aspects to his being: (1) the Divine, (2) the Ideal, (3) the Prophet, (4) the Message-bearer, (5) the Teacher. Four of these aspects have been terminated, so that now only one is distinguished, which is the Teacher.
95.	
a) Notebooks 1921 :	Saying. Every moment of life is an opportunity and who profits by it is wise.
b) MS. in an unidentified handwriting, together with other sayings with some add. and a corr.	Saying. - - - - - - - - - - - - - .

Cont. b)

ORIGIN and elaboration :	DIFFERENT VERSIONS:
Cont. b) by Inayat Khan, found with the "Gayan" documents.	

96.

a) Notebooks 1921 :	Saying. The reserve gives a weight to the personality. 1)

Note 1): For elaborations and different versions see Sayings I: "Gayan" - Bola 150 under a), b) and d).
Cf. Sayings II : Part Two no. 265.

97.

a) Notebooks 1921 :	Saying. The one who says no is often stronger than the one who says yes.
b) MS. in an unidentified handwriting, together with other sayings with some add. and a corr. by Inayat Khan, found with the Gayan documents. The alterations already appear in the unidentified handwriting.	Saying. The one who can say : no is often stronger than the one who can say : yes.

98.

a) Notebooks 1921 :	Gamaka. People set 1) through me a chill when they show me their feeling against another.
b) Copied by Ng. from (?).	______ People send through me a chill, when they express to me their feelings against another.

Note 1): Probably 'set' was written mistakenly for 'send'.

99.

a) Notebooks 1921 :	Saying. Every person has his own way in life and that particular way is most suited to him.
b) MS. in an unidentified handwriting, together with other sayings found with the Gayan documents, in which Inayat Khan wrote some add. and a corr. The alteration already appears in the unidentified handwriting.	Saying. - way is more suited to him.

ORIGIN and elaborations:	DIFFERENT VERSIONS:
100.	
a) Notebooks 1921 :	Saying. The greater your sacrifice, the greater your reward.
b) MS. in an unidentified handwriting, together with other sayings, found with the Gayan documents, in which Inayat Khan wrote some add. and a corr.	Saying. - - - - - - - - - - - - - .
Inayat Khan added one word.	- - - - - - - - - - - - - - - - the greater is your reward.

Cf. Sayings II : Part Two no. 113.

101.	
Notebooks 1921 :	Saying. In the path of sacrifice the further you proceed the greater is your gain.

Cf. Sayings II : Part Two no. 113.

102.	
a) Notebooks 1921 :	Saying. Satan has no power over you unless you give your wrist in his grip.
b) MS. Ng.	Saying. -your wrist into his grip.
c) Copied by Gd., together with other sayings, mostly meant for publication in the "Gayan".	______ -your wrist in__ his grip.

103.	
a) Notebooks 1921 :	Message. Saum and Salat are not man-made prayers, they have descended from above and there is every power and blessing in them for those who believe.
b) Copied by Gd. from (?).	Message. -. They - - - - - - - - - - - above as in every period of ~~religious~~ spiritual reconstruction the prayer was given and there is every power and blessing in them, especially for those who believe.
c) A typewritten copy of sayings meant for publication in the "Vadan" (Gd.'s bookpreparation of the "Vadan").	Chala. - •They have descended from above, as in -the prayer

Cont. c)

ORIGIN and elaborations:	DIFFERENT VERSIONS:
Cont. c)	was given; and there is - - - - - - - - - - - - - in them_ especially - - - - - - - - - - - - .
d) A typewritten copy of five sayings under the heading 'The Message', found with Gd.'s book-preparation of 'The Unity of Religious Ideals', a compilation prepared by her.	The Message. - - - - - - - - - - - - - - .

104.

a) Notebooks :	Battle with self and make peace with others.
b) Copied by Sk., probably from her own MS., together with other sayings meant for publication in the "Vadan".	Bola. Make battle with oneself and - - - - .

105.

a) Notebooks 1921 :	Saying. The sense of honour is the sign of the noble, the one who has no respect for another indeed has no respect for himself.
b) Copied by Gd. from (?), together with other sayings meant for publication in the "Gayan".	- noble. The one - - - - - - - etc.

106.

a) Notebooks 1921 :	Psychology. You see the beautiful side of a person's nature when you are in a habit to see good and when your habit is to see evil, then the evil side of man comes before you.
b) MS. Gd., together with other sayings meant for publication in the "Gayan" and the "Vadan".	Philosophy. -are in the habit of seeing it, but when - - - - - - - - - - evil_ in a person _ then the evil side of man's nature must manifest before you.
c) Sangatha I-12	- - - - - - - - - - - - - .

107.

a) Notebooks :	By silence comes inspiration, by fasting is produced ecstasy and by devotion is sweetened the personality,

Cont. a)

ORIGIN and elaborations:	DIFFERENT VERSIONS:
Cont. a)	by purification is brought a healthy life and by abstinence psychic and occult power - by higher deeds the heaven is brought on earth, and by knowledge can be united with God.
b) A typewritten copy, over which was typed: 'in Kismet's handwriting'.	By silence comes inspiration, by fasting is produced ecstasy, and by devotion is sweetened the personality, by purification is brought a healthy life, and by abstinence psychic and occult power, by higher deeds the heaven is brought on earth, and by knowledge one can be united with God.

108.

a) Notebooks 1921 :	Saying. The cold silence is preferable to the hot words between friends which lead to lack of dignity and result in disagreement.
b) MS. in an unidentified handwriting, together with other sayings, found with the Gayan documents.	Saying. - - - - - - - - - - - - - - - - - - etc. lead to indignance and result - - - - - - - - - - - .
Crossed out two words, probably by Inayat Khan.	The cold silence is preferable to the hot words ______ ______ which lead to - - - - - - - - - - - - - - - etc.

109.

a) Notebooks 1922 :	Saying. Be resigned to the things of the past which cannot be helped now.
b) Copied by Ek. from (?), and copied by Km.	Saying. - - - - - - - - - - - - - - - .
c) A typewritten copy with sayings meant for publication in the "Gayan". (Gd.'s bookpreparation).	Saying. - - - - - - - - - - - - - - - .

110.

a) Notebooks possibly 1923 :	It is not enough to find out the ultimate Truth, what is most necessary is to hold the consciousness of reality.
b) Copied by Gd. with other sayings under the heading "Vadan".	Chala. - truth; what - - - - - etc.

ORIGIN and elaboration:	DIFFERENT VERSIONS:
111.	
a) Notebooks 1921 :	Teaching. If you will preserve my words as I have spoken, it will be as saving my life.
b) Sangita I-17, Wasiat.	- -spoken them, it will - - - - - .
112.	
a) Notebooks 1921 :	Saying. Words can never express what the eyes can speak.
b) MS. in an unidentified handwriting.	Saying. - - - - - - - - - - - - - - .

Cf. Sayings II : Part Two no. 32.

113.	
a) Notebooks 1921 :	Saying. In the path of renunciation the further you proceed the greater your reward.
b) MS. in an unidentified handwriting, together with other sayings, found with the "Gayan" documents.	Saying. - proceed, the greater - - - - .
Inayat Khan added one word.	- the greater is your reward.

Cf. Sayings II : Part Two nrs. 100 and 101.

114.	
a) Notebooks 1923 :	With no one am I intimate for no one do I long my body, heart and soul to you I offer for your song.
b) MS. Sk., dated Winter 1922/1923.	- - - - - - - - -intimate, For - - - - - - long. My - - - - - - - - - - - - You - - - - - - Your song.
115.	
a) Notebooks 1923 :	You have brought to me God's secret my secret is to love ~~No-one~~ You of which no one on earth knows ~~except~~ but ~~angels~~ heavens from above.
b) MS. Sk., dated Winter 1922/1923.	- - - - - - - - - - - - - - - - -secret, My secret is to love. You of which - - - - - - - - - - - But Heavens - - - - - - - .

ORIGIN and elaboration:	DIFFERENT VERSIONS:
116.	
a) Notebooks :	There is no one who does not work for some profit, selfish or unselfish.
b) Copied by Gd., together with other sayings meant for publication in the "Vadan", then crossed out, probably by herself.	Bola. There is no-one who ____ ___ works for nothing, selfish or unselfish.
117.	
a) Notebooks :	Saying. Innocence with intelligence is a true sign of spirituality.
b) Copied by Ek. from (?).	Saying. - - - - - - - - - - - - - - - - - is the true - - - - - - - - - - - - .
Cf. Sayings II : Part One under 27th February.	
118.	
a) Notebooks 1921 : Also found in Inayat Khan's letter to Mahtab van Hogendorp, Wissous, 7th July 1921.	On Viladat Day 1921. The years of my life are passing, leaving me behind to live a fuller and everlasting life after the Message I give.
b) Copied by Gd. from (?).	Poetry. 1921. The years of my life are passing_ leaving me behind to live a fuller and everlasting life after the message I give.
119.	
a) Notebook 19th April - 12th May 1923 :	Saying. If not saint, satan, take some model to mould your life.
b) Copied by Ng. from (?).	Heathen Saying. If not Saint, Satan ! Take some model to mould your life.
120.	
a) Notebooks 1921 :	Message. The absence of the ideal facilitates the idealistic devotee to expand his ideal, but the presence of the ideal most often hinders the devotee in building his ideal, for the ideal of imagination always excels the ideal who is living the life of limitations.
b) In slightly different words this sentence appears in an undated lecture 'The Message', of which parts were published in January 1922	The absence of the Ideal often makes it easier for the devotee, and the presence of the Ideal makes it more difficult for him; for the Ideal that grows and expands in his imagination will always excel that enshrined in a

Cont. b)

	ORIGIN and elaborations:	DIFFERENT VERSIONS:
	Cont. b) in the pamphlet 'The Message'.	personality, however great, who is living on earth the life of limitations.
	c) A typewritten copy, with Gd.'s bookpreparation of 'The Unity of Religious Ideals' (a compilation prepared by Gd.).	The absence of the ideal makes it easier for the idealistic devotee to make his ideal greater; but the presence of the ideal most often hinders the devotee in strengthening his ideal. For the ideal that grows and expands in the imagination of the devotee, will always excel the ideal personality which is living on earth the life of limitations.
121.	Notebooks 1921 :	Saying. It is absurd for one to be always wise and not be foolish even once in a while.
122.	Notebooks 1924 :	I am that to every one, what he thinks of me, for I am each and I am all.
123.	Notebooks :	Saying. Perfect aristocracy is the true democracy.
124.	Notebooks :	Saying. Even he who can fight an army, finds it difficult to fight the self.
124A.	Notebooks :	Blessed is he who has seen his Life's purpose.
		Cf. Sayings I : "Gayan" - Sura 1.
125.	In Inayat Khan's handwritten notes of approx. 1911, handed down by Murshida Martin to one of her mureeds, Mrs. Duce, who sent them partly to Sirdar van Tuyll, and partly to the Biographical Department on the latter's request in 1977.	The various aspects of Sufism can be gradually revealed to the initiated, by the Murshad, the ever incarnating universal reason, according to the intellectual development of the age in which he incarnated himself.
126.		Tassawuf. To leave aught undone for the esteem

Cont.)

ORIGIN:	VERSION:
Cont.)	of men is hypocrisy, and to do aught for their esteem is idolatry.
127.	Tassawuf. Much is he beguiled who serves God for fear or hope, for His true service is for mere love. Serve God because you cannot help serving is for mere love's sake.
128.	Sufism. Steering a mid-course between the atheism on the one hand and the deism on the other, the Sufi's cult is the religion of beauty, where heavenly perfection is considered under the imperfect type of earthly loveliness.

---

129. Notebooks :

Sex.
The beauty of the immanence of God is most admired in the opposite sex.

---

130. Notebooks 1921 :

Saying.
Beauty you must regard from a distance, by touching and tempering with it, either you will cause harm to the beauty or will bring ruination to yourself.

---

131. Notebooks 1922 :

Saying.
There is no beauty which cannot be surmounted.

---

132. Notebooks 1921 :

Saying.
To a spiritual being the whole world's burden is light to lift, but to the material person his own burden is too heavy for him to lift.

---

133. Notebooks 1921 :

Sura.
Verily the believers are blessed.

---

134. Notebooks :

My blessing extends to all (those ... hearts)
in the heart that is open, it enters
and (it waits / (~~it stands waiting~~ at the gate of
those whose heart is closed.

ORIGIN:	VERSION:
135. Notebooks :	I have drunk the bowl of poison which the seeker after perfection must drink.

---

136. Notebooks 1921 :	Saying. Born of a thorny branch the beautiful rose blooms.

---

137. Notebooks :	Whose brows are smiling and whose eyes have great lustre and who has an open visage, Gentle in action and thoughtful in speech, he is a saintly soul, he is a sage. Whose heart is tender and who has great compassion, who stands alone and who gives others courage know then he is the man who is friend of all, He is a saintly soul, he is a sage. Whose brows are smiling and whose eyes have great lustre and who has an open visage, Gentle and thoughtful in all things he says and does, He is a friend of all, he is a sage. Who knows all things, yet is so simple, he suffers with all and gives them courage. He shares his good with the others.
Notebooks :	Gentle and thoughtful in all things he says and does, he is a saintly soul, he is a sage. Wise and simple, who gives to the sorrowful console(ation) and comfort and courage. Life on earth to him is as a bird in a cage. His brows are smiling and his eyes have great lustre and he has an open visage, Gentle and wise he is in all he says and does, life on earth to him is as a bird in a cage, Knowing all things and yet he is so simple, that he suffers with all and gives them courage.

---

138. Notebooks 1922 :	I bring to you the message of peace and leave you alone to calmly enjoy it.

Cont.)

ORIGIN: VERSION:

Cont.) We so fondly rise to welcome you, O wind, and so readily respond to your call, then we are ~~forsaken~~ left by ourselves to await your next coming.

I come to you with the message ~~of peace~~ from above and pass away to let the sea be calm.

Note: It may be assumed that this is a dialogue between the wind and the waves.

Notebooks : Waves.
We rise and go forward to welcome thee and readily respond to thy call, then thou goest and we are left alone by ourselves.

We so fondly respond to your call, o wind, but you go away and leave us in a gloom.

Wind.
I come unto you with wisdom's message and leave you alone to solve the riddle by yourselves.

The Wind:
I come from above with wisdom's subtle message and leave you alone to solve the riddle by yourselves.

Cf. Sayings I : "Vadan" - Tanas 10 and 18.

139.
Notebooks 1923 : If Christ child is accepted who came from a Jewish mother, you will certainly not refuse the divine message conceived in the womb of the Sufi esoteric school of ancient wisdom and born as the call to humanity to unite in one brotherhood.

140.
Notebooks 1921 : Py.
When Christ was crucified, it was God Who was judged in the court of man.

141.
Notebooks 1921 : Claim of perfection for the man with all sincerity and trueness, seems beyond his reach and it is best it was not claimed, but realised only.

142.
Notebooks : Complexity results into simplicity.

ORIGIN:	VERSION:
143. Notebooks 1923 :	Gamaka. Wherever I happen to be I feel it to be in my own country, for I see my Beloved everywhere and I am with Him home.
144. Notebooks :	Saying. By judging that what one learns, one becomes a critic instead of a student.
145. Notebooks :	Death, who overcomes thy sting? The knower of life who is conscious.
146. Notebooks :	There is no death after once you die.
147. Notebooks :	A good deed is that which begins in pleasure, continues in joy and results in happiness.
148. Notebooks :	Tana. Devil, where do you find your location. In the head 1) a clever man In the eyes of a fascinating woman In the hands of a greedy youth, And in the legs of a mischievous child. 2)

Note 1): Here one word was omitted.
2): Cf. Sayings I : "Gayan" - Tana 20.

149. Notebooks 1921 :	Saying. As the dewdrops help the bud to bloom, so the joy-tears help the heart to bloom.
150. Notebooks 1914/1915 :	The disorder in the health is caused by the irregularity of the ether, one of the five elements, also either by congestion or by over-circulation.
151. Notebooks 1921 :	Saying. Observe all that is beautiful, but stay at a distance; by getting close to it you limit your vision of beauty.

ORIGIN:	VERSION:
152. Notebooks 1921 :	Sangatha. Py. In the dream the mind is like a mechanism which works on by itself without the direction of the engineer.
153. Notebook April - May 1923 :	Tana. Earth, are you made to be my throne? Yes, but your crown also.
154. Notebook April - May 1923 :	Tana. From where do you bring your beautiful jewels? I lay my heart open to heaven so that the beauty of the heaven may be reflected in my heart.

Note: The sayings written just before and after this one in the Notebooks are beginning with the word 'Earth,'.

ORIGIN:	VERSION:
155. Notebook April - May 1923 :	Tana. Earth, how do you attract heaven? I send him my love with the vapour and he sends his answer (in (by his tears.
156. Notebook April - May 1923 :	Tana. Earth, what is trodden beneath our feet? What have you done to be trodden beneath our feet? Tana. Earth, what does make you lie beneath our feet in such humiliation? The unsteadiness of my character. Tana. Earth, what have you done to be trodden beneath our feet? I have deserved it for the unsteadiness of my character.
157. Notebook April - May 1923 :	Tana. Earth, what makes you lie beneath our feet? It appears so to you, in reality I raise even your feet above your head.

ORIGIN:	VERSION:
158. Notebook April - May 1923 :	Tana. Earth, you are the floor of my house, but the roof also.
159. Notebooks :	Alankara. Earth, you produce jewels, my heart produces ideas.
160. Notebooks 1921 :	For Magazines. The modern education teaches to make the students best fitted to guard their own interest in life, instead of showing them how dependent is the interest of an individual upon the general interest.
161. Notebooks 1921 :	Question: When the end of the world will come, can you tell me? When the horns of the animals will turn into wings, When the beaks of the birds will become two lips, When the heart of man will turn into a blooming rose, And when woman's soul will become an eye, Then the end of the world will come.
162. Notebooks :	Saying. All that ends well must begin well.
163. Notebooks :	No one would do evil if he knew he was doing it.

Cf. Sayings I : "Nirtan" - Bola 43.

164. Notebooks 1921 :	Phy. At every fault the ego pushes the reason forward, put the fault on someone else, but at every thing rightly done, the ego readily raises its head to be crowned with the victory.

ORIGIN:	VERSION:
165. Notebooks :	Gamaka. I do not accuse anyone of his fault, for I leave him free to choose his own way, as I wish myself to be free.
166. Notebooks 1921 :	Saying. Favours from the undesirable sources have their interest a hundred times more than the amount received.
167. Notebooks :	Prayer. Fear comes in my heart when I half cover my eyes by dropping my eyelids and look down to earth and see the holes and the pits, but I have no fear when I raise my eyes and look to Thee.
168. Notebooks :	Saying. The one who fools his fellowman, will be fooled a thousand times over in return.
169. Notebooks 1914/1915 :	In Fikar the word repeated in the breath is engraved upon the soul as a record.
170. Notebooks 1924 :	Pour out floods of love, yet keeping your garment of detachment from being wet.
171. Notebooks :	Saying. Verily the one who fools another, maketh himself a fool.
172. Notebooks :	Foolish turns truth into false, wise turns false into truth.
173. Notebooks 1921 :	By forgiveness man goes forward, by thought of revenge he goes backward and by remembering the harm done to him by someone, man stands still.

ORIGIN:	VERSION:
174.	
Notebooks 1914/1915 :	The form of every creature is made according to the needs of life.
175.	
Notebooks 1921 :	Saying. Your best friend may harm you more than your worst enemy.
Notebooks 1922 :	Saying. Most loving friend may act as your bitterest enemy.
176.	
Notebooks :	Gamaka. My best friend and worst enemy is my love.
177.	
Notebooks :	Saying. Tread not love's path so far that ye may have to draw back. Saying. Tread not the path of intimacy so far ..... Do not go so far in friendship that you may have to step backwards in disappointment.
178.	
Notebooks :	Thanks to Thee, o Gardener, for the thriving of (my plant. (the plant of my life.
179.	
Notebooks :	When the globe turns its back, the sun spreads its light through the heart of the moon.
180.	
Notebooks 1921 :	Saying. Do not fear God, but be conscientious lest you may ~~displeasure~~ displease in any way.

Note: See for origin, elaborations and different versions Sayings I : "Gayan" - Bola 56.

181.	
A printed card which Inayat Khan sent to the mureeds for Christmas 1925.	God grant you: Thought that expandeth, Feeling that deepeneth, Friendship that lasteth long, Love that changeth not,

Cont.)

ORIGIN:	VERSION:
Cont.)	A treasure that ever groweth, Happiness that endeth not, Faith that reason cannot shake, Devotion that endureth all tests, Light that continually burneth, Life that liveth for ever. I.K. Blessings from Murshid.
182. Notebooks 1924 :	God is beyond all praise, if you wish to praise Him, you must make think of Him as an ideal man.
183. Notebooks :	If ever God is seen on the earth, it is in the one who hath spirit divine. If ever is God seen in the world, it is in you who reflect spirit divine.
184. Notebooks 1921 :	Saying. Heathen. If you have not a God, create one.
185. Notebooks :	Saying. Rather God be without a temple than a temple without God.
186. In 'Notes and Fragments' in Inayat Khan's handwriting, approx. 1911 :	Sufi Saying. They whom the God approaches most nearly, are the most severely tried.
187. Notebooks 1921 :	Saying. Those who imagine God as a just God, limit Him.
188. Notebooks :	Even to carry out God's great work tact and common sense is necessary.
189. Notebooks 1921 :	Heathen Saying. God-ideal is the best ideal that human mind can create.

ORIGIN:	VERSION:

190.
Notebooks :

Alankara.
Gold : I am the light of the earth.

191.
Notebooks :

He who shares his good with his fellows and sympathizes with them in their pain, constant in friendship, he who always keeps his word, sincere and faithful, who is above loss or gain

He who shares his good with his fellows and who sympathizes with them in their pain,
Constant in friendship, he who always keeps his word, patient and poised through every loss or gain,
He who is wise in all he says and does, who in a moment man's character can gauge,
Ever forgiving and so loving, he is the friend of all, he is the sage.

.... and does in their pleasures and pain by them stand.

Notebooks :

He who defends himself against an accusation has justice weighing upon his head.
He who owns his faults as he shares his good with others, he is the friend of all, he is the sage.

192.
Notebooks 1921 :

Sura.
We have blessed you by extending Our hands from the trees in the forest, did you not see the thousand hands blessing?
How the branches of the tree greet thee bending and stooping down to the earth, in complete humility they prostrate before that divine spirit which is in the form of man.

193.
Notebooks 1923 :

If you can bring happiness
and joy in someone's life,
If you really think you can
please him by being his wife,

then do not lose one moment.

194.
Notebooks 1926 :

One gives happiness in order to buy pleasure.

Pleasure costs happiness.

Cf.)

ORIGIN: VERSION:

Cf. Sayings I : "Nirtan" - Bola 8.

195.
Notebooks 1914/1915 : Harmony.
The best moral is to learn from all which to us sounds inharmonious that we may not use that for the other, and that which sounds harmonious to us, to use the same for the others. Thus the ears should be trained.

196.
Notebooks : Gamaka.
I voice 1) in the heart of my sincere mureed the word of God.

Note 1): An obsolete form for to speak, to utter, to proclaim. (Oxford Dict.).

197.
Notebooks 1921 : Saying.
Create heaven or hell, whatever you may, since both are your creations.

198.
Notebooks : Alankara.
Heaven: These are not raindrops, these are my tears dropping in sympathy for my hungry children on earth.

199.
Notebooks Autumn 1924 : What begins with howling ends in crying.

200.
Notebooks 1922 : Be good, kind and considerate and be conscious of your husband's honour and of your life's privilege.

201.
Notebooks : Saying.
Do not try to force your broad ideas upon the narrow-minded, it is like trying put ~~a lion into a narrow trap~~ something large in a small bag, which cannot hold.

Cf. Sangita I - 59.

202.
Notebooks : To express my ideas fully my own words are necessary. When they are
Cont.)

ORIGIN:	VERSION:
Cont.)	interpreted, they seem clothed in clothes which don't belong to them.

Note: This saying appears in Sangita I-42 under the heading 'Nasihat'.

203.
Notebooks 1921 :

Saying.
Whom I love and adore is my ideal, it matters not if he is man or God.

204.
Notebooks :

Monogamy.
With the breaking of the ideal whole life's plan is broken. The downfall of Napoleon is dated from the day he deserted his beloved mate.

205.
Notebooks :

Not only among the monogamous people, but even among the prostitutes whose life has been with so many men, are instances to be found that they have come in the end to monogamy in which alone they have at last found their heart's satisfaction.

206.
Notebooks :

Sex. Monogamy.
When a person has gone from one to two, then he has crossed the barrier of ideal that kept him intact and when once he has crossed it, he would not mind with how many he becomes intimate. Of course the tie of marriage obliges him to limit the number.

207.
Notebooks 1921 :

Saying.
Every impulse is a movement of God directed to accomplish a certain purpose which is often beyond human comprehension.

208.
Notebooks :

Alankara.
My infirmity, thou givest weapons - a weapon - in the hand of my adversary and a handle in the hold of my friend.

Gamaka.
My ~~faults~~ shortcomings become weapons in the hands of my adversaries and
Cont.)

ORIGIN:	VERSION:
Cont.)	tools in the hands of my loving friends.

209.

Notebooks 1914/1915 :	Inharmony is produced by the peculiarity of people's evolution through different grades and directions.

210.

Notebooks 1914/1915 :	Everyone judges according to one's own interest, that is why the justice of God is right. Divine law and divine justice.

211.

Notebooks 1923 :	Jesus came to raise mankind from sin.

212.

Notebooks :	They want to know which is which and what is what and they wish to be reassured that this is this and that is that.

213.

Notebooks 1924 :	One who knows truth can be a worse guide than the one who did not know it if he only knew truth not the psychology of human nature.

214.

Notebooks 1924 :	The knower of the Light cannot be a spiritual guide if he did not know the psychology of human nature.
Notebooks 1924 :	By knowing truth alone one cannot be a teacher, in order to be a teacher one must have the knowledge of human nature.

Cf. Sayings I : "Vadan" - Chala 114.

215.

Notebooks :	To I. we gave the law, to M. we taught its practice, to C. we showed the way and to S. came the realization of truth.

216.

Notebooks 1924 :	It must take a certain length of time to be able to gain a person's confidence.

ORIGIN:	VERSION:

217.
Notebooks 1923 :

Tala.
The length of one's heart man shows by his tolerance.
The width of one's heart man shows by his endurance.
The height of one's heart man shows by his power of understanding.
The depth of one's heart man shows by the capacity of assimilating all.

Cf. Sayings I : "Vadan" - Tala 50.

218.
Notebooks :

A hard life often serves to bring out all that is best in man.

219.
Notebooks 1923 :

Life around us appears passing, when in fact we are passing ~~through~~ 1).

Note 1): See for complete elaborations and different versions: Sayings I : "Vadan" - Tala 23.

220.
Notebooks :

Life never dies, it is death which is dead.

It is death which dies, not life.

Cf. Sayings I : "Vadan" - Sura 15, only the second sentence.

221.
Notebooks :

Gamaka.
My life cannot afford to have someone in my immediate surroundings who cannot fit in, in the circle of my friends who is indiscreet, among my comrades who is domineering and as my collaborator who is too clever for me.

222.
Notebooks 1923 :

Gamaka.
My life feels the strain of being held fast by the heavens above and being pulled down by the earth below.
My life feels the strain.

223.
Notebooks :

Saying.
No one gets in life what he doesn't deserve. 2)

Note 2): See for elaborations and different versions: Sayings I - "Gayan" - Bola 79.

ORIGIN: | VERSION:

224.
Notebooks 1922 :

Magazine lecture.
Political and social life must go
hand in hand,
Domestic and educational
Religious and theatrical
Science and moral
Industry and art
Commercial and spiritual
This can produce a new civilization.

225.
Notebooks :

Saying.
Those who love to make their life
dramatic, turn every situation of
life into a romance.

226.
Notebooks 1921 :

Saying.
The wiser you become, the more you
realize that you have to (live your
(make
life among fools.

227.
Notebooks :

While in life's ~~endless~~ sea we are
sailing toward the goal of our soul's
desire we must pass by all that
meets us patiently ~~courageously~~ and
~~continue~~ always ~~to~~ aspire.
Let our heart as compass guide us ~~in
the-sea~~ and our boat our faith will
steer.
Day or night through the wind or storm
We must (keep near Yaveh
(row and need not fear.

~~Soon-the-lighthouse-on-port-we'll-see.~~
~~Before-long-we-will-reach-the-shore.~~

One who hath seen his life's purpose
as light seen on port from sea
~~The-dawn-is-promising-sunrise~~
~~Surely~~ He will fulfil his life's
mission
~~Trust-in-him-for-blessed-is-he~~
Courageously whatever it be.

While in life's sea we are sailing
toward the goal of our souls' desire
We must pass by all that meets us
and patiently always aspire.
Let our heart as compass guide us
and the boat our faith will steer.
Day or night through the wind or storm
We must row and need not fear.

ORIGIN: **VERSION:**

228.
Notebooks :

We take with us memories of joy,
leaving pains and troubles behind.

229.
In Inayat Khan's handwriting on a loose sheet of paper.

Motherhood.
The praise of the beauty in all phases of life is truly due to the Mother, from the spirit to the matter and from the mineral to the human evolution.

230.
Notebooks 1922 :

Thy light which riseth in my heart,
in the hearts of my mureeds may shine.

The juice that hath made me so drunken,
O Sāqī, give my mureeds that wine.
Surround my mureeds with Thy beauty,
Create in their lives harmony divine.
Give them sympathy for one another
Raise them above Life's mine and thine.

Thy light which riseth in my heart,
may in the hearts of my mureeds shine.
The juice that intoxicated me so,
O Sāqī, give my mureeds that wine.
Surround my mureeds with Thy beauty,
Create in them Thy harmony Divine,
Give them sympathy for one another
May they forget world's mine and thine.

231.
Notebooks :

Gamaka.
I found many who love me and many still more who hate me, but .....

Many there are who like me and many more there are who do not like me, but .....

I find many who like me and many more who do not like me, but there are few who understand me and fewer still who know me well.

232.
Notebooks :

As I forward myself so I know my limitation, my King, but as I withdraw myself from the world, so I enter into Thy Kingdom.

233.
Notebooks 1924 :

Close your lips and open ears, close ears and open eyes, close eyes and
Cont.)

ORIGIN:	VERSION:
Cont.)	open your heart. When you close your lips, your ears will open. When you close your ears, your eyes will open. When you close your eyes, your heart will open, and when your heart is closed to all the outside influences your soul will unfold and manifest to your view.

234.
Notebooks 1924 :

We shall be able to make a living as your capital will fertilize my labour.

235.
Notebooks :

No loss is greater than the loss of one's soul.

236.
Notebooks :

Love can bring out what is worst and best in man.

237.
Notebooks 1922 :

Saying.
Love is nectar as long as it is in the spiritual spheres, but as it descends to the material plane, it turns into poison.

Notebooks 1922 :

Saying.
The spiritual love is a nectar, but as soon as it is (brought to material
(plane,
(mixed with matter,
it becomes a sweet wine mixed with a bitter poison.

238.
Notebooks 1921 :

Saying.
Too much love is like a searing sun.

239.
Notebooks 1921 :

Saying.
Enviable is he who loveth and asketh for no return. 1)
(Pitiable is he who loveth not, but
(wanteth love from another.
(Pitiable is he who hath no love, but
(seeketh the love from another.
Trader is he who loveth and seeketh a response for his love.

Cont.)

ORIGIN:	VERSION:
Cont.)	Contemptible is he who seeketh not and receiveth not love from another.

Note 1): This sentence was published in Sayings I : "Gayan" - Sura 18.

Notebooks 1921 :	Saying. He is the lover who loves and asks for no return. Trader is he who loves and asks for love in return. Player is he who loves, but changes sides every season. He who loves and asks for love in return is a trader in love. He who loves, but changes his love every season is a player in love.

240.

In Inayat Khan's handwriting on the fly-leaf of a copy of 'In an Eastern Rosegarden', presented by him to Lakmé P. van Hogendorp, dated 5th March 1921.	Love produces harmony and harmony creates beauty, therefore the chief motto of life is 'Love, harmony and beauty'. Love in all things and beings the beloved God, in harmony with all in the right understanding, and beautify your life, by observing the beauty within and without. By love, harmony and beauty you must turn the whole life into a single vision of Divine glory. May your life, your music, and your soul, be blessed. Inayat Khan 5 March 1921.

241.

Notebook 19th April - 12th May 1923 :	Touch me not I 2) who am such an untrue 2) lover whose ...... 3) is made by artificiality, you might break my vow of chastity.

Notes: 2) The handwriting of this passage in the Notebooks has become illegible.
3) The word after 'whose' is not well legible, although Sk. read it as 'character'.

242.

Notebooks 1924 :	I neither believe in nor follow a man, I only worship the formless God, Who is beyond anyone's reach, Whom I myself do not know.

243.

Notebooks :	If it has cost you all you ~~possessed~~ had, to become a real man, it is a bargain.

ORIGIN:	VERSION:
244. Notebooks 1921 :	Heathen Saying. If man would have been perfect there would have been no God.
245. Notebooks 1922 :	It is man who maketh with his own hand an idol which he worshipeth and then it is the man again who breaketh the idol with his own hands, which he once had worshipped.
246. Notebooks 1921 :	Saying. Man always expects more than the life has to give.
247. Notebooks 1921 :	Sura. Man himself is the best judge of his own doings, no one else can judge better.
248. Notebooks 1922 :	Saying. Man is the greatest mystery there is.
249. Notebooks :	Saying. A man of friendly nature will always have friends.
250. Notebooks 1921 :	Saying. Man rebels, seeing his fellowman in an enviable position, not recognizing, how hard it is to get, it is harder still to keep it.
251. Notebooks :	Alapa. Man shows Our nature, but woman signifies Our art.

Cf. Sayings I : "Gayan" - Alapa 5.

252. Notebooks 1922 :	Saying. Man who has no (reputation (character? hath no feeling for the (reputation (character? of another.

Cf. Sayings I : "Gayan" - Chala 45.

ORIGIN:	VERSION:
253. Notebooks :	Man who lives in beauty and progresses through beauty, rises from external beauty to the inner beauty, the beauty of sentiment and virtue.
254. Notebooks :	Sura. The wisest man in the world may do a most foolish thing in an instant. Know by this the imperfection of man and trust in the Guidance from above.
255. Notebooks :	Sura. However greatly man's heart may seem drawn to the spiritual ideal, the moment question of money arrives, he shows himself if his treasure was residing in heaven or on earth.
256. Notebooks Autumn 1924 :	Men will always divide themselves into groups - it is human nature.
257. Notebooks 1922 :	Saying. Heathen- Manifestation is the grave of God and resurrection is His birth.
258. Notebooks :	Saying. With its maturity a seeking for God is born in the soul, the soul seeks after the truth and wisdom is the outcome of it.
259. Notebooks :	His Message is every Message ~~but when it comes from all sides~~ and it is given by all, but it is in its fulness, when given by Himself.
260. Notebooks :	My mind is calm in the thought of God My heart is tranquil in the peace of God.
261. Notebooks 1921 :	Saying. Every moment in life is an invaluable opportunity given to make life worth

Cont.)

ORIGIN: VERSION:

Cont.) while; who disregards this has lost his chance; who considers this has gained.

Cf. Sayings II : Part One under 29th February.

262.
Notebooks 1922 : Gamaka.
I was born a musician in a musical family and nourished by music was brought up in a musical atmosphere. I lived in music, I loved music and until music began to appear to me as only a miniature expression of the life which is all music. I then sought for the Musician in Whom I found my life's source. It is this pursuit which busied me.

263.
Notebooks : Narciss hath drunk out of Thy cup, Thy glance cast spell on it.

Notebooks : Narciss hath caught a magic spell since Thy glance did fall upon it. The flame became a haunted moth.

264.
Notebooks : It is nature which I love, though art I admire.

265.
Notebooks 1921 : Saying.
The reserved nature gives weight, but makes the personality heavy.

Cf. Sayings I : "Gayan" - Bola 150.
Cf. Sayings II: Part Two no. 96.

266.
Notebooks 1923 : Tana.
Ocean, why are you bitter?
I have taken the bowl of poison which the seekers after ....1)

Note 1): This saying was found unfinished in Inayat Khan's Notebooks.

267.
Notebooks 1921 : Sign of the Sufi.

(A tendency to friendship and dis-
(inclination to hostility.
(Inclined to friendship and dis-
(inclined to hostility.
Ready to forgive and unwilling to take offence.

ORIGIN: VERSION:

268\.
Notebooks : Pain with resignation and pleasure with thanksgiving.

269\.
Notebooks 1921 : Saying. Heathen-
When you rise above passion you know what is love,
When you rise above love you know what is God,
but when you rise above the God ideal then you know yourself.

270\.
Notebooks : Forget the past, think not of the morrow, but mind the now present now.

271\.
Notebooks : Trouble not about the past, worry not over the future, but concern yourself with the present, for it is the present which is the picture of the past and the design for the future.

272\.
Notebooks : If you are rich, people envy you, if you are poor, they have contempt.

273\.
Notebooks : Message.
Most people want the world Teacher to come as a full moon, being ignorant of the fact that when the moon is full, it begins to decline.

274\.
Notebooks : There are some people, such-that if they are once allowed to whisper in your ears, they will take liberty too and they will whisper next in your mouth.

275\.
Notebooks : Western people have tendency toward doing something which can bring practical result. Faná or Laya, having no substantial gain, it does not agree with them. To the Eastern the value of nothingness is known, so he goes along this without being sceptical or disappointed, not expecting from his hard work any result but that nothingness which is everything.

ORIGIN:	VERSION:

276.
Notebooks 1921 :

Saying.
Towards the One, the Perfection of Love, Harmony and Beauty, the Only Being.

United with all the illuminated souls, the rays of the Master spirit.

One with all the illuminated souls.

United with all the illuminated souls, who form the embodiment of the Master, the Spirit of Guidance.

Notebook 1921 :

Towards the One, the Perfection of Love, Harmony and Beauty, the Only Being, united with all the illuminated souls who form the embodiment of the Master, the Spirit of Guidance.

277.
Notebook 19th April - 12th May 1923 :

Saying.
As much good a person is, so much capacity he has to be the contrary.

278.
Notebooks 1921 :

Phy.
An intuitive person often makes a mistake, not because he had no intuition, but because he did not listen to it.

Cf. Sayings I : "Gayan" - Gamaka 11.

279.
Notebooks 1914/1915, in Begum's handwriting :

A spiritual person may experience the life through senses in the organs of body, still not take a delight in anything material, his joy being centered in spirit. Neither food, drink nor comfort would enslave him, his joy being independent of all.

280.
Notebooks :

Beautiful personality is the proof of the real prophet.

281.
Notebooks 1921 :

Saying.
Some plants burn by the sun, so some people are spoilt by love.

282.
Notebooks :

Saying.
The hard times show the holes in human nature.

ORIGIN:	VERSION:
Notebooks :	Poverty shows holes in human nature.

283.

Notebooks 1914/1915 :	Two powers are working through the world, creative and responsive.

284.

Notebooks 1921 :	Py. Offering prayer to God is bringing to God consciousness of His perfection.

285.

Notebooks :

Your presence gives me exquisite joy and an unearthly passion doth rise in my heart.

Your presence lifts me up with joy and an unearthly passion does rise in my heart.

I become raised above small things of life and my burden is lightened.

My burden lightens and I rise above all things, cares of my life at that moment depart.

Your eyes inspire me with trust and confidence and make me drunken with heavenly wine.

Thy presence filleth me with joy, and an unearthly passion does rise in my heart.
My burden lighteneth, I rise above all things, cares of my life in Thy presence depart.
Thine eyes inspire me with trust and confidence and make me drunken with celestial wine.

Cf. Sayings I : "Vadan" - Gayatri Pir and Nabi, which may date from the same period.

286.

Notebooks 1921 :	Saying. The very presence of the wise answers the problems of life.

287.

Notebooks 1921 :

My false pride falleth down on earth before thee in prostration in the morn with thy rise, oh sun, I found myself as a twinkling star in the midst of the darkness of night, and by Thy mild light, o crescent moon, my vanity quickeneth and I thought I

Cont.)

ORIGIN:	VERSION:
Cont.)	was something, I was somewhere, I was somebody.

288.

Notebooks :	Who is the promised one? It is he who realizes that promise within himself and inspires others with same.

289.

Notebook 19th April - 12th May 1923 :	Saying. The purity of the water is in its passivity for all dirt that comes to the sea, it receives 1) without any resistance and sends it down to the bottom 2) but the tank resists it, so it stands on the face of the earth. Resist not evil.

Note 1): Added 'it' by Sk.
2): After 'the' in Inayat Khan's Notebook only a line is still visible where Sk. read 'bottom'.

290.

Notebooks 1921 : with Inayat Khan's explanation of the word 'barzakh'.	Saying. Sangatha. Purpose is like a barzakh 3); as barzakh appears before the eyes, so purpose is before mind and as barzakh is in fact not existent, so is purpose in reality.

Note 3): Barzakh: an interval, partition, bar, the interval of time, according to the Qur'ān, between the death of a man and the resurrection; a picture of the imagination.

291.

Notebooks 1921 :	Saying. There is a purpose behind all things.

292.

Notebooks :	Saying. There is a purpose for everything known or unknown, but beyond this purpose there is no purpose and that non-purpose is the purpose of all.

293.

Notebook 1914/1915 :	The quickening of the heart is the prize of life's pain.

Cf. Sayings II : Part One, under 15th August, and
Sayings I : "Gayan" - Bola 157.

ORIGIN: VERSION:

294\.
Notebooks 1914/1915 : The reality of the Arif 1) is unreal to an average person and that which is real to him is unreal to the Arif.

1) 'Ārif': Hindustani word for wise, a holy man. As a Sufi term it means gnostic.

295\.
Notebooks 1922 : Raga.
They say I have lost my reason, for I seek after the unseen, but Thou art manifest to my view by Thy Grace since my sight is keen.

296\.
Notebooks : Think no further than your reason allows you to think,
Feel no deeper than your heart can bear,
Say no more than ~~that-what-is-momentary wise-to-demand~~ what is necessary to be said,
Act no more once your purpose is accomplished.

297\.
Notebooks : Where relativity ends, reality begins.

By rising above relativity, one touches reality.

Cf. Sayings I : "Vadan" - Bola 151.

298\.
Notebooks : Philosophy.
The one who becomes wise with rise,
becomes wiser with fall,
but the one who with a rise becomes foolish,
will become a greater fool with a fall.

299\.
Notebooks 1921 : Sura.
When the rocks are asleep, leaving Us to use them for whatever purpose We may, when the trees are resigned to Our will to bear whatever fruit We may want them to bear,
when the animals are carried along with their passions and appetites,
We have made you partner in Our dominion and have given you a share in Our mercy, compassion, wisdom and righteousness, that your heart may expand so that it may rise to Our own perfection.

ORIGIN:	VERSION:
300. Notebooks :	I am a rose of Thy garden, and o Thou, the seed, the root, the origin, Thou art hidden through the darkness of night.

Cf. Sayings I : " Gayan" - Raga 22.

---

301. Notebooks :	O rosebud, why have you so many thorns around you? To test my lover.

---

302. Notebook 19th April - 12th May 1923 :	Tana. Roseplant, from where do you get your flowers and thorns? Flowers I inherit from the heaven and thorns from the earth.

---

303. Notebooks :	Loving ones must make sacrifices, and loveless must submit to their punishment.

---

304. Notebooks :	Sea-green, what do you signify? I am the same thing in the water as the jealousy in the human heart. Tana. Sea-green, what do you signify? The confusion of the brain of the sea.

---

305. Notebook 19th April - 12th May 1923 :	Verna. The sea : What do you bring me that swings my soul with joy? The new moon : Good tidings.

---

306. Notebooks :	Verna. Sea to the morning breeze : What does thy gentle kiss mean express? Good morning. What have you come to tell me? Rise before the sunrise.

---

307. Notebooks :	Verna. The sea : What doest thou bring me that giveth me such ecstasy? The morning breeze : The breath of life.

ORIGIN:	VERSION:
308. Notebook 19th April - 12th May 1923 :	Verna. The sea : What does make you sweet and me bitter? River : My devotion and your conceit.
309. Notebooks :	In the search of truth all one has lost is not really lost, only it has cost.
310. Notebooks 1914/1915 :	For the seer of the light the dark is a dark and for the waker in the dark the light is dark just like the sun blind.
311. Notebooks :	Bola. Being by oneself is being one's self.
312. Notebooks 1923 :	W 1) Gamaka. My self is higher than every claim that can be made, therefore ~~I claim to be nothing~~ I make no claim.

Note 1): W probably stands for "Wadan" (= Vadan).

ORIGIN:	VERSION:
313. Notebooks 1921 :	When I look at Thee I fly heavenwards, when I look at my little self I drop down. When Thou art before my vision I fly, my burden becometh light, but as I see my little self I drop down and upon me falleth all the load of the earth.
314. Notebooks :	Chala. By controlling one's sentiments one becomes a reservoir of power. By controlling your sentiments you become a reservoir of power.
315. Notebooks, probably 1924 :	A service without wages, love without reciprocity, merit without gift, beauty without appreciation.

ORIGIN: VERSION:

316\. Notebooks 1922 :

Saying.
It is your physical shadow reflected in the heart of another which becomes doubt.

Cf. Sayings I : "Gayan" - Chala 140.

317\. Notebooks 1924 :

He who is ready to observe the funny side of things, who is **ready** inclined to sympathize with the sorrowful, who is inclined to admire beauty in all its expressions, who is inclined to observe all that is deep and subtle is indeed an awakened soul.

318\. Notebooks 1921 :

Saying.
The one who agrees the most, sees all sides of the question, and the one who disagrees, sees but one side.

319\. Notebooks 1923 :

Chala.
Sin is something which does not cope with one's life and character, its effect on life is like the effect of some food one has eaten which one cannot digest.

320\. Notebooks :

Saying.
Looking at the sinful makes the sin embarrassed, when the sinner looks at his sin, he becomes ashamed of himself.

321\. Notebooks 1921 :

Saying.
Every situation of life is a preparation for some purpose.

Note: See Sayings I : "Gayan" - Bola 128.

322\. Notebooks 1921 :

Situations are involved under circumstances.

323\. Notebooks 1921 :

Raga.
The song of Thy glory so many singers have sung in all ages, and yet it is never finished.

ORIGIN: VERSION:

324

Notebooks 1921 : Saying.
Sorrow tunes a person to a higher pitch.

325.

Notebooks : Every soul is to be illuminated by My spirit.
Every heart is open to My call.
Every soul awaits My glance.

Cf. Sayings I : "Vadan" - Alapa 6.

326.

Notebooks 1921 : Phy.
The soul is linked directly with all that concerns it and its reflection falling upon all it concerns directs affairs of life accordingly.

327.

Notebooks : Speech of a sage is inspiring, but his silence illuminates souls.

328.

Notebooks : My lionlike spirit has been closed in prison bars,

(My soul is soaring, holding
(My soaring soul is holding a beg-

gar's bowl in hand.

329.

Notebooks : The spirit of discontentment will never be satisfied, but will demand more and more ~~satisfaction, if you offered it at all,~~ even if you gave it all that is in the earth and in the heaven.

330.

Notebooks : There are seven steps to the staircase of Love: 1. passion, 2. affection, 3. admiration, 4. adoration, 5. devotion, 6. service and 7. sacrifice.

1. attraction, 2. control, 3. support, 4. use, 5. govern, 6. raise, 7. renunciation.

1. observe, 2. penetrate, 3. analyze, 4. conceive, 5. distinguish, 6. express, 7. synthesize.

1. observation, 2. penetration, 3. perception, 4. conception, 5. analy-

Cont.)

ORIGIN:	VERSION:
Cont.)	sation, 6. assimilation, 7. synthesisation.

331.
Notebooks :

Let your strength be the force of truth.

332.
Notebooks 1921 :

Phy.
When the strongminded takes counsel of the weakwilled and when the wise listens 1) the advice of the foolish, then affairs go wrong.

Note 1): 'To listen' without preposition: see Oxford Dictionary.

333.
Notebooks :

Saying.
Study begins in observation and ends in examination,

334.
Notebooks :

1. ~~Seek the truth, not success~~
   Seek not success, but truth.
2. Trust even your worst enemy.
3. Forget the past; give up the thought for the morrow, only make the best of ..... 2)
4. Work for the work, not for success.
5. Value the nobility of the soul ~~more than money~~ most of all things.
6. Respect every soul, worthy or unworthy.
7. Don't forgive yourself for not forgiving the others.
8. Consider no loss greater than losing one's soul.
9. Arrest every impulse and examine before it is expressed.
10. If you believe in no God, worship ~~beauty~~ nature.

Note 2): an open space in the Notebook.

335.
Notebooks, probably 1924 :

A Sufi must always recognize in God the source of all things and the origin of all beings.

336.
Notebooks, probably 1924 :

A Sufi must observe in the continual unfoldment of the spirit the birth of the soul.

ORIGIN:	VERSION:
337. Notebooks :	Verna. The rising sun : What offering do you bring me? The roses : Our tears.
338. Notebooks 1914/1915, in Begum's handwriting :	Sun is formed by the grouping of vibrations of Noor, the light, and moon the shadow of the sun. The planetary system is formed of the limited groupings of the vibrations of sun's light by its activity and the world is the result on the surface of the activity of the sun. The colours are the illusions which take place during a certain replacement of the vibrations appearing to our sight under the influence of time and space.
338A. Notebooks 1914/1915, in Begum's handwriting.	The human race at each step of evolution added a special beauty until it arrived from animal likeness to a beautiful human structure and then here a time comes that the store and stock of the most beautiful forms and merits should thus be sacrificed to the machines. Had it been better if the war would have come a little later when the machinery would have been perfected enough to fight together in the place of man with his brave and beautiful heart.
339. Notebooks 1914/1915, in Begum's handwriting.	The sweet eater wants attention The sour eater wants argument The salt eater wants beauty The pepper eater wants ....1)

Note 1): an open space in the Notebook.

340. Notebooks :	Saying. The teacher creates appetite in the pupil for the knowledge which cannot be taught.
341. Notebooks 1923 :	Message. The great teachers have been the examples for souls bound to perfection.

ORIGIN: VERSION:

342.
Notebooks : Gamaka.
Every thing in life that strikes against my heart acts like turning of a switch that puts the light on.

Cf. Sayings I : "Vadan" - Gamaka 6.

343.
Notebooks : There is one thing which has no answer and that is: "Why".

Notebooks : Why, - I have no answer for thee.
Why, - Thy self art the cover over the answer.
Why, - Thou art an appetite which in the morning is fed; in the eve asks for food.

Notebooks : Tana.
Match-stick, what did you say when I struck thee ?
Why?

Cf. Sayings I : "Gayan" - Tana 21.

344.
Notebooks : Saying.
All things lead to some good.

345.
Notebooks 1921 : Saying.
All things that make man long for them, deprive him of his freedom.

346.
Notebooks 1921 : Saying.
It is easy to believe and it is easier still to disbelieve without troubling to know about the things.

347.
Notebooks : There is nothing which is wrong, ~~wrong is only that which is not in its place~~ things seem ~~to be~~ wrong when not in their proper place.

Cf. Sayings I : "Vadan" - Tala 46.

348.
Notebooks 1921 : Saying.
Things you would never like to do, circumstances compel you to do.

ORIGIN:	VERSION:

349.
Notebooks 1921 :

Philosophy.
Three things of the Bible are less understood by the generality: the self-denial, the vain repetition, and the sacrament.

350.
Notebooks :

Saying.
To talk about inner things to an unmatured soul is like singing romance to a babe in the cradle instead of lullaby.

351.
Notebooks 1921 :

Phy.
While holding things you are held by them, but as you lose your hold on them so they will be attracted to you as steel to the magnet.

A typewritten copy of Sangatha I-12.

Tassawuf.
When holding things you are held by them; ___ as - - - - - - - - - - - etc. as steel is attracted to a magnet.

352.
Notebooks :

Prayer.
I am friendless among friends and I am lost on finding Thee.
My life's safety is in clinging fast to Thy rope and when I let it loose my life is in danger.
I am fearless in Thy thought when I took to this in all times.

353.
Notebooks 1921 :

Saying.
A thousand worldly clever people cannot make one real wise man.

354.
Notebooks 1921 :

Saying.
Even the trees cover under their leaves and branches what must be covered and when man boldly brings out his infirmities and is proud over them, certainly his soul has not come to life yet.

355.
Notebooks 1921 :

Saying.
Going after truth considering it false is worse than going after falsehood.

Cont.)

ORIGIN:	VERSION:
Cont.)	Going after truth thinking it might be false is worse than treading the path of falsehood.

356.
Notebooks :

Truth is my backbone,
Love is my heart,
Imagination is the wings I have,
and on the legs of reason I stand,
Duty is my hand,
Life is my voice
and my word is God.

357.
Notebooks :

When truth is not recognized by the people, falsehood takes its chance.

358.
Notebooks 1924 :

Roseflower, why do you open your mouth?
To tell you of my glorious past.

Cf. Sayings I : "Vadan" - Tana 9.

359.
Notebooks 1924 :

Roseflower, what are you saying with your lips open?
I am speaking of my glorious past.

Cf. Sayings I : "Vadan" - Tana 9.

360.
Notebooks :

Tulip, where is your reserve gone?
My reserve has passed with the moments of vanity and I am left here.

Cf. Sayings I : "Gayan" - Tana 5.

360A.
Notebooks :

It is most essential to distinguish between want and need.

Cf. Sayings I : "Vadan" - Chala 10.

361.
Notebooks :

Saying.
The uncovering of the error is discovering of the path.

362.
Notebooks 1914/1915 :

The universe is formed by the five elements which alone sustain it and in the same it is absorbed.

ORIGIN:	VERSION:
363. a) Notebooks 1921 :	W. of P.M. The general unrest in the world at the present moment is an outcome of wrong mentality and the only way out of it is the changing of the attitude of mind from wrong to right.
b) Copied by Gd.	Words of Pir-o-Murshid The general unrest in the world at the present moment is an outcome of wrong mentality, and the only way out of it is the changing of the attitude of mind from wrong to right.

---

364. Notebooks, probably 1924 :

Tala
Who has once sinned is a venturer, who has twice sinned is an explorer, but who has thrice sinned is a sinner.

---

365. Notebooks :

There are many ways which lead to illusion, but there is one way that leads to truth.

---

366. Notebooks 1921 :

Saying.
Do not put your weight on others unnecessarily, for they, in their turn, will throw you down and tread upon you.

Cf. Sangita I-8.

---

367. Notebooks 1921 :

Amusing idea.
In the West feet do not exist, they are buried in the boots.

---

368. Notebook 19th April - 12th May 1923 :

How charming is your gentle whispering, o morning breeze, it thrills my heart, vibrating through my whole being.
It is the glad tidings I bring you, the sun will soon rise.

---

369. Notebooks 1921 :

Saying.
The wise is more ready to believe than the foolish one.

---

370. Notebooks :

~~Every word gives rise to a question.~~
Words raise argument as dust raised by the wind, but as the water keeps
Cont.)

ORIGIN:	VERSION:
Cont.)	dust down, so is the power of silence upon the restless mind.

371.
Notebooks 1921 :

Question:
Please tell me what are you, what is your work, and what is your aim?

I am what I know myself to be, and also I am what you think I am, my work is whatever I do and my aim is to be what I must be.

372.
Notebooks 1921 :

Question:
Please tell me what you are?

I have three aspects to my being:
First I am what I am,
Second I am what I know myself to be,
Third I am what you take me to be.

Please explain all three aspects you just mentioned in detail.

The first aspect of my being is beyond significance,
The second aspect can be only in my knowledge,
and the third aspect you already know.

373.
Notebooks :

Tana.
Workman, you were sleeping, I suppose?
No, I was sawing wood.

Note: 'To saw wood' (fig.) means: to work while others deliberate (U.S.slang, 1909). See Oxford Dictionary.

374.
Notebooks 1914/1915, in Begum's handwriting :

Bad you be you are cruel to the world,
Good you become you crush yourself.
Therefore Sufi forms his principle according to the standard of the world's evolution according to the trend of the thought of the land in order to serve his environments and surroundings in whichever way he may bring peace.
Therefore his inner life is different from the outer which he calls mysticism.

375.
Notebooks 1921 :

Phy.
If you are displeased with yourself

Cont.)

ORIGIN:	VERSION:
Cont.)	then the whole world is displeased, even God is displeased with you, but if you are satisfied with yourself, then what else do you need?

376.

In Inayat Khan's handwriting, found together with sayings copied by Mt., and classified by Inayat Khan as 'Gamak'.	Gamaka. There is nothing in the world that I specially care for, though everything in life interests me.

377.

Notebooks :	Gamaka. There is nothing in the world which I cannot do, but many things there are which I must not do.

378.

Notebooks :	The world is large, but I am larger still.

379.

Notebooks 1921 :	Phy. The world within you is reflected in the world without and it is the action and reaction between the two worlds that makes your life.

380.

Notebooks :	Saying. It is better not to be than be in the wrong.

381.

Notebooks 1922 :	Message. To be so fine as to keep tuned to that high pitch that He may at any moment find His lute ready to strike and at the same time to be as strong as the steel to endure the constant wear and tear of this earthly life. It is to be in heaven and at the same time on earth, which is beyond the power of every man except the one with the supernatural power who beareth the Message from above and walketh on this earth. He walketh on the thorny path barefooted, over doubts, suspicions, criticisms, oppositions, treachery, deceit and all evils (of the human nature. (the human nature breeds.

Cont.)

ORIGIN: | **VERSION:**

Cont.)

He fighteth every fear, risketh every danger of life and yet unshaken in his faith and with unbroken courage, with closed eyes and open heart, he passeth unimaginable distances, on the land, in the water, through the air toward the sky.
He who is seen by all and yet not seen, known to all and yet unknown, living amidst all and yet far away, speaketh to all and yet perfectly silent, walketh most gently and humbly on the earth, such is the being of the Messenger. To the eyes of men he is a man and in the being of God he is God.

Most attached and yet detached, most interested and yet indifferent, sad and yet most joyful, rich and yet so poor, comrade of the old and friend of the ~~children~~ young, Master of both the worlds and yet the servant of all. Himself a beautiful personality, yet a worshipper of beauty, Himself the singer of heavenly lore and yet a great lover of song, Himself a prophet, yet enjoying all poetry, the Messenger is born of beauty, he lives in beauty, he spreads beauty all over and yet the same he must renounce.

Note: Although parts of these words appear in different compilations (Pamphlet 'The Message', 1922 and the book 'The Unity of Religious Ideals') the whole of them was not found elsewhere in the archives to-date.

382.
Notebook 1914/1915 :

A Western person does a thing at his immediate desire, he never waits to dream.

383.
Notebook 1914/1915 :

The Western person does not allow himself to render an undue help specially to a stranger, nor he expects the same from a stranger.
Surrender self to stranger.

384.
Notebook 1914/1915 :

Saying.
He who speaks bad of any one, he knows him but a little, and he who speaks good of any one, he undoubtedly knows him better, but he who knows and says nothing about any one, knows him the best, for he is the knower.

ORIGIN:	VERSION:

385.
Notebook 1914/1915 : The reward for man's virtue and punishment for his sin is first produced within his own mind, which in his life time is his courage or fear and heaven and hell after death.

386.
Notebook 1914/1915 : If a spiritual person tries to take another person on the path of the ditch digger, he cannot be succesful in it for he has a torch in his hand; it shows the person the ditch or pit before coming to it; but (if) a person whose soul is darkened can cause another to fall in a pit in one moment's time for he carries darkness with him, which overwhelms everybody that comes in his contact.

Cf. Sayings II : Part Two nrs. 84 and 85.

387.
Notebook 1914/1915 : In all ages woman has been considered as the ideal figure of beauty, though the sight of man and woman both together forms the most perfect picture of all creation.

388.
Notebook 1914/1915 : Love is the fire that burns all infirmities.

389.
Notebook 1914/1915 : Hurting with harsh words is worse than hitting with hard stone.

390.
Notebook 1914/1915 : An immoral person is preferable to the illmannered one.

391.
Notebook 1914/1915 : You cannot admire a beautiful person with ugly personality.

392.
Notebook 1914/1915 : Do not imagine what you do not wish to happen.

393.
Notebook 1914/1915 : Do not say what you do not wish to be done.

ORIGIN:	VERSION:
394. Notebook 1914/1915 :	A donkey is more useful than an ass among men.
395. Notebook 1914/1915 :	Trying to make a fool understand is as knocking one's head against a wall.
396. Notebook 1914/1915 :	Look for the satan in the crowd and search for God in the solitude.
397. Notebook 1914/1915 :	City is the home of the satan and wilderness is the abode of God.
398. Notebook 1914/1915 :	Sex. There is nothing after which man goes as blindly as after a woman. Adam would have easily left heaven for earth if Eva had only desired of him.
399. Notebook 1914/1915 :	Sex. It is the goodness of woman that makes man pray upon her and it is the tyranny of woman that makes man love.
400. Notebook 1914/1915 :	Sex. Poligamy. The progress of man and woman in different lines and in different speeds bring difference in the married couples.
401. Notebook 1914/1915 :	Sex. How inconsiderate it is of man who does not recognize any woman body as sacred as the womb of his mother.
402. Notebook 1914/1915 :	Sex. To a person with changeable nature, monogamy as a principle would become nothing but an imprisonment.
403. Notebook 1914/1915 :	Sex. Courtship. What respect that man has who cannot

Cont.)

ORIGIN:	VERSION:
Cont.)	respect a woman.

404\. Notebook 1914/1915 :

Saying.
She is a precious pearl that forms in the shell of heart and is found in the soil of the spirit, and that is sincerity.

Cf. Sayings I : "Gayan" - Bola 40.
Cf. Sayings II: Part One "The Bowl of Sâki", 28th January.

405\. Notebook 1914/1915 :

No ideal proves to be ideal in the end because it is not the creation of your own mind.

406\. Notebook 1914/1915 :

Saying.
Good manner is much more becoming than good dress.

407\. Notebook 1914/1915 :

The treasure of virtue is an imperishable treasure.

408\. Notebook 1914/1915 :

Misti. 1).
The nature of the trees to spread their branches and the forms of animals, birds and especially of man, all shows a light with its rays spread around; it is therefore star is the symbol of the form of man.

Note 1): Hindustani word for drunkenness, intoxication, lust.
In Persian poetry it is used to convey that the (Divine) beloved does not pay heed to the lover.

409\. Notebook 1914/1915 :

The brackets were put by Inayat Khan.

Saying.
Looking down in shame for one's fault is as kissing the feet (of the one offended) with one's eyes.

410\. Notebook 1914/1915 :
The brackets were put by Inayat Khan.

There is no better penalty (for one's fault) than repentance.

ORIGIN:	VERSION:
411. Notebook 1914/1915 :	Greeting one with a happy smile is as presenting one with most beautiful flowers.
412. Notebook 1914/1915 :	Power wants the eyes of justice.
413. Notebook 1914/1915 :	Be generous with your own but considerate with the property of another.
414. Notebook 1914/1915 :	Be forward in giving but backward in taking things from another.
415. Notebook 1914/1915 :	The heart of man is the shrine of God; take care when you touch it lest you may hurt the Unseen Dweller within.
416. Notebook 1914/1915 :	He who speaks things, he himself knows all, who listens knows but a little but the third person knows nothing.
417. Notebook 1914/1915 :	Justice is done by law and the law is made by man whose life is based on looking for his own interest.
418. Notebook 1914/1915 :	Selfdenial is the first step to saintliness.
419. Notebook 1914/1915 : The brackets were put by Inayat Khan.	Life is a (playground) stage to the thoughtless and a school to the thinker.
420. Notebook 1914/1915 :	Who receives an honour is honoured and who refuses it is above the honour.
421. Notebook 1914/1915 :	Saying. It is a blow that awakens from sleep,

Cont.)

ORIGIN:	VERSION:
Cont.)	not a caress.
422. Notebook 1914/1915 :	Saying. An action forced by a principle is not necessarily a virtue.
423. Notebook 1914/1915 :	Saying. Do not turn any one against anybody for you may teach him some day to turn against you.
424. Notebook 1914/1915 :	Teach yourself to suit the world instead of trying to make the world suit you, which can never be done.
425. Notebook 1914/1915 :	He who pities himself and looks for sympathy from others has failed and he who forgets himself sympathizing with others is the one whose life is a success.
426. Notebook 1914/1915 :	Saying. With things unchangeable, situations unalterable and people firm in their habit, you can do nothing but to put up with.
427. Notebook 1914/1915 :	You can break rocks, cut the wood and melt metal, you can direct animals and birds, but with man who does not learn, you cannot do anything.
428. Notebook 1914/1915 :	Saying. Life provides you with a substitute for all you have lost.
429. Notebook 1914/1915 :	World becomes bitter, life becomes hard and mind becomes weary, when misfortune overtakes man.
430. Notebook 1914/1915 :	Thoughts are the fruits of the seed man sows in his mind.

ORIGIN:	VERSION:
431. Notebook 1914/1915 :	Saying. The more I know, the more I realize how little I know.
432. Notebook 1914/1915 :	Why worry about another's fault, his fault itself is his own enemy.
433. Notebook 1914/1915 :	Saying. Honour sold for money and soul sold for honour, in all the cases the seller is at a loss.
434. Notebook 1914/1915 :	If your friend does not see from your point of view, do not argue, keep quiet, he will perhaps not understand you just now.
435. Notebook 1914/1915 :	Saying. Work for the sake of reward is a labourwork but work done for the sake of work is a piece of art.
436. Notebook 1914/1915 :	The tail of the scorpion has poison and poison is in the teeth of the snake, poison is in the tongue of man who hurts another by his harsh word but he who is bittered against another has a poison in his heart.
437. Notebook 1914/1915 :	Saying. The rich in the kingdom of God pity him whose kingdom passes away.
438. Notebook 1914/1915 :	Sound is the sign of life in the temples of Gods and Goddesses in Hindu churches . . . . . 1) bells ringing show life even in the silence. 2)

Notes: 1) may be an open space in the Notebook or an illegible part of the sentence.
2) the last four words are not clearly legible.

439. Notebook 1914/1915 :	Saying.

Cont.)

ORIGIN and elaboration :	DIFFERENT VERSIONS:
Cont.)	Love is without a head, beauty is without a heart.

440.

Notebook 1914/1915 :	Pain is as water to the plant of love.

441.

a) MS. Sk., dated Summer 1922. In shorthand; the first two sentences were written in longhand.	Error is made by a wrong aim. Every activity is as hitting at a target, when a man has not hit it rightly it is gone astray. Personally I consider to err not only natural but interesting. I think the persons who do not make an error will not do right also; he is not capable of either. Who does not ride will not fall also off the horse. It is the rider who will have a chance of falling. It is the person who is courageous himself to act, who will . . . .
b) Copied by Sk. from her shorthand.	Error is made by a wrong aim. Every activity is a hitting at a target; when one has not hit it rightly it is gone astray. Personally I consider to err not only natural, but interesting. I think the person(s?) who do not make an error will not do right also; he is not capable of either. Who does not ride will not fall also off the horse. It is the rider who will have the chance of falling. ___ ___ ___ ___ ___ ___ ___ ___ ___ ___ ___ ___

442.

Copied by Gd. from (?).	In absence of success, vanity finds support in failure. A donkey, being accustomed to whips, cannot feel the joy of being patted.

443.

MS. Gr., together with other sayings, mostly meant for publication in the "Gayan".	There are three paths : path of saintliness - of mastery - and the prophetic path. In the path of saintliness continual resignation is necessary. In the path of mastery constant struggle is required. In the prophetic path resignation to the past and struggle for the future is necessary.

Cont.)

ORIGIN and elaborations:	DIFFERENT VERSIONS:
Cont.)	Saying. There are three possible attitudes towards evil impressions. 1. In the path of saintliness one must consider it to be Karma and therefore be resigned to it. 2. In the path of mastery think it to be the evil force and fight against it. 3. In the prophetic path that which has happened think it was from Karma - and what will happen - think that you will struggle against it.

Cf. Part 2, no.620.

---

a) Some sentences in the lecture 'Psychology - Attraction and Repulsion' of 24th August 1925, reported by Sk. Sk.'s shorthand reads:	For the love is the plant of God. It needs no water to grow. It is life itself. It has power in itself to grow and expand.
b) Sk.'s transcription of her shorthand at a later date.	For ___ love - - - - - - - - - God; it - itself, it has - - - - - - - - - - - .
c) A typewritten version, found together with other sayings under the heading 'Written down by memory during the Summer School 1925'.	___ Love is - - - - - - - - - -God, it - - - to make it grow, __ __ ____ ______ _ it has the power within itself - - - - - - - - - - - - - - - - - - .

---

a) A sentence in the lecture 'Mysticism' of 4th September 1925, reported by Sk. Sk.'s shorthand reads:	The godly is not always the self-realized one. But the self-realized one is godly.
b) Sk.'s transcription of her shorthand at a later date.	- -one; but - - - - - - - etc.
c) A typewritten version, found together with other sayings under the heading 'Written down by memory during the Summer School 1925'.	The godly is not always ___ self realised, ___ but the self realised ___ is always godly.

---

a) A sentence in the lecture 'Mysticism' - 'The Path to God' of 10th July 1925, reported by Sk. Sk.'s shorthand and her	Then the man becomes God-man, God-conscious. Outwardly he is in the universe, inwardly the universe is in him. Outwardly he is smaller than a drop, (inwardly) he is larger than the ocean.

Cont.)

ORIGIN and elaborations:	DIFFERENT VERSIONS:
Cont.) transcription of it; in the latter the brackets were omitted.	
b) A typewritten version, found together with other sayings under the heading 'Written down by memory during the Summer School 1925'.	The God conscious man seems to be in the universe, in reality the universe is in Him. He seems to be smaller than a drop. in reality he is larger than the ocean.

447.

a) A sentence in the lecture 'Mysticism - When considering virtue ...' of 7th August 1925, reported by Sk. and published in the book 'Philosophy, Psychology, Mysticism', year not known. Sk.'s shorthand and her transcription of it:	Sacrifice begins renunciation but it is the point of perfection which may be called renunciation.
b) A typewritten version, found together with other sayings under the heading 'Written down by memory during the Summer School 1925'.	Sacrifice is a preparation for renunciation.

448.

a) Some sentences in the lecture 'It is the spirit of all souls ...' (= Religious Gatheka 2), Summer 1922, reported by Sk. Sk.'s shorthand and her transcription of it:	The belief in God is natural; but in life art and nature both are necessary. So God, Who exists independent of us making Him, must be made by us for our own comprehension.
b) Copied by Gd. as 'Gatheka No. 2', to which in Sk.'s handwriting was added 'Religious'.	- - - - - - - - - - - - - - .
Two alterations made by Gd. in her copied text.	- -life both art and nature are necessary. - - - - - - - - - - - - - - - - - - - of <u>our</u> making Him, -.
c) Copied by Gd. with other sayings meant for publication in the "Gayan".	___ Belief - - - - - - - - - - etc.

449.

a) MS. Gd., dated October 14th, 1917, 5 a.m.	Alapa. We have opened the book of life before thy sight and have taught thee

Cont. a)

ORIGIN and elaboration: DIFFERENT VERSIONS:

Cont. a) The word 'Alapa' was added later on.

from it the lesson. Is it a small boon for all thy pains? This book of life is open to all but known to few. Almost all turn the pages of this book day and night and yet every page in it is as a blank paper to them. There are many who can read this book like a parrot and cannot understand the meaning, but there are some blessed ones who turn the pages of this book bearing the divine torch in the hand. They alone can see into it clearly and read it properly and can understand Our teaching thoroughly.

b) A typewritten copy with five Alapas under the heading "Wadan". (Gd.'s bookpreparation for the "Vadan".)

Wadan.
Alapa.
- -
- - - - - - - - - - - - - - - taught thee,
from it, the - - - - - - - - - - etc.
- - - - to all, but - - - - - -etc.
- - and night, and - - - - - - etc.
- - - - - - - - - - - - - - - - - -book, like
a parrot, and yet cannot understand
the meaning. But there - - - etc.
- - - - - - - - - - - - -torch in ___ hand.
- - - - - - - - - - - - - - - - - - - -etc.

450.
a) MS. Gd., dated October 11th, 1917, 10 p.m.

The word 'Alapa' was added later on.

Alapa.
We have disclosed the hearts of people before thee, that thou mayest distinguish between false and true. It is not that thou mayest become indifferent to people, but that thou mayest become independent in the trust of thy Lord.

b) A typewritten copy with five Alapas under the heading "Wadan". (Gd.'s bookpreparation for the "Vadan".)

Wadan.
Alapa.
- - - - - - - - - - - - - - - -

451.
a) MS. Gd., dated October 11th, 1917, 10 p.m., second part of the previous sentences.

Alapa.
The universe is like unto a harp in Our hands and all in the universe are as its strings. Their high and low works therein are as the notes We strike upon Our harp. When We are pleased We can favour through thy ~~enemies~~ adversaries, when We are displeased We can disfavour through thy friends. All thy pain and pleasure is absolutely in Our hands. It is thy mistake that thou attributest the good and bad done unto thee to the

Cont. a)

ORIGIN and elaboration: | DIFFERENT VERSIONS:

Cont. a)

others, who are nothing but Our ~~in-struments~~ tools to work. As thou prayest thou just as well mayest see with open eyes Our might and Our works.

b) A typewritten copy with five Alapas under the heading "Wadan". (Gd.'s bookpreparation for the "Vadan".)

Wadan.
Alapa.
The universe is like unto a harp in Our hands, and all in this universe are as its strings. Their high and low works therein are as the notes We strike upon Our harp. When We are pleased We can favour through thine adversaries, when We are displeased We can disfavour through thy friends. All thy pain and pleasure is absolutely in Our hands. It is thy mistake that thou attributes the good and bad done unto thee to the others, who are nothing but Our tools to work with. As thou prayest, thou mayest just as well see with open eyes Our might and Our works.

452.

a) MS. Gd., dated October 12th, 1917, 6 a.m.

The word 'Alapa' was added later on.

Alapa.
To those whom We wish to torment We can torture their life even when they are in the midst of all environments of comfort and happiness and those whom We wish to make happy, in them We ~~send Our peace~~ open Our fountain of peace even if they are surrounded by ~~the~~ all miseries and discomforts. Do not look therefore to the seeming source of comfort and to the apparant means of happiness with a view to attain peace. Let not the miseries frighten thee nor let discomforts make thee disheartened. Look at Us. It is Our smile which brings 1)
and it is Our glance of wrath 2)
all the torture there is. We may turn the whole world for one into heaven. We may change in a moment's time heaven into hell. He who cannot see Us he is not living, he is dead, and to him We are as dead; and he who can see Us, he is living and to him We are alive.

Notes 1) and 2): an open space in the MS.

b) A typewritten copy with five Alapas under the heading "Wadan". (Gd.'s bookpreparation of the "Vadan".)

Wadan.
Alapa.
__ Those - - - - - - to torment, We can torture their lives even - - - -
\- - - - - - - - - - - - - - - - - - - -

Cont. b)

ORIGIN and elaboration:	DIFFERENT VERSIONS:
Cont. b)	- - - - - - - - happiness, and - - etc. - - - - - - - - - - - - -Our fountain of peace, even - - - - - - - - - - etc. Do not look, therefore, to - - - etc. - - - - - - - - - - - - - -We may turn the whole world for one into Heaven, We may change in a moment's time Heaven into Hell. He who cannot see Us, he is not living, he is dead, and - - - - - - - - - - - - - - - - - - -etc.

453.

a) MS. Gd., dated October 14th, 1917, 10 p.m. The word 'Alapa' was added later on.	Alapa. We have laid bare thy ideals before thee, that thou mayest for thyself see what is in them that is worth your while. Nothing ~~is-the-answer~~ except Our being in everything which is the only ideal there is. Therefore depend not upon any one save Us. We alone are your protector, your sustainer, your helper and your saviour. Have trust in Us, have faith in Us, depend only upon Us, and look upon Us for all things thou desirest. Verily all that the earth possesseth and all that the heavens contain is absolutely in the mighty hand of thy Lord, the all powerful, supreme, King of the whole being.
b) A typewritten copy with five Alapas under the heading "Wadan". (Gd.'s bookpreparation of the "Vadan".)	Wadan. We have laid bare thine ideals - etc. - - - - - - - - - - - - - - - - - -worth thy while. Nothing except Our Being in everything, which - - - - - - - - - - - - - - - - - - -etc. - - - are thy protector, thy sustainer, thy helper and thy saviour. -look to Us - - - - - - - - - - - - - - - - - - etc. - - all that the Heavens - - - - etc. - - - - - - - - - - - - - - - supreme King - - - - - - - - - - .

454.

a) Copied by Gd. from (?).	Message. The claimant of Christhood living on earth must surely be searched by numberless searchlights constantly falling upon him. Men can only see the limitations of his human life and can never ~~fathom~~ probe the hights of his dinivity, except some few ~~who-are~~ whose number is comparatively small ~~in-number~~.

b)

ORIGIN and elaborations:	DIFFERENT VERSIONS:
b) A typewritten copy, found with Gd.'s bookpreparation of 'The Unity of Religious Ideals', Chapter 'The Messenger', together with some other sayings under the heading 'The Message'.	The Message. The claimant of Christhood, living on earth, - - - - - - - - - - - - - - etc. - - - - - - - - - - - - Men can see only the - - - - - - - - - - - - - - - - -etc. - - - - - except some, who are few ____ ____ __ comparatively, ____ in number.
c) Another typewritten copy (Gd.'s bookpreparation of the "Vadan".)	Wadan. ~~Bola~~ Chala. - - - - - - - - - - - - - - - - - - -etc. - - - - - - - - - - - - - - - - - - -are few_ comparatively_ in number.

455.

Copied by Gd. from one of Inayat Khan's lectures, together with other sentences meant for publication in the "Vadan", under the heading 'Sayings (to be read to Pir-o-Murshid)'.	Chala. It is for our convenience that we say "thing" and "being"; in reality there are no things, they are all beings.

456.

a) A sentence in the lecture 'Concentration' (Gatha Series II no. 2, 'Everyday Life') of 28th July 1922, in Miss R. Jones's handwriting.	All faculties in man become invaluable when a person is able to use them at will.
b) Copied by Gd. 'from Gathas' and meant for publication in the "Gayan". In Mc.'s handwriting 'valuable' was written over 'invaluable'.	All faculties __ ___ become invaluable when - - - - - - - - - - - .

457.

a) A sentence in the lecture 'The Message' (Religious Gatheka 20) of 10th March 1921, reported by Mrs. Iris Reelfs.	The fatalist makes human beings as chairs and tables, the mystic makes even chairs and tables living beings.
b) Copied by Gd.	- - - - - - - - - - - - - .

458.

a) A sentence in the lecture 'It is the spirit of all souls ...' (Religious Gatheka 2), Summer 1922, reported by Sk.,	God cannot be two - God of each is God of all - but in order to comprehend that God we each have to make our own God.

Cont. a)

ORIGIN and elaboration:	DIFFERENT VERSIONS:
Cont. a) Sk.'s shorthand and her transcription of it.	
b) Copied by Gd. and meant for publication in the "Gayan".	God cannot be two; the God of each is the God of all, but - - - - - etc.

459.

a) MS. Gd.	Gamaka. The more pendent I have become the more I have suffered, owing to the indiscretion of people.
b) A typewritten copy with sayings meant for publication in the "Vadan". (Gd.'s bookpreparation).	Gamaka. The more independent - to people's indiscretion.

460.

The last sentence of 'Questions and Answers' after the lecture 'Metaphysics' of 10th July 1923, in Sr.'s handwriting.	The key of the mind lays in God realization.

461.

The beginning of the lecture 'Art', Summer 1921, reported by Sr. (Sr. and Sd. van Tuyll had it painted on the top of the walls of Sd.'s studio, 78 Anna Paulownastraat, The Hague, Holland).	Life is as the movement of lines. The beauty of lines is the wisdom and the beauty of life. Who understands lines, understands God's plan. The colour is a later creation than the line. The colour is the fulfilment of the line. The line is God's power (mind), the colour His softness (mercy, wisdom), the light is his everduring life.

462.

A separate sentence or may be an answer to a question, dictated by Inayat Khan to Sr. together with the lecture 'Art', Summer 1921.	Symbology means to understand every form, every colour, every light. To understand this in its ever creating action, is to understand the language of symbology.

463.

a) Copied by Gr. from (?).	Chala. All that man sees is his own thought; man out of his thought can produce a ghost, a satan or a devil; or he can produce God, the most Merciful and compassionate.
b) A typewritten copy with sayings meant for publi-	Chala. - - - - - - - - - - - - - - - - - - -thought.

Cont. b)

ORIGIN and elaborations:	DIFFERENT VERSIONS:
Cont. b) cation in the "Vadan". (Gd.'s book-preparation).	Man -a Satan or a devil, or - etc.

464.

a) A sentence in the lecture 'Intuition', 22nd May 1922, in M.lle Lefèbvre's handwriting. (A reporting of the simultaneous translation in French).	C'est l'insincérité, l'amertume, ... 1) porter rancune, à pouvoir 2) empêcher l'intuition.

Notes: 1) one word illegible.
2) not clear in the MS. It could be 'pouvoir'.

b) Copied by M.lle Lefèbvre from her own reporting.	C'est le manque de sincérité, l'amertume, la tendance à la rancune, qui empêchent l'intuition.
c) Copied as a saying by Gd.	C'est le manque de sincérité, l'amertume, une disposition rancunière qui empêche l'intuition.
d) An English translation of the lecture in Sadaruny's handwriting.	It is insincerity, bitterness, artificiality and spite which keep intuition away.

465.

a) The last sentence in the lecture 'Intuition', 22nd May 1922, in M.lle Lefèbvre's handwriting. (A reporting of the simultaneous translation in French).	Puisque l'homme, ce n'est pas son corps, mais son mind, c'est la santé du mind qui est la vraie santé, et le résultat de cette santé, c'est l'intuition. 3)

Note 3): Translation by compiler:
As man is not his body, but his mind, it is the health of the mind which is the real health, and the outcome of that health is intuition.

b) An English translation of this sentence as a separate saying, in Sadaruny's handwriting.	As man is not his body, he is his mind. Mind is the real health. The outcome of this health is intuition.

466.

a) A sentence in the lecture 'Sufism', 23rd July 1922 (Social Gatheka no. 7), reported or copied from (?) by Miss R.Jones.	If man is himself, the whole world is his own. If he is not himself, then even his self does not belong to him.
b) Copied by Gd. 'From Gathekas' and meant for publication in the "Gayan". Four words were crossed	- - - - - - - - - - - - - - - - - -world ~~belongs to him~~ is his own. If he - - - - - - - - - - - - - - - etc. Bolas III.

Cont. b)

ORIGIN and elaboration:	DIFFERENT VERSIONS:
Cont. b) out, probably by Mc., who wrote 'Bolas III' over it and in the margin: 'similar to another'.	- - - - - - - - - - - - - - - - - - is his own, if __ __ not _______ _ ____ even his self - - - - - - etc.

467.

a) Words spoken during an Evening Class on 14th August 1922, in an unidentified handwriting. (Sangatha II - 50).	When man says, "I have done this", or "I can do it", or "I will do it", the One perfect in power and wisdom smiles, as a grown-up person would smile at a child saying "I will remove mountains."
b) Copied by Gd. 'From Sangathas' and meant for publication in the "Gayan". In Mc.'s handwriting was written 'Omit' in the margin.	- - - - - - - - - - - - - - .

468.

a) The last part of the lecture 'Healing' of 28th July 1924, reported by Sk. Sk.'s shorthand and her transcription of it.	The best medicine is a pure diet, nourishing food, fresh air, regularity in action and repose, clearness of thought, pureness of feeling, and confidence in the perfect Being with Whom we are linked, and Whose expression we are.
b) Copied by Ng. as a saying, together with other sentences from lectures.	- - - - - - - - - - is _ pure diet, _________ ____ _ _____ ___ _ regularity in sleep and action, fresh air, clear thinking, purity of feeling_ and perfect confidence in the Divine Being with Whom we are linked_ and Whose essence 1) we are.

Note 1): Sk.'s shorthand has 'expression'; the next sentence in the lecture 'Healing', however, reads: 'That is the essence of health'. Therefore 'essence' under b) may have been taken erroneously for 'expression'.

469.

a) MS. Fm.	Gamaka. Who, do you think, give me over to my scornful opponents: Who eagerly await such opportunity; most often my own loving friends.
Alterations by Inayat Khan:	- opponents: who - - - - - - - - - - -opportunity; ____ _____ My own loving friends.
b) Copied by Gd. with other sayings,	_______ - - - - - - - - - etc. - - - - - - -

Cont. b)

ORIGIN and elaboration:	DIFFERENT VERSIONS:
Cont. b) meant for publication in the "Nirtan".	- - - - - - opportunity? - - - etc.

470.

a) The last sentence in the lecture 'The God Ideal', 22nd November 1921 (Religious Gatheka no. 31). No reporting of it has been found in the archives to date, only a typewritten copy.	It is not the path of freedom that leads to the goal of freedom, but the path of the God-Ideal that leads to the goal of Truth.
b) Copied by Gd., together with other sentences, meant for publication in the "Vadan", under the heading 'Sayings (to be read to Pir-o-Murshid)'.	Bola. - of freedom; but it is the - - - - - - - - - - - - - - etc.
Gd. crossed out the first part of the sentence (14 words) and three words of the second part.	___ It is the path of ___ God _____ that leads to the goal of Truth.

471.

a) MS. Sk.	Reaching perfection is contemplating on perfection.
b) Crossed out by Gd. who replaced it by:	Saying. One reaches perfection by contemplating on perfection.

472.

a) Copied by Gd. from (?).	Chala. Why are people so stupid? Because they enjoy being so.
b) A typewritten copy of sayings meant to be published in the "Vadan". (Gd.'s bookpreparation).	Chala. - - - - - - - - - - - - - - .

473.

a) A sentence in the lecture 'Heya' - Moral Culture (Gatha Saluk III No. 8), Summer 1922, reported by Sk. (Sk.'s shorthand and her transcription of it).	A modest person in comparison to the immodest one is like a plant standing by the side of a rock.
b) Copied by Gd. 'From Gathas' together with other sayings meant for publication in the "Gayan".	A modest person, in comparison with the immodest one, is - - - - - etc.

c)

ORIGIN and elaborations:	DIFFERENT VERSIONS:
c) Another copy found in Gd.'s handwriting.	The modest person, compared to the immodest - - - - - - - - - - - - etc.
474. Copied by Gd. 'From Gathekas', together with other sayings meant for publication in the "Gayan".	In the progress of the world ideal is the principal thing. What the world needs is not a certain religion, it needs the spirit of religion.
Mc. replaced 'ideal' by 'idealism', then crossed out the whole saying.	
475. A sentence in the lecture 'The Prophet' (Religious Gatheka No. 10), 19th August 1922, in Miss Jones's handwriting.	The Prophet is an interpreter of the divine law in human tongue.
See Sayings I :	"Gayan" - Chala 27 under a), first saying.
476. MS. Fm., together with other sayings meant for publication in the "Gayan".	Message. The Prophet's charm is his personality.
Copied by Km.	
Add. by Inayat Khan to MS. Fm.	Message. Bola (also). - - - - - - - - - - - - - - .
477. MS. Sk. In her handwriting is written underneath: 'As dictated by Murshid in answers to letters to different persons. Sakina.'	Please take no discouraging remarks from friends or foes to be effective. Think Whose Cause it is, and be sure that all will be well in the end. If F. did not come, Z. will come; if M. will not help, N. will support. We recognize only one help and one support, and that is the help of God. If the whole world failed us still we shall maintain our faith that the One, Whose service we do, will not fail us. All the outside things matter little; it is, that something which is hidden behind, counts.
478. MS. Sk. In her handwriting is written underneath: 'As dictated by Mursnid in answers to letters to	I do not take things seriously to heart, you do not need to worry about it. I have forgiven, from the day I called you my brother, all you did,

Cont.)

ORIGIN and elaboration:	DIFFERENT VERSIONS:
Cont.) different persons. Sakina.'	you do and that you may do. For I know it all comes from love, and it is the love of one being, and that is God. I continue to pray for you.

479.

a) MS. Gr.	A straight road before the soul that he may reach the goal.
b) Copied by Gd., together with other sayings, mostly meant for publication in the "Gayan".	- - - - - - - - - - - - - .

480.

Copied by Gd. 'From Q. and A.' 1), together with other sayings meant for publication in the "Gayan".	What does it matter if the scientist calls his religion science, if the literary man calls his, ideals and morals?
A few alterations in Mc.'s handwriting:	- science <u>or</u> if the - - - - - - - - - - - -his, <u>idealism</u> and <u>morality</u>?
Then the whole sentence was crossed out and in the margin was written in Mc.'s handwriting: 'Omit.'	

Note 1): 'Q. and A.' means: Inayat Khan's answers to questions. These have not been found as such in the archives to date.

481.

Copied by Ng., probably from her own MS., together with other Suras, meant for publication in the "Gayan".	Sura. Our deep sentiments we cannot tell to anyone; Truth is the deepest sentiment of the soul, therefore it cannot be told.

482.

MS. Ng. Copied by Km.	Heathen Saying. A tenderhearted sinner is better than one who is hardened by piety. 2)

Note 2): For complete elaborations and different versions see Sayings I : "Gayan" - Bola 37.

483.

a) Copied by Gd. from (?).	Bola. It is the slave who gives in, the Master struggles, but the Lord rises above all conditions of life.

ORIGIN and elaboration:	DIFFERENT VERSIONS:
b) A typewritten copy, together with other sayings meant for publication in the "Vadan" (Gd.'s bookpreparation).	Bola. - - - - - - - - - - - - - .
484.	
a) Copied by Gd. from (?), together with other sayings meant for publication in the "Nirtan".	Bola. Someone much sought for becomes costly.
b) A typewritten copy with sayings prepared by Gd. for publication in the "Vadan".	Bola. - - - - - - - -sought after becomes costly.
485.	
a) Two sentences in the lecture 'The liberal and Conservative Point of View' (Social Gatheka no. 9), 30th July 1922, in Gd.'s, Kf.'s and Miss R.Jones's handwriting.	Therefore the conservative spirit is the individualizing spirit, which is the central theme of the whole creation. But there is always a danger of this spirit, if increased, producing congestion.
b) Copied by Gd. 'From Gathekas', together with other sayings meant for publication in the "Gayan". In Mc.'s handwriting the 'b' of 'but' was replaced by a capital B, making it again two sentences and the last word was changed.	________ The conservative -the whole creation, but there - - - - - - - - etc. The conservative - - - - - - - - etc. - - - - - - - - - - - - - - - - creation. But there is - stagnation.
486.	
a) Copied by Gd. from (?).	If anyone talks to me against another out of spite my heart instantly goes out to the one of whom ill words have been spoken.
b) A typewritten copy with sayings meant for publication in the "Vadan" (Gd.'s bookpreparation).	Bola. - - - - - - - - - - - - - - .
487.	
MS. Gd. Found together with other sayings with the "Gayan"-documents.	The stillness of the idol stills the mind of the idol worshipper.

ORIGIN and elaboration:	DIFFERENT VERSIONS:
488.	
MS. Gd., together with other sayings meant for publication in the "Gayan".	Gamaka. The struggle of life in the world is the one thing which I dread the most, yet destiny has placed me in the very midst of it.
Two words crossed out by Mc.	- thing _____ I dread ___ most, - - - - - - - - - - - - - - - - - etc.
489.	
a) A sentence in the lecture 'Sufism' (Social Gatheka no. 7), 23rd July 1922, in Miss R. Jones's handwriting.	Success is natural, failure is unnatural.
b) Copied by Gd. 'From Gathekas', together with other sayings found with the Gayan-documents.	- - - - - - - - - - - - - .
490.	
Two sentences found as a separate saying in an undated lecture about 'Sufism', of which only typewritten fragments have been found in the archives to date.	The Sufi holds that the perfection of life is perfecting oneself not only spiritually, but in all different aspects of life. The man who is not capable of attending to all life's needs is certainly ignorant of the true freedom of life.
491.	
a) Copied by Gd., probably from her own MS. Inayat Khan wrote in the margin: 'Put on separate page'.	What is the religion of the Sufi? Natural life. What is the manner of the Sufi? Simplicity. What is the goal of the Sufi? Self-realization. What is the God of the Sufi? His very being. What is the path of the Sufi? Friendship. What is the art of the Sufi? Humility. What is the charm of the Sufi? Personality. What is the moral of the Sufi? Beneficence. What is the cross of the Sufi? Forgiveness. What is the Beloved of the Sufi? God. What is the ideal of the Sufi? Man.
Mc. altered 'moral' (8th line) into 'morality'.	What is the <u>morality</u> of the Sufi? Beneficence.

b)

ORIGIN and elaborations:	DIFFERENT VERSIONS:
b) Published in the magazine 'Sufism', June 1923.	Sufi Characteristics.
9th question:	What is the attitude of the Sufi?
11th (last) question:	What is the Ideal of the Sufi?

Note: version b) also became Sangita III-6.

2.

a) A typewritten copy with other sayings about a Sufi, in the form of questions and answers, part of which became a Sangita.	What is a Sufi? One who does not separate himself from others by opinion or dogma, and who realises the heart as the shrine of God. What does he desire? To remove the false ego and discover God within. What does he teach? Happiness. What does he seek? Illumination. What does he see? Harmony. What does he give? Love to all created things. What does he get? A greater power of love. What does he find? God. What does he lose? Self.
b) Printed at the beginning of each issue of 'The Sufi Quarterly', Sept. 1926-March 1933.	A Sufi Dialogue
2nd answer:	To remove the false self and - - - .
8th question and answer:	What does he find? GOD.
9th question and answer:	____ ____ And lose? self.

2A.

MS. Gd. and a stencilled H.Q. copy.	Who has lost Me is lost; who has found Me has found himself.

Cf. Sayings I : "Vadan" - Gamaka 19.

2B.

a) Copied by Ng. from (?).	Tala. Love from above is forgiveness. From below is Devotion. From within is kindness and from without is affection.
b) Copied by Ek. and classified by Inayat Khan as 'Tal'.	Tala. - - - - - - - - - - - - - - .
c) Only the first two lines were published in the "Gayan" - Tala 3.	

93.

a) A sentence in the lecture 'Concentration' - Everydaylife (Gatha II-	All things that deprive one of one's freedom in life are undesirable.

Cont. a)

ORIGIN and elaboration:	DIFFERENT VERSIONS:
Cont. a) No. 2), 28th July 1922, in Miss R.Jones's and Kf.'s handwriting.	
b) Copied by Gd. 'From Gathas', together with other sayings meant for publication in the "Gayan".	- - - - - - - - - - - - - - .
Two words altered by Mc.	- - - - - - - - - deprive man of his freedom - - - - - - - - - - - - .

494.

a) Copied by Gd. from (?), together with other sayings meant for publication in the "Vadan".	Tala. Tone continues, time expires.
b) A typewritten copy. (Gd.'s bookpreparation of the "Vadan").	Tala. - - - - - - - - - - - - - - .

495.

Copied by Gd. from (?), together with other sayings meant for publication in the "Vadan".	Tala. Tone lives on time; time assimilates tone.

496.

a) The last sentence in the lecture 'The Way how the wise make life in the world,' of 22 Aug. 1922, not known by whom reported. Only Sk. hwr. copy, a typed and a stencilled copy are in the archives. (= Religious Gatheka no. 11.)	Verily, truth is the treasure that every soul is seeking.
b) Copied by Gd. 'From Gathekas'. The whole saying was crossed out, probably by Mc.	Verily_ truth is - - - - - - etc.

497.

a) Two sentences in the lecture 'The Message' 1), 16th June 1925, reported by Sk. (shorthand and and her transcription).	The real meaning of initiation is to be reborn, to be born again. The first birth is the birth of the person, the next birth is the birth of the soul.
b) From nine typewritten sayings (= sentences in lectures and Questions and Answers) under the	Initiation is in reality __ __ ______ _ to be born again. The first birth is the birth of the person, the second birth is the birth

Cont. b)

ORIGIN and elaboration:	DIFFERENT VERSIONS:
Cont. b) heading 'Written down by memory during the Summer School 1925'.	of the soul.

Note 1): This same lecture is also Sangita I-116 'The Message - Wakening to the Message'.

498.

A sentence in the lecture 'Saluk', Moral Culture - Respect (Gatha III no. 4), Summer 1922, reported by Sk. (shorthand and her transcription).	A true worshipper of God sees His presence in all forms and in respecting others he respects God.

See Sayings I : "Gayan" - Chala 16 for elaboration and different version.

499.

On a stencilled Head Quarter's copy, prepared by Gd., with sayings meant for publication in the "Vadan".	Chala. In the vastly prevailing flood of feeling the spirit of action becomes drowned.

500.

a) The last sentences of the lecture 'The soul's manifestation', 1st September 1923, reported by Sk. Sk.'s shorthand and her transcription of it. The lecture was published in 1924/1925 in the book 'The Soul Whence and Whither?' - Manifestation, Chapter 3.	The man who will shut up himself from all men, however high spiritual he may be, he will not be free in the Malakut, in the higher sphere. He will have a wall around him keeping away djinns, even angels when in the angel world; and so his journey is exclusive. It is therefore that Sufism does not only teach concentration and meditation which help one to make one onesided 2), but the love of God which is expansion, opening of the heart to all.

Note 2): one shorthand sign illegible.

b) A typewritten version together with other sayings, taken from the Magazine 'The Sufi Quarterly' of June 1932, under the heading 'Unpublished Sayings, preserved by Nargis.'	The man who shuts himself away from all men - however high spiritually he may be, he will not be free __ ___ _______ _ in the higher spheres. He will have around him a wall keeping away the genii from the sphere of djinns, and even the angels of the angelic heavens. ___ So his journey is exclusive. It is therefore that Sufism does not only teach concentration and meditation, which help one to make ___ onesided progress, but also the love of God, which is expansion - the opening of the heart to all beings, which is the Way of Christ and the Sign of the Cross. Note)

ORIGIN and elaboration:	DIFFERENT VERSIONS:
	Note : See Sayings II : Part Four no. 318 (the first sentence only).

501.

a) A sentence in the lecture 'The Purpose of Life', 28th July 1924, reported by Sk. Sk.'s shorthand and her transcription of it. The lecture was published in the book 'The Purpose of Life' (1927), Chapter 7.	The true religion is living and being conscious of this sense of duty that we have toward man and towards God.
b) In Ng.'s handwriting, together with other sentences from lectures, as separate sayings.	___ True religion is "living" , and being conscious of the ___ ___ duty ___ man has toward man and towards God.

502.

a) Part of two sentences in the lecture 'The Prophet' (Religious Gatheka no. 10), 19th August 1922, in Miss R. Jones's handwriting.	The Prophet is an interpreter of the Divine law in human tongue, he is an Ambassador of the spiritual hierarchy for he represents to humanity the illuminated souls who are known and unknown to the world, who are hidden and manifest, who are in the world, or on the other side of the world. The Prophet is an Initiate and Initiator, for he is an answer to the cry of humanity, of individuals, and of the collectivity.....
b) From a collection of sayings under the heading: 'Murshid's sayings passed on by Nargis.'	The Prophet is an Ambassador of the Spiritual Hierarchy for He represents to humanity the Illuminated Souls who are known and unknown to the world, who are hidden and manifest. The Prophet is an Initiate and an Initiator. An answer to the cry of humanity, individually and collectively.

Cf. Sayings I : "Gayan" - Chala 27 and Sayings II : Part Two, no. 475.

503.

a) The last sentence in the lecture 'Healing by Suggestion', (Gita Healing, Series III-7), 1920, of which only old typewritten copies and a handwritten copy by Miss R. Jones probably of a later date, have been found in the ar-	When the healer thinks he is healing, his power is as small as a drop, when he thinks God is healing, and when from his thought his own self is forgotten and he is only conscious of the self of God, then his power becomes as large as the ocean.

Cont.a)

ORIGIN and elaboration:	DIFFERENT VERSIONS:
Cont. a) chives to date. Published in 1931 in the book 'Health', Part II.	
b) From a collection of sayings under the heading: 'Murshid's sayings passed on by Nargis.'	- a drop. When he thinks - - - - - - - - - and when from his thought ___ ___ self is forgotten, and - - - - - - - - - - - - of the Self of God, - Ocean.
504.	
a) A sentence in the lecture 'Fulfilment of the Obligations of Human Life', 4th September 1922, taken down by a professional shorthand writer and published in 1923 in the book 'Inner Life', Chapter 3.	Friends, there is nothing in this world, wealth or rank, position, power or learning, that can give such conceit as the slightest little amount of spiritual knowledge, and once a person has that conceit then he cannot take a further step; he is nailed down to that place where he stands, because the very idea of spiritual realization is in self- -lessness.
b) From a collection of sayings under the heading: 'Murshid's sayings passed on by Nargis.'	Friends, there is nothing - - etc. - - - - - - - - - - - knowledge. ___ Once - - - - - - - - - - - - - - -etc. - -nailed down to the place - etc. - - - - - - - - - - - - - selflessness.
505.	
a) A sentence in the lecture 'The Purpose of Life', 28th July 1924, reported by Sk. (Sk.'s shorthand and her transcription). Published in the book 'The Purpose of Life' - Chapter 7 (1927).	In duty one finds a road which leads to the final purpose of life.
b) A typewritten copy with sayings under the heading 'Written down by memory during the Summer School 1924'.	In duty one finds the road which leads us to the goal which is the _____ purpose of life.
506.	
a) A sentence in the lecture 'The Message' (Religious Gatheka no. 45), 22nd June 1921, found only typewritten.	Now the question "What is pain" may be explained thus that pain is the fullest aspect of life.
b) In Sr.'s copybook of 1921 was written as a separate sentence:	Pain is the fullest aspect of life.

ORIGIN and elaboration:	DIFFERENT VERSIONS:
507.	
a) A sentence in the lecture 'The Message' (Religious Gatheka no.45), 22nd June 1921, found only typewritten.	Man's real being is his heart, and in pain the heart becomes living and without pain man seems to be living on the surface.
b) In Sr.'s copybook of 1921 was written as a separate sentence:	- - - - - - - - - - - - - heart_ and in pain his heart - - - - - - - - - - - - - - - pain he (lives (seems to live on the surface.
508. Three sentences, added to the Bolas in later editions of the "Nirtan".	The more you depend upon God, the more God becomes dependable.
509.	Love's reward is love itself.
510.	The essence of reason is the knowledge of God.
They do not appear in the "Nirtan" as first published by Kismet Stam, nor in the following edition published by the Sufi Movement. It may be assumed that these sentences were taken from Inayat Khan's lectures.	
511.	
a) Two sentences in the lecture 'The Way of Attainment' (Sadhana), 1921/1922, found in Gd.'s handwriting.	The great minds, the masters think that behind their thought, their will, there is the will of God. They have confidence in that will, and whatever they think is done.
b) As a separate sentence, in an unidentified handwriting; it was found with Gd.'s bookpreparation of 'The Unity of Religious Ideals'.	The great minds, the Masters, know that behind their thought and their will, ____ is the Will of God, they have confidence in that Will, and whatever they think, is done.
512.	
a) Three sentences in the lecture 'The Way of Attainment' (Sadhana), 1921/1922, found in Gd.'s handwriting.	It may be asked whether all things cannot be attained by psychic power alone without any physical means. But, as we exist on the physical plane and have the physical body, it is better to work with the physical means also, to work by the thought and with the body. In this way the aim is attained by all means.

ORIGIN and elaboration:	DIFFERENT VERSIONS:
b) As a separate saying, in an unidentified handwriting, it was found with Gd.'s bookpreparation of 'The Unity of Religious Ideals'.	It may be asked whether all things cannot be attained by psychic power alone, without any physical means, but as we exist on the physical plane and have a physical body, it is better to use ____ ___ physical means also. To work by the thought and with the body, in this way the aim is attained by all means.

513.

a) Two sentences in the lecture 'The Spiritual Hierarchy', (1917-1920) reported and revised by Dr. Gruner as published in the book 'In an Eastern Rosegarden', 1st ed. 1920/1921.	The warner, the master, the messenger of to-day will not claim; he will only work. He will leave his work to prove for itself whether it is true or false.
b) Copied by Ng. under the heading 'Some sayings of Murshid'.	The Warner, the Master, the Messenger of to-day, will not claim, he will only work. He will leave his work to prove for itself, whether it is true or false.

514.

a) Three sentences (two of which partly) in the lecture 'The Development of Ego' (= Gatha Moral Culture - Saluk II No. 8), 9th May 1921, in Miss R. Jones's handwriting.	When a person wishes to keep away from all jarring influences, he had better not try to live, It does not require strength to stand against the jarring influences of life - it is a small piece of wood, little and light that can fall and rise with the waves, be always above them uninjured and safe. The lighter, the smaller man's ego becomes the more power of endurance it has.
b) Copied by Ng. under the heading 'Some sayings of Murshid'.	When a person - - - - - - - - etc. - - - - - - - - - - - live. It does not - - - - - - - - - - etc. life. It is a small piece of wood, little and light, that can rise and fall with the waves, __ always above them, uninjured and safe. The lighter_ and smaller man's ego becomes, the more power and endurance it has.

515.

a) A sentence in the lecture 'About Discipleship', 18th May 1921 (Sangatha III-30) in	Even in the case of a Teacher the devotee may make a mistake by halting at the feet of the teacher and not progressing to God.

Cont. a)

ORIGIN and elaboration:	DIFFERENT VERSIONS:
Cont. a) Kf.'s handwriting.	
b) Copied by Ng. under the heading 'Some sayings of Murshid'.	Even in the case of the teacher, the - - - - - - - - - - - - - - - - - - etc.

516.

a) Two sentences in the lecture 'About Discipleship' (Sangatha III-30) 18th May 1921, in Kf.'s handwriting.	The secret of discipleship is not study or contemplation, but devotion. At that moment it is not Murshid but God Who is seen, the door is unlocked, the shrine opened, it is no more Murshid but God.
b) Copied by Ng. under the heading 'Some sayings of Murshid'.	The secret of discipleship is not in study - - - - - - - - - - - - - - - - . At the moment - - - - - - - - - - - etc. the shrine is opened, it is no more Murshid, but God.

517.

a) Two sentences in the lecture 'About Discipleship' (Sangatha III-30), 18th May 1921, in Kf.'s handwriting.	For the Teacher one has gratitude but love and devotion is for God. God alone deserves all love and the freedom of Love is in giving it to God.
b) Copied by Ng. under the heading 'Some sayings of Murshid'.	For the Teacher one has gratitude, but love and devotion are for God alone, Who deserves all love; and the freedom of love is in giving it to God.

Note: The second part of the saying was published in Sayings II : Part One, "The Bowl of Sãki" under 16th September.

517A.

Notebooks 1922 :	Be either false or true but not both if you wish success. /if you wish to be successful.

Note: The first part of the saying was published in Sayings I, "Gayan", Bola 7.

PART THREE

HITHERTO UNPUBLISHED SAYINGS AND WORDS OF PIR-O-MURSHID INAYAT KHAN,

found in the handwriting of some of his early mureeds.

INTRODUCTION TO PART THREE.

These additional sayings and other words of Inayat Khan are so far unpublished 1), just as are the sayings and other words in Part Two. For this reason the unpublished sayings and words of Part Two and Part Three were consecutively numbered.

In most cases it cannot be ascertained if these sayings were dictated by Inayat Khan to his pupils. They were found in the handwriting of some of his early mureeds; the sub-title over each group of sayings gives some further particulars. Dr. Gruner handed down typewritten copies of the sayings transmitted by him and probably destroyed his shorthand notes.

Note 1): An exception was made for some sayings, published in old Sufi Magazines and pamphlets and for two sayings, quoted by Ng. in her book 'The Way of Return'. These publications are mentioned in the left column.

PART THREE.

The following sayings and other words of Pir-o-Murshid Inayat Khan were received, collected and transmitted by some of his early mureeds :

Written down and preserved by Miss Angela Alt.

518. I wish that my mureeds everywhere should work towards the enlightenment of humanity.

519. All that begins in unhappiness and ends in discontent is wrong. And all that begins in happiness and culminates into content is right.

(given privately)

520. The heart is as the angelic body, the soul's finest body, yet only a temporary hotel of soul.
The heart is the shrine of God.

521. With indifference, one still must have sympathy and love, be more and more sensitive as one evolves.

522. Nirvana Faná Vairagia
Indifference independence dispassion.

523. I come from a perfect Source.
I am going to a perfect Goal.
The light of the perfect Being is kindled in my soul.
And in Him I live and move and have my being. 1)

Note 1): Another version was found in Miss Reza Jones's handwriting (see no. 642).

In Begum Inayat Khan's handwriting.

524. An Eastern person is inclined to give even to material things a spiritual meaning.
A Western person, on the contrary, is inclined to give every spiritual thing a material form.

Partly taken down, partly copied, collected and passed on by Miss Nargis Dowland.

525. It is the desire to learn, not to teach, by which one becomes a Teacher.

526. The explanation of a God-ideal is: closed lips.

527. Every lesson learnt in the inner life must be brought down and practised on earth before it is of real value on the path of discipleship. This is not generally realized, but only thus is true progress achieved.

528. As soon as a disciple says: "I know" he loses ground. All great Teachers of humanity have been great Pupils; learning from an innocent child, from situations, etc., he learns sympathy, harmony and beauty.

529. Meditation is for a purpose, not an end in itself.

530. Initiation signifies the entrance of a stranger into the bond of human brotherhood, so that the usual consideration of earthly distinctions and differences which separate man from man may be abolished.

531. Mysticism is an experience; it cannct be studied, it cannot be put into words, it cannot be explained or talked about. Those who write explanations of it, or talk about colours, spirits, visions, experiences etc., are not true mystics.

532. What is necessary just now is not only that brotherhood should be taught as morals, but as spirit, as a spiritual law. This whole manifestation is one whole mechanical working wherein every soul has its place. There is not one soul in the whole universe, which is a foreign soul. It is this Brotherhood which must be realized.

533. When a person attains seership, he rises above such things as palmistry, crystal gazing etc. etc.; for him they have no use.

534. It is the Call from above which strikes the note of the day.

535. If you believe in no God, worship Nature.

536. On the Spiritual Path one unlearns what one has already learnt; it means emptying oneself.

537. The secret of Peace is hidden under the cover of the ego.

538. Rising above a religion does not mean giving up the religion, it means being fully benefitted by it. Those who say they have given up their religion, are <u>not</u> above it; they alone are above it who have reached a full understanding of the Spirit of Religion.

539. The more we sympathize with ourselves, the heavier becomes the burden of the soul to lift.

540. The aim of the Sufi is not power or inspiration although by contemplation and meditation both will come as he proceeds forth. His only aim is to tread the Path until he can arrive no matter how long it may take. He does not worry about what sacrifice he will have to make. He desires one thing, be it God or Goal, the attainment of which is his perfection.

541. (Personal development).
Life is blinding, and it keeps man busy and engaged finding fault with others.
He does not find the "thorn" in himself; he always sees it in others.

542. Do not let your doubt stand against your trust.

543. Do not forgive yourself for not forgiving others.

544. Value the nobility of soul above all things.

545. Respect every soul - worthy or unworthy.

546. Work for the work - not for success.

547. Arrest every impulse to examine it before it is expressed.

548. When we try too much, we miss the joy in the agony of doing.

549. Care of the body is the first thing, and without it spirituality has very little significance.

550. Imagination is the stepping-stone to realization.

551. When I leave the earth, I would rather be known as the Consoler than the Teacher.

552. One kindled soul proves greater in power than ten thousand souls groping in darkness.

553. If in working we seem to fall, it is to rise still higher and with greater force.

554. You must have in your hand a staff of Faith and hold a lantern of Truth. You must tolerate all, endure all things, forgive all; then with the strength of selfconfidence and unshakable faith in the Message, you can serve with sincere devotion the Great Cause, which is striking the note to-day.

555. Say little, serve all, pass on.
This is true greatness: to serve unnoticed and work unseen.

556. We rise by treading the Path of Faith.

557. Some day we shall realize what God is, but that only comes after the first lesson has been learnt.

558. My work is not to stay beside you, but to open your heart to receive the Light.

559. The task of the Teacher in the past age was like walking on the ever moving water.
The task of the Teacher in the present age is like walking barefooted on unsheathed swords.

560. The chief object of creation is the formation of the Bodhisattva.

561. The Lord Maitreya, the Bodhisattva Spirit or Spirit of Guidance, working in man, fulfils his mission in a planet. On the fulfilment of his mission he is crowned Rassoul. (Note: one in every cycle.) 1)

Note 1): This addition was found with the saying.

562. All the essence which rises from the intelligence of humanity, merges into the Spirit of Guidance, the Bodhisattva; and all waste matter coming from the Spirit of Guidance goes to make the intellect of man.

563. All Masters and Saints are group-souls. The souls belonging to a group-soul are not equal, but each is different and has a different purpose to fulfil. The Master is not complete until all souls in the group are perfected.

564. We shall never know ourselves as part of God until we first realize that every mind is part of ourselves and that we are part of every mind.

565. Intelligence of humanity is the all pervading undifferentiated Spirit of God. (Chaitanya)

-566-

566. Every man on leaving this world, takes with him his own heaven or hell. 2)

Note 2): Dated: 2nd June 1921.

567. When treading the right path, if one wonders whether it be really right, that is worse than treading a wrong path with certainty. For all paths must lead sooner or later to the same Goal. 3)

Note 3): This saying was published in 'The Sufi Quarterly' of June 1932.

568. All that begins in doubt, continues in difficulty, and ends in unhappiness, is wrong.
All that begins with faith, continues in faith and ends in joy, is right. 4)

Note 4): This saying was published in 'The Sufi Quarterly' of June 1932.

569. Murshid's blessing:
May your heart be filled with heavenly joy,
May your soul be illuminated with divine light,
May your spirit uphold the divine Message,
May you go on in the spiritual path,
May God's peace abide with you for ever and evermore. 5)

Note 5): These lines were also found in Angela Alt's handwriting but incomplete.

570. Your work you are doing,
My work I am doing.
And it is the co-operation of both out of which comes something. 6)

Note 6): Dated 12th May 1922.

571. It is the destiny of the Message to awaken humanity to a new spiritual consciousness.

572. Our sympathy, our love for one another, our devotion to the Cause, our faith in God - with this organization we will work hand in hand.

573. Action leads to perfection. 7)

Note 7): A typewritten version has 'Bola' over it.

574. To accuse a person of his wickedness is a worse wickedness.

575. All a Teacher can do is to prepare the vessel and pray that it may be filled with divine grace, but the vessel can only be filled after it is entirely empty, and only the pupil can do that.

576. That which is a station to the novice is a veil to the adept. The real is a ceaseless experience; maya is to cease from that experience in order to talk about it.

577. Greatness is in humility
Wisdom is in modesty
Success is in sacrifice
Truth is in silence.

Murshid
Given at Suresnes, August 13 1923
as an address to Cherags; later
made into Gatheka 23.

578. All the studies in Sufism are to teach us how to govern life's subtle forces.

579. Brain is the instrument through which thought works. Thought is far greater than the brain. Imagination is uncontrolled thought. Thought is controlled imagination.

580. The soul is pure of characteristics, it takes them as it passes through the spheres.

581. It is not every soul who is developed enough to see God in wood, and stone, and in all things; when one has reached this realization, he has touched perfection.

582. Faith is a sacred thing, because it cannot be given, it must be developed within oneself.

583. Verily he is blessed, who can rest in the thought of God.

Verily he is blessed, to whom God's call comes.

Verily he is blessed, whose eyes have seen the Beauty of God.

And Verily he is twice blessed, who speaketh of God, with closed lips. 8)

Note 8): Dated 28th May 1922. These four sentences were found in Ng.'s handwriting as one saying, of which the first, third and fourth were published in Ng.'s book 'Between the Desert and the Sown'. Inayat Khan wrote 'Suras' over it.

Dictated to and preserved by Miss Sakina Furnée.

584. Mastering means not killing the senses.
Mastering means conquering the senses, using the senses as one likes and not to be used by them.

585. Man's heart is visualized in the Shrine of God and even a small injury in thought, word and deed against it, is considered as a great sin against God, the Indwelling One.

586. So much good as a man has in him, so much bad he has, (Wagner - English people did not understand his harmony, throwing with stones at him during a performance of his music.) So what is called bad is only what does not go in with the vibrations of a certain surrounding. Therefore two things are important in life: to advance in wisdom and to keep it secret in the heart; and to try to cope with others, whatever be their stage of evolution.

587. Death is a greater joy to me than life.
But the fulfilment of the purpose, a still greater joy.

588. It is worse than death to me to have to tell a mureed his fault. It is as if I tell from having committed that fault myself.

-589-

589. Sound is hidden under words and words are hidden under sound. When one perceives the words, one does not perceive the sound underneath, and when one perceives sound, one does not perceive the words underneath. When the poet perceives word, the musician perceives sound underneath. The mystic perceives even in that sound a word which was God.

590. Rebelling against what our soul knows to be wrong, is right.

591. Incense: that which has gone through the fire, rises to God; incense is from the earth, enters by breath into our being, where is the Kingdom of God.

592. Life, like every other blessing, derives its value from its use alone.

593. Meditation means uniting with the Self. Hands on knees, lower part in connection with higher part.

594. Symbology 1).
The heart of man is as a rosebud and as the bloom of the rose comes from the sunny cross, so the heart, as a rose blooms when it has met with life's cross.

Note 1): Inayat Khan added 'Sangatha Series I', which was crossed out by Gd. and replaced by 'Saying' in her handwriting.

595. Congestion comes from closing of circulation. (natural restrain or excess of expressing natural tendencies).

596. Freedom of action is a good thing, but it must be considered with the freedom of result.

597. Vanity is the deepest depth of the nature of the Spirit. Without vanity no art would have been.

598. Moral is nothing but a law of adjustment. To a metaphysician it is of no importance at all what the moral can teach; it is allright for a priest.

Note: These sayings were dated: Summer School 1921.

599. Humanity has learned enough to fight very well-perfected. Not what is needed is fight with oneself. All energy and strength must be given to fight one-self. Oneself is one's enemy. Then there will come peace.

600. Spiritual line is the line, not scientific.

601. The only things that hinder in the spiritual path are enmity, spite and bitterness. All other sins don't matter.

602. For those who seek after spiritual truth, association with friends in the same path is more precious than anything in the world. 2)

Note 2): This saying was published in the Magazine 'The Sufi' of July 1938.

Preserved and transmitted by Murshida Sharifa Goodenough.

603. A mystic's God is Reality.

604. Man's aim is the aim of the whole world - consciousness, to be conscious, to know. This is the aim of the mineral world, the vegetable and the animal world. The tree, in its decay, in its annihilation, becomes many thousand germs and worms. The worms and insects become birds and animals and the animal becomes man.

605. A painter paints a little picture. It is sold for thousands of dollars. He is admired as so great an artist, and no one thinks how great an Artist is He Who made that on the model of which the painting is made.
The justice existed in the Consciousness before our justice was made.

606. We cannot say that the carpenter creates the tables and chairs. He takes wood of which to make them. We cannot say that we create anything.

607. Perfection is applicable only to God and never to man so long as he remains man.

608. We do not wish to interfere with world politics, but certainly work for the unity of nations and wish to spare no effort in ~~abolishing~~ helping to destroy the moral degeneration of the present time, our only object being to bring about a better understanding between the different creeds, nations, and races, thus working toward the formation of one human brotherhood.

609. God lost in the manifestation is the state which we call waking.

610. To have consideration for another is the root of all religious laws.

611. Love is a great inspirer of law. 1)

Note 1): In an old typewritten copy the last two words were omitted.

612. Virtues are virtues because they give joy if they are once practised. If a virtue does not give a joy, it is not a virtue.

613. A wise person thinks another 2) knows as much as he knows, and a foolish one thinks another person 2) knows as little as he knows.

Note 2): In another copy Gd. suggested to replace 'another' and 'another person' by 'one'.

614. If we make the best of life, life will show its best side to us. 3)

Note 3): Another version has: 'life will show us its better side.'

615. That is not devotion which does not expand the heart.

-616-

616. When a person sees that another does not stand where he himself stands, he generally thinks the other has not that point; he does not think that the other has passed it. And when he finds that another is not looking at what he himself is seeing, he most often supposes the other cannot see it, not that he is not interested in looking at it.

(Another version:)

When a person sees that another is not looking at what he himself sees, he mostly thinks that he cannot see it; he does not think he is not interested in looking at it.
And when a person sees that another is not in that place where he himself is standing, he mostly thinks he has not reached it **yet**; not that he has passed it.

617. Looking at the past and finding one's errors is like cracking nuts and finding a shrivelled kernel.

618. Looking at the past and recognizing one's mistakes is like mounting the steps of a staircase.

619. The light is reflected through the current that links all the Murshids upon the mureed in accordance with his response.

Handed down by Murshida Sophia Saintsbury Green.

620. There are three possible attitudes towards evil impressions.
1. In the path of saintliness one must consider it to be karma and therefore be resigned to it.
2. In the path of mastery - think it to be the evil force and fight against it.
3. In the prophetic path that which has happened think it was from karma and what will happen - think that you will struggle against it.

Note: See Sayings II : Part Two - no. 443.

621. Human beings living in their shells are mostly unaware of the privilege of life, and so are unthankful to the Giver of them. In order to see the Grace of God, man must open his eyes and raise his head from his little world, and then he will see above and below, to right and to left, before and behind, the Grace of God reaching him from everywhere in abundance.

622. If we try to thank God, we might thank for thousands of years, and it would never be enough, but if man stays in his own little shell, he does not find the Grace of God, he finds misery, injustice, ugliness, coldness.

623. When one looks down, one sees the mud; when one looks up, one sees the sun, moon and planets. It all depends how we look, upwards or downwards.

624. Every man has his own little world, so little sometimes that it is like a doll's house; and in that little world he is not concerned with the world outside, or with the universe, he just lives in his small world so full of illness, misery and ill luck. He cannot come out of it, for he has built a little shell in which he lives, a shell of misery for himself; he likes to live in it, for it is his own home.

625. Balance must be maintained between what is physical and what is eternal, by being conscious of both. One must not dive so deep into eternity that one does not know what time is, nor be so immersed in the physical, that one is unaware of immortality. As there is night and day, so there is the change of consciousness from the physical to the spiritual, and from the spiritual to the physical. By keeping a balance between these two conditions, a person leads a complete life.

Reported and transmitted by Dr. O.C. Gruner.

626. To say "the Kingdom of God is at hand" is to say it is at your hand! So why look over the whole universe or 1) for a future life, when that which you seek is within - quite close, "at hand"!

Note 1): In a later typewritten version (probably also Dr. Gruner's) under the heading "The Voice of Inayat Khan - Sayings", was added: (and) wait.

627. The Sufi path is to seek the Unity, and not get lost in variety. People may 2) take up philosophy, theosophy and the like, if they please. It is no concern 3) of the Sufi. He does not restrict them, even if they choose to be restricted. His path is direct to the Unity. The 4) path is the path of balance.

Notes: In a later typewritten version (probably also Dr. Gruner's) under the heading "The Voice of Inayat Khan - Sayings" is mentioned:
2) 'can'.
3) 'But these are not the concern'.
4) 'His'.

628. The object of the Sufi is to enter the Silence - to leave the form and the external and the attributes, and to cease striving for anything but the Goal.

629. Good concentration is like a hot pan: the oil in it is always fluid, enabling things to cook quickly. Do not let the pan cool by extraneous occupation. If the mind is intensely concentrated on one thing, everything else that comes in the way will also be achieved.

630. If a person considers two pictures and believes one is good and the other poor it is his choice. Why arouse the fire in his ego faculty by comments; it is for him to choose. Some day he will understand (see). 5)

Note 5: In a later typewritten version (probably also Dr. Gruner's) under the heading "The Voice of Inayat Khan - Sayings" the first sentence reads:

If a person compares two pictures and believes one good and the other poor, it is his choice, let him be.

In another typewritten version the whole saying reads:

If a person compares two pictures and calls one good and the other poor, let him be. There is no gain if the fire in his Ego-faculty be aroused. Some day he will see,

631. God is not in Time; therefore He is in the Silence. Sound is part of the world of Time.

632. The object of meditation is to raise the soul above both body and mind. 6)

Note 6): A later typewritten version (probably also Dr. Gruner's) under the heading "The Voice of Inayat Khan - Sayings" has:

'above the body and the mind'.

633. The basis of every religion is the matter of saving the self or killing it. 7)

Note 7): Another typewritten version (probably also Dr. Gruner's) under the heading "The Voice of Inayat Khan - Sayings" has:

The basis of every religion is 'to save the self' or 'to kill the self'.

634. Self-realization is not the same as self-expression. It is not "work", it is not "art", it is not a realization of a mental or artistic self. It is not the creation of a thing that lives for ever like Shakespeare or Beethoven. It is realizing God. It is union with God. It is attainment.

635. Divine perfection is perfection in all powers and mysteries. These are manifested without specially striving for them.

Note: These sayings may be dated between 1918 and 1920.

Preserved and transmitted by Mrs. Mahtab van Hogendorp.

636. Have faith in your own ideal.

637. Many followers, but rare it is to find a devotee.
Many workers, but rare it is to find a trustee.
Many worshippers, but rare it is to find a lover of God.
Many students, but rare it is to find one who glorifies the Lord.

With most hearty blessings

Inayat Khan

27 October 1923. 1)

Note 1): These lines were found in Pir-o-Murshid Inayat Khan's handwriting on the fly-leaf of a copy of the Gayan, given by Murshid to Mahtab van Hogendorp.

From some of Miss Reza Jones's copybooks:

638. By realizing the divine in one's self, one begins to respect one's self and others. This is the commencement of the Kingdom of God.

639. Man's best cure is reliance on that Being Whose creation he is and Who expresses Himself through him.

640. When Jesus Christ was asked: "Where is the proof of the truth of your Message?", his answer was: "In the hearts of my disciples." He did not say: "In the miracles."

641. The word "Nirvana" means "no colour".
The colours change into the one pure white light, the Light of God. 1)

Note 1): This saying was dated: 19th August 1923.

642. I come from a perfect Source
And I return to a perfect Goal.
The light of that Being is kindled in my soul.
I live and move and have my being in God.
Nothing in the past or the present has power to touch me. I rise above all. 2)

Note 2): This is another version of the saying under 523.

From one of Mrs. Kefayat LLoyd's copybooks:

643. Occultism is to know the inner reason or cause of

-Cont.)-

Cont.) what the average man only sees as a result. 1)

Note 1): Dated: 13th June 1921.

Found in Miss Kismet Stam's handwriting.

644. There are people who act as they act because they do not know why they act as they act. But if you could make them know why they act as they act, they would be worse.

645. Murshid once said in a letter:
"My teaching has no particular teaching. In other words, I teach what cannot very well be put into words. Besides, my way is not to urge, but to bring before humanity what is good and beautiful, and let them choose for themselves what they will."

From some of Mr. Sirdar van Tuyll van Serooskerken's notebooks.

646. The life of the disciples will always be to go through different tests. It is by going, strong by their faith, through the tests, that they develop and show the peace of the Message.

647. All the tragedy in life is caused by self-consciousness. Every pain and depression is caused by this, and anything that can take away the thought of the self helps to a certain extent to relieve man from pain, but God-Consciousness gives a perfect relief.

From a personal talk with Murshid,
Wissous, 1921.

648. On tiredness.

If it is a nervous thing, eat more meat.
If it is muscular, do physical exercise.
If it is brain, oil the head every night.
If it is (something else), it must be cured by the physician.

649. In every problem you must see the line instead of the points. That is Sufism.
There are two points, but one line joins them.
If you seek the point you will go to the one or to the other end, but if you hold the line, you understand the whole.

650. The Prophet sleeps as the crescent moon. As the bow, that shoots the arrow, the arrow being God.

(for the description of the life of the prophet.)

651. Never hurt the human feelings in thought, word or deed. The human heart is so delicate, it is like a

-Cont.)-

Cont.) fine tissue. And when once there is a tear in the tissue you can repair it, yet the tear remains and so it is with the human heart. Once there is a tear in it, it can never be healed.

September 1922.

It is not known by whom these sayings have been passed on. They were found in the archives of the Nekbakht Foundation.

---

652. All that is born, built, sprung or made, must one day be destroyed.

653. Revelation is different from intuition, vision or inspiration. These are but for a time, but revelation is the continual outpouring of divine bliss.

654. God is not kind only to a few, to those who are good. We can see that He sends the rain to all the trees and plants, not to a few only, the sun shines upon all, all are given food. Because His kindness is perfect.

655. What is most necessary in order to acquire healing power? Will-power.

656. Barriers are for those who cannot fly. 1)

Note 1): On a Sufi pamphlet from Brighton and on the cover of the Magazine "Sufism" (May 1921 - December 1924) edited by S.E.M. Green.

657. The mind recognises the body, and the soul recognises the mind, because the body stands before the mind, and the mind stands before the soul, but the soul cannot recognise itself, because behind the soul there is nothing. It is all consciousness. The soul sees the mind and the body, it cannot see itself.

658. There are three Lights. God, the Light of the Teacher, and the manifested Word.
The Consciousness makes from itself the other two Lights, by which it experiences Life. This is the meaning of the Christian Trinity. My definition of Light is "that which appears", all that appears can only appear by the radiance of the Light that is in it.

659. Pir-o-Murshid told a mureed:

The colour of Christianity is red.
The colour of Islam is green.
The colour of Buddhism is yellow.
The colour of Judaism is blue.

.-.-.-.-.

P A R T F O U R

SAYINGS PUBLISHED AS "APHORISMS".

INTRODUCTION TO PART FOUR.

This part gives a selection of sayings collected by Mrs. Kefayat LLoyd from Inayat Khan's lectures. They were published under the title 'Aphorisms' in the 'Sufi Quarterly', a philosophical review, edited by Ronald A.L. Mumtaz Armstrong. In seven successive numbers of this review appeared a chapter containing Aphorisms (December 1927, March 1928, June 1928, September 1928, December 1928, March 1929 and June 1929). About the way Kefayat LLoyd used to collect sayings from Inayat Khan's lectures and the latter's approval of it, something was told in Kefayat's Biographical sketch in the Biography of Pir-o-Murshid Inayat Khan, published by East-West Publications in 1979.

In 1929/1930 Mumtaz Armstrong published a stencilled booklet, called 'The Aphorisms of Inayat Khan', in which the above mentioned seven chapters were put together, in the same sequence as in 'The Sufi Quarterly'. To this collection he added 70 more aphorisms. It is not known if these too were selected by Kefayat LLoyd; no indication about it was made by Mumtaz Armstrong in his preface to the booklet. Besides sentences from Inayat Khan's lectures, this last part of the booklet contains three sayings from the "Vadan" (Aphorisms 308, 315, 316), some parts or different versions of the Unpublished Sayings (see under Part Two of this book) and a few different versions of previously included Aphorisms (Aphorisms 296, 336, and 346).

In the first edition of this book, it was requested that those familiar with the lectures of Pir-o-Murshid Inayat Khan and the books in which they have been published undertake to trace the origins of the Aphorisms. One correspondent found the origin of a few Aphorisms in the books "Character Building" and "The Soul Whence and Whither?" Since the lectures from which these books were made have now been published as originally spoken in The Complete Works of Pir-o-Murshid Hazrat Inayat Khan, 1923 II, a comparison of the Aphorisms with the extensive index in that volume allowed the identification of the sources of a considerable number of Aphorisms. A more careful and extensive comparison will no doubt yield the origin of many more, and as the publication of the Complete Works continues it should be possible eventually to find the origin of virtually every Aphorism. Since that process is far from complete, in this edition we are adding to this Introduction a list of the origins identified to date, all from the Summer School in Suresnes in 1923. In a later edition, when the identification of sources is more complete, we will include a full comparison of the original words with the published version, as we have done with "The Bowl of Sâki".

Meanwhile, we would like to urge those interested to continue this work of finding the origins, and to communicate their findings to the archives in Suresnes (see end of Preface for the address).

Origins of Aphorisms:

The number of the Aphorism is on the left, followed by the title and date (all 1923) of the lecture or class from which it was taken and the page number on which the origin appears in *The Complete Works of Pir-o-Murshid Inayat Khan*, 1923 II, July-December, London and The Hague, 1988.

19, 20, 21. : "God Ideal", 23 July, p. 182.

22. : Questions and Answers, 14 July, p. 110.

23. : Questions and Answers, 14 July, p. 111.

27. : "Tasawwuf", 18 July, p. 140.

31, 32, 33. : "Tasawwuf", 20 July, p. 156.

38. : "Metaphysics. Mind", 11 July, p. 87.

39. : "Metaphysics. Mind", 11 July, p. 87-8.

48. : Questions and Answers, 14 July, p. 110.

50. : "Tasawwuf. The Soul towards Manifestation", 10 August, p. 335.

52, 53. : "The Soul towards the Goal", 10 September, p. 627.

55. : "The Soul towards the Goal", 11 September, p. 635.

59. : "Conventionality", 21 July, p. 163.

60. : "Conventionality", 21 July, p. 164.

62. : "Tasawwuf", 23 July, p. 177.

63, 64, 65. : "Tasawwuf", 23 July, p. 178.

66. : "The Spiritual Hierarchy", 24 July, p. 189.

70. : "The Spiritual Hierarchy", 24 July, p. 190.

77, 78. : "Character Building", 20 August, p. 420.

79, 80. : "Tasawwuf. The Soul towards Manifestation", 18 August, p. 415.

81. : "The Soul towards Manifestation", 20 August, p. 429

82, 83. : "The Soul towards Manifestation", 20 August, p. 430.

88. : "Tasawwuf. The Soul towards Manifestation", 18 August, p. 414.

93. : Question Class, 8 August, p. 324.

96. : "Character Building", 11 August, p. 341.

98, 99. : "There is a custom...", 10 August, p. 332.

100. : "The Character Building", 13 August, p. 356.

101. : "Character Building", 11 August, p. 343.

102. : "The Character Building", 13 August, p. 352.

109. : "The God Ideal. God, the Infinite", 7 August, p. 314.

127. : "The God Ideal. The Self and the Merit of God", 28 July, p. 233.

128. : "God Ideal", 25 July, p. 212.

173. : "The Prophet. What Is Asked of a Prophet," 7 August, p. 307.

175, 176. : "The Message", 6 August, p. 295.

177. : Question Class, 8 August, p. 322.

178. : "The God Ideal. God, the Infinite", 7 August, p. 309.

179. : "The God Ideal. God, the Infinite", 7 August, p. 310.

180. : "The God Ideal. God, the Infinite", 7 August, p. 311.

183. : "Character Building", 18 August, p. 402.

184. : "Character Building", 18 August, p. 405.

185. : "Character Building", 18 August, p. 404.

186. : "Character Building", 18 August, p. 406.

187. : "Character Building", 11 August, p. 341.

188. : "Character Building", 18 August, p. 402.

189, 190. : "Character Building", 11 August, p. 341.

191. : "Character Building", 14 August, p. 367.

193. : "The Character Building", 13 August, p. 356.

195, 196. : "Character Building", 20 August, p. 420.

197. : "Character Building", 20 August, p. 421.

199, 200. : "Character Building", 17 August, p. 391.

221. : "Character Building", 20 August, p. 424.

230. : "The Soul's Manifestation", 6 September, p. 586.

A P H O R I S M S

1. Illusion is the cover of things: reality is the depth of things. The body is the illusion; the soul is the reality. The flower is the illusion: the fragrance is the reality. The fragrance is the spirit of the flower; it persists.

2. Man is not made by God as the wood is cut by the carpenter; for the carpenter and the wood are different, while God and man are the same. Man is made of the substance of God: man is in God: and all that is in God, is in man.

3. Belief cannot be taught: it cannot be learned; it is the grace of God. To affirm a belief is one thing; to realise belief is another.

4. The aim of the mystic is to stretch his range of consciousness as widely as possible, so that he may touch the highest pride and the deepest humility. The only fall for a mystic is to fall beneath the level of his ideal.

5. A man who has no imagination, stands on the earth; he has no wings: he cannot fly.

6. When we are face to face with Truth, the point of view of Krishna, Buddha, Christ, or any other Prophet, is the same. When we look at life from the top of the mountain, there is no limitation: there is the same immensity.

7. To every question that arises in the heart of the mystic, he finds the answer in the life before him.

8. The false shows itself; all that is true proves itself.

9. That which is not beautiful in its effect, cannot be real beauty.

10. It is those who have touched the Inner Beauty, who are able to appreciate beauty in all its forms.

11. The Beauty which the knower knows and the lover appreciates, the mystic worships.

12. The difference between Spirit and soul is like that of

-the-

the sun and the ray. The ray is the ray of the sun, but at the same time the sun is the sun, and the ray is the ray.

13. God is the essense of beauty; it is His love of beauty, which has caused Him to express His own beauty in Manifestation.

14. Beauty is God's desire fulfilled in the objective world.

15. Beauty is the depth of the soul; its expression in whatever form is the sign of the soul's unfoldment.

16. When an individual becomes a person, the beauty hidden in the individual, which is divine, develops: and that development of beauty is personality.

17. Beauty is hidden in every soul, however wicked; and our trust and confidence in the beauty of the soul helps to draw out that hidden beauty, which must shine out one day.

18. Most unbelievers have a very near horizon, like birds in a covered cage, who do not know that there is anything beyond.

19. The wonderful thing is that the soul already knows to some extent that there is something behind the veil, the veil of perplexity: that there is something to be sought for in the highest spheres of life: that there is some beauty to be seen: that there is some One to be known, Who is knowable.

20. This desire, this longing is not acquired; it is a dim knowledge of the soul, which it has in itself. Therefore, disbelief in God is nothing but a condition brought about by the vapours arising from this material life and covering, as clouds, the Light of the soul which is its life.

21. If this world offers to a person all it possesses, even then the soul is not satisfied, because its satisfaction is in its higher aspiration; and it is this higher aspiration which leads to God.

22. If the mind did not stand as a hindrance to the intuition, every person would be intuitive, for intuition is more natural and more easy than the reasoning of the mind.

23. What comes from without is not intuition; intuition is something which rises from one's own heart and brings a sense of satisfaction, of ease and happiness.

24. The life of man, however great and spiritual, has its -limitations-

limitations. Before the conditions of life the greatest man on earth, the most powerful soul, will for a moment seem helpless; but it is not the beginning which counts: it is the end.

25. It is the last note that a great soul strikes which proves that soul to be real and true.

26. There can be no better sign of spiritual development than control over passion and anger. If one can control these, one can control life.

27. The secret of seeking the will of God is in cultivating the faculty of sensing harmony; for harmony is beauty and beauty is harmony, and the lover of beauty in his further progress becomes the seeker for harmony; and by trying always to maintain harmony, man will tune his heart to the will of God.

28. If it were not for pain, one would not enjoy the experience of joy. It is pain which helps one to experience joy, for everything is distinguished by its opposite.

29. If it were not for pain, life would be most uninteresting, for it is by pain that the heart is penetrated.

30. Since the nature of life is action and reaction, every outer experience has a reaction within and every inner experience has its reaction in the outer life.

31. In the spheres of conscience the soul of man and the Spirit of God meet and become one.

32. To a soul which is wide-awake, the Judgment Day does not come after death. For that soul, every day is a Judgment Day.

33. Every step forward gives a certain amount of freedom of action, and, as one goes further and further in the path of Truth, the freedom is greater at every step.

34. The more one regards the feelings of others, the more harmony one can create.

35. The heart in its depth is linked up with the Divine Mind: so in the depth of the heart there is greater justice than on the surface.

36. Inspiration comes when knowledge and the Inner Light, falling on one's own conception of things, come together in the conscience, which is the Court of God, where He Himself

-sits-

sits on the throne of Justice.

37. Happiness is our birthright: in our happiness is the happiness of God.

38. Thought has its birth and death as a living being, and the life of a thought is incomparably longer than that of a living being in the physical body.

39. The mind is a world, a world that man makes - in which he will make his life in the hereafter, as a spider lives in the web it has woven.

Cf. Aph. 296.

40. To what does the love of God lead? It leads to that peace and stillness which can be seen in the life of the tree, which flowers and bears fruit for others and expects no return.

41. Verily he who pursues the world, will inherit the world; but the soul who pursues God, will attain in the end to the presence of God.

42. A material person has a silent craving in his heart to probe the depth of the spiritual ideal which he disowns.

43. There is nothing in this world which does not speak. Every thing and every being is continually calling out its nature, its character, and its secret: and the more the inner sense is open, the more capable it becomes of hearing the voice of all things.

44. When once the inner sense has broken the walls around it, it breathes the freedom and happiness which is the soul's own property and which the soul then attains.

45. The sign of the enlightened soul is readiness to understand.

46. The soul comes to a stage of realization where the whole of life becomes to him one sublime vision of the immanence of God.

47. The brain may be said to be the seat of the Intelligence, and the heart to be the throne of Wisdom.

48. Wisdom may be called spiritual knowledge.

49. The real place where the Heavens are made, is within man.

50. The soul is the ray of the Sun, which is the infinite Spirit.

51. The soul is the action of the heavenly Sun. It manifests and returns, as man exhales and inhales.

52. God is Love: so God is beyond the Law. Love is above the Law.

53. If we come to any solution of our everrising questions, it is never by studying the Law that we find satisfaction, but by diving deep into Love, and letting Love inspire us.

Cf. Aph. 346.

54. If one has learned while on earth how to create joy and happiness for oneself and others, in the other world that joy and happiness surround one: and if one has sown the seeds of poison, one must reap those fruits there: and thus one sees that justice is the nature of life.

55. The Judgment Day is every day, and one knows it as one's sight becomes more keen. Every hour, every moment in life has its judgment.

56. What connection has the soul, which has passed from the Earth, with those still on this plane? The connection of the heart still keeps intact, and it remains unbroken as long as the link of sympathy is there.

57. To create happiness for oneself and others is the whole philosophy of religion.

58. What is Sufism? It is wisdom. To learn wisdom, at every step on the path of life, is the only work of the Sufi.

59. The one who is the slave of conventionality, is a captive; the one who is the master of conventionality, is the possessor of that kingdom which is mentioned in the Bible: "Blessed are the meek, for they shall inherit the kingdom of the Earth."

60. As soon as a person begins to regard the pleasure and displeasure of God in the feelings of every person he meets, he can only be refined, whatever his position in life.

61. The human soul is by nature perfect, but the life of limitation on Earth brings imperfection to it.

62. The sense of Shame is a channel which leads to that Goal which is called Perfection.

63. Beauty, in all its aspects, is beyond price.

64. Often the sense of shame works like a sharp knife upon a feeling heart, but it only makes it like a cut diamond: for by it we come to the realization that what is most precious in life, is feeling.

65. The heights of every civilisation show the fineness of human feeling, which is the highest of all aspects of culture.

66. What the moon seems to give as light, is not its own; it is the light of the sun. So it is with the divine Messengers of all times.

67. When a soul arrives at its full bloom, it begins to show the colour and spread the fragrance of the Divine Spirit of God.

68. The one who does not seek God, has, in the end of the journey of illusion, a great disappointment; for, throughout his whole journey, he has not found the perfection of Love, Beauty, and Goodness on the Earth; and he does not believe in, or expect to find, such an ideal in Heaven.

69. Every soul seeks for happiness, and, after running after all the objects which for the moment seem to give happiness, finds out that nowhere is there perfect happiness except in God.

70. All souls in the world are receptacles of the Message of God; not only human beings, but even the lower creation convey the Message of the One and Only Being.
= also Aph. 122.

71. No sooner has the heart become living, than the law of Justice manifests.

72. God is noth Judge and Forgiver. He forgives even more than He judges; for justice comes from His intelligence, but forgiveness comes from His Divine Love.

73. When God's Divine Love rises as a wave, it washes away the sins of the whole life in a moment, for Law has no power to stand before Love: the stream of Love sweeps it away.

74. The very thought of the love of God fills the heart with joy and makes it light of its burden.

75. The kingship of God manifests in the blossoming of every soul.

76. The finest things are to be felt: words cannot express them. Noise only spoils their beauty and robs them of preciousness.

77. The attitude of looking at everything with a smile is the sign of the saintly soul.

78. As the sunshine from without lightens the whole world, so the sunshine from within, if it were raised, would illuminate the whole life, in spite of all seeming wrongs and all limitations.

79. Fear is a shadow cast upon the light of the soul: the shadow of something the soul does not know, which is strange to the soul.

80. Fear comes from ignorance. For instance, the soul is frightened on entering the body of matter: and the soul does not know death, and so it is afraid.

81. The illuminated soul finds its way through darkness, both within and without.

82. In spite of all his limitation, a wonderful power is hidden in man's soul. What makes man helpless, is ignorance of his free-will. Free-will is the basis of the whole life.

83. Free-will is the mighty power, the God-power, hidden in man, and it is ignorance which keeps man from his divine heritage.

84. Many seem wide-awake to the life without, but asleep to the life within; and, though the chamber of the heart is continually visited by the hosts of Heaven, they do not know their heart, for they are not there.

85. Man can only be really happy when he connects his soul with the spheres of Heaven.

86. The more closely a person is drawn to Heaven, the more the things of Earth lose their colour and taste.

87. The religions have always taught self-denial; but the soul which naturally rises to Heaven, does not need to practise renunciation.

88. The moment the soul compares its own limitation with the perfection of God, it has begun to progress.

89. At the cost of the happiness of Heaven, the soul comes to the great fulfilment of life, which even angels are not blessed with: for manifestation in human form is the utmost boundary of manifestation, the furthest that any soul can go.

90. Every difficulty in life is owing to man's limitation, which covers the divine spark in him until in time it becomes obscured from his view, and this culminates in the tragedy of life.

91. Not only human beings, but animals, birds, insects, trees and plants all have a spiritual attainment. No creature that has ever been on earth will be deprived entirely of spiritual bliss.

92. There is nothing in this world without purpose, and, though the place of one in the scheme of life may seem different from that of another, yet, in the sum total of things, we and the lower creation, together with the djinns and angels, have our purpose, and that purpose is the realization of Truth; and it comes to all in the form of bliss.

93. Wisdom is Love, and Love is true Wisdom. The cold-hearted man is never wise, and the truly warm-hearted person is never foolish, for love comes from Wisdom and wisdom from love.

94. One must not make even principles so set that one cannot break them.

95. Every soul inclined to serve has a scope for service on every plane; and the one who is able to serve here, is able to serve on the higher planes even more.

96. Self-pity is the worst poverty. When a person says, "I am to be pitied" - before he says anything more, he has diminished, by half, what he is: and what is said further, diminishes him totally.

97. Out of the heart that is happy, springs a fountain that pours water from above and in time brings flowers and fruits.

98. A person need not be unworldly in order to become spiritual. We may live in the world and yet not be of the world.

99. Spirituality is in no way a hindrance to worldly progress. A worldly success, gained through the power of spirituality, has a stronger foundation.

100. Virtue, forced upon oneself or another, is not a virtue; it loses its beauty. There must be willingness - virtue must not be forced.

101. The true Ego does not know sorrow; its true being is happiness, for the real Ego is God and God is Happiness.

102. Once a soul has awakened to the continual music of life, that soul will consider it as his responsibility, his duty, to play his part in the outer life, even if it be contrary to his inner condition at the moment.

103. The knowers of Truth close their lips, for they cannot say one thing or another from the point of view of Absolute Truth.

104. There are many names for the seas and rivers and streams, but they all contain water - and there are various names for religion, but they all contain the same Truth, spoken in different forms at different times.

105. It is the love element developing in the animals, which brings them together in flocks and herds.

106. We must not observe a principle only, but we must consult our own ideals in everything we do.

107. I think the knower of the Truth will find truth in the symbols of the Roman Catholic Church, and will find the same truth in the absence of symbols in the Protestant Church.

108. If the soul were awakened to feel what the birds feel when singing in the forest at dawn, man would know that their prayer is even more exalting than his own, for it is more natural.

109. Trees are more holy and spiritual than some men. Their purpose is to give some contribution to life, and they are continually busy fulfilling their purpose. They feel that joy and satisfaction which man cannot feel until he attains to their stage of stillness and peace.

110. Where there is form, there is shadow - so, where there is human love, there is jealousy.

111. Tolerance is the sign of an evolved soul. A soul gives the proof of its evolution in the degree of tolerance it shows.

112. Death does not belong to the soul - so it does not belong to the person. Death comes to what the person knows: not to the person himself.

113. There is no scripture in which contradiction does not exist. It is the contradiction which makes the music of the Message.

114. None of the Great Ones have called themselves Masters, nor have they ever considered themselves to be so. What they have known in their lives, is their privilege in opening their heart wider and wider to reflect the Light of The Master, Who is God Himself.

115. For all faces are His faces, and from all lips it is His word that comes. But those who can respond to Him, they become as His appointed servants.

116. God has chosen all, for all souls are near and dear to the Creator.

117. The greater a person is in spiritual advancement, the more unassuming he becomes.

118. The Great Ones are initiated by God Himself, and they prove their initiations, not by their claims, but in their works.

119. Everything has its purpose, but knowledge of the purpose makes us able to use it to the best advantage.

120. Beauty is created out of variety.

121. Truth is the heritage of Man - the human soul, whether in the East or West, possesses the Truth.

122. All souls in the world are receptacles of the Message of God, and not only the human beings but even the lower creation, all objects and all conditions, convey to us the Message of the One and Only Being.

= also Aph. 70.

123. There is nothing in the world which is not the instrument of God.

124. Evil and ugliness are in man's limited conception. In God's great Being they have no existence.

125. Evil is only the shadow of goodness. As the shadow is non-existent, so is evil.

126. It is the knowledge of the purpose of life which gives man the strength with which he stands in the midst of the opposing forces of life.

127. God knows Himself by His manifestation. Manifestation is the self of God, but a self which is limited - a self which makes Him know that He is perfect, when He compares His own Being with this limited self which we call Nature. Therefore, the purpose of the whole creation is the realization that God Himself gains by discovering His own perfection through His manifestation.

128. Merit is not creative. Merit is something which is possessed. Therefore attributes are not important - the importance is in the possessor of the attribute.

129. We are too limited to see the justice of the Perfect One.

130. We often suffer because we do not understand. Understanding is a great thing - once we understand, we can tolerate.

131. The soul of every individual is God; but man has a mind and a body, which contain God according to his accommodation.

132. The water of the ocean is ever pure, in spite of all that may be thrown into it. So the Pure One consumes all impurities, and turns them into purity.

133. The soul is the Divine Breath. It purifies, re-vivifies, and heals the instrument through which it functions.

134. The soul is on a continual journey. On whatever plane, it journeys all the time, and on this journey it has a purpose to accomplish.

135. Nothing that the human heart has once desired, remains unfulfilled. If it is not fulfilled here, it is accom-

-plished-

plished in the hereafter.

136. The desire of the soul is the wish of God.

137. The Source of the soul is perfect, and so is the Goal.

138. No soul perishes - the soul was not born to perish.

139. The one who loves fairness, blows the spark of justice to a flame, in the light of which life becomes clear to him.

140. The one who judges himself, learns justice - not he who is occupied in judging others.

141. There comes a stage in life, the stage of life's culmination, when man has nothing to say against any one, unless it be against himself; and it is from this point that he begins to see the Divine Justice hidden behind Manifestation.

142. The wise see in every form the Divine Form - in every heart they see the Divine Light shining.

143. When we judge others, we are certainly judging the Artist Who has created them. If we realized this, it would not be difficult to feel the presence of God everywhere.

144. When we go more deeply into the phenomena of life, we shall come to a place where the whole nature of Being will unveil itself, and we shall be able to say: "There is nothing but God."

145. Noisiness comes from restlessness, and restlessness is the destructive rhythm.

146. Those who have made any success in life, in whatever direction, it is by their quiet working.

147. Enthusiasm is a great thing in life: it is creative; but too much of it sometimes spoils things.

148. When one devotes one's time and thought to trying to know what one need not know, one loses the opportunity which life offers of discovering the nature and secret of the soul, in which lies the fulfilment of the purpose of life.

149. Life's mysteries apart, the less words used in the little things of everyday life, the more profitable it is.

150. People think that many words express things better. They do not know that most often so many words spoken are so many veils wrapped around the idea.

151. He who holds himself close to Heaven, he is guided from Heaven.

152. He who disconnects himself from the heavenly spheres, is like the broken fruit fallen from the tree.

153. He who clings to the light from Heaven, has a light to warn and guard him at every step, according to his desire for guidance.

154. The angelic souls who are in direct touch with the Spirit of God, and who have no knowledge of the false world which is full of illusion - who live and know not death, whose lives are happiness, whose food is divine light - make around the Divine Spirit an aura which is called the highest Heaven.

155. Death is the unveiling of a cover, after which many things will be known to the soul, which have been hitherto hidden in regard to its own life and in regard to the whole world.

156. Innocence is the natural condition of the soul, and the lack of innocence is a foreign element which the soul acquires after coming upon earth.

157. Death, for the spiritual souls, is only a gate through which they enter into that sphere which every soul knows to be its home.

158. Souls which have become conscious of the angelic spheres, even in the smallest degree, hear the calling of that sphere, and the discomfort they have in this world is that of home-sickness which the call of the angelic spheres gives.

159. Intelligence is the Light of Life, the Life of Life, and the Essence of the whole Being.

160. Rhythm cannot exist without tone, nor tone without rhythm. They are interdependent for their existence, and it is the same with time and space.

161. The mystic contemplates upon the Being of God, and so raises his consciousness above the limitations of time and space, and liberates his soul by lifting it to the divine spheres.

162. The blessing of life is in the consciousness of the blessing.

163. Man will find, in the end of his search on the spiritual line, that all beings, including trees and plants, rocks and mountains, oceans and rivers, all are prayerful - and all attain to that spiritual summit which is the real longing of all souls.

164. Only when man learns to serve and do his duty without the thought of appreciation - only then will he attain.

165. That self-denial cannot be a virtue, which comes as a result of helplessness and culminates in dissatisfaction.

166. The soul's happiness is in itself - nothing can make the soul fully happy but self-realization.

167. The life which everyone knows, is this momentary period of the soul's captivity.

168. Spirit is matter and matter is spirit. The denseness of spirit is matter, and the fineness of matter is spirit.

169. According to the width of his motive, man's vision is wide; and according to the power of his motive, man's strength is great.

170. Such souls as are conscious of their relation to God as that between a child and his parents, are especially cared for. They are always guided, because they ask for guidance.

171. There is nothing in this world which is void of form, except God, Who is formless.

172. The limitless God cannot be made intelligible to the limited self, unless He is first made limited. That limited ideal becomes as an instrument, as a medium of God Who is perfect and Who is limitless.

173. What is religion? In the outer sense of the word, a form given for the worship of God, a law given to the community that it may live harmoniously. And what does

-religion-

religion mean in the inner sense of the word? It means a staircase made for the soul to climb to reach that plane where Truth is realized.

174. Many do good - but how few do it wisely! To do good wisely is the work of the Sage.

175. The one who lives in his mind, is conscious of the mind; the one who lives in his soul, is conscious of the soul.

176. Truth is unlimited and incomparable - therefore Truth alone knows, enjoys, and realizes its own existence.

177. The soul is Light, the mind is Light, and the body is Light - Light of different grades - and it is this relation which connects man with the planets and stars.

178. The Infinite God is the Self of God; and all that has manifested under name and form, is the outward aspect of God.

179. All men who join in prayers, may not be so sincere as the birds in the forest, for not one among them says its prayers without sincerity.

180. Spirituality is attained by all beings - not only by man, but by beasts and birds, for they each have their religion, their principles, their law and their morals.

181. The pride that says, "I am so spiritual", is not spiritual pride; it is earthly pride: for where there is spirituality, there is no proud claim.

182. Spiritual realization can be attained in one moment in rare cases, but generally a considerable time of preparation is needed.

183. Fineness of nature is the sign of the intelligent.

184. Fineness can be acquired by love of refinement.

185. In the heart of man the whole universe is reflected: and, as the whole universe is reflected in it, man may be called the heart of the universe.

186. Subtlety produces Beauty. It is Subtlety which is the Curl of the Beloved.

187. In order to acquire spiritual knowledge, in order to receive inspiration, in order to prepare one's heart for the inner revelation, one must try to make one's mentality pliable - like water, rather than a rock.

188. Once peace is made within, one will have gained sufficient strength and power to use in the struggle of life, within and without.

189. Life is a continual battle. Man's constant struggle with things outside gives a chance to the foes who exist in his own being.

190. The first thing necessary is to make peace for the time being with the outside world, in order to prepare for the warfare which is to be fought within.

191. The one who is able to keep his equilibrium without being annoyed, without being troubled, gains that mastery which is needed in the evolution of life.

192. The heart, when it is not living and making its life a life of love, feels out of place; and all the discomfort of life comes from this.

193. Nothing, however good it appears, is a virtue unless it is willingly done - because, in the willingness of making even a sacrifice, one experiences the breath of freedom.

194. When a person is absorbed in self, he has no time to build his character; but when he forgets himself, he collects all that is good and beautiful. This is the key to the whole life - to worldly success and to spiritual attainment.

195. God is happiness, the soul is happiness, and spirituality is happiness. So there is no place for sadness in the kingdom of God.

196. That which deprives man of happiness, deprives him of God.

197. The light - which comes from the soul, rises through the heart, and manifests outwardly in man's smile - is indeed the Light from Heaven. In that Light many flowers frow and many fruits become ripe.

198. We help God to forgive us by forgiving ourselves.

199. He who realises the relation of friendship between one soul and another - the tenderness, delicacy, and sacredness of this relationship - he is living, and in this manner he will one day communicate with God.

200. The same bridge, which connects two souls in the world, when stretched becomes the path to God.

201. Nirvana is as a star in our hearts, which we develop; and as we develop it, it becomes brilliant: and its brilliance consumes all the wrong of life until nothing is left but that purity which is the Divine Light.

202. It must be remembered as the first principle of life, that manifestation was destined for keener observation of life within and without.

203. The soul is happy by nature: the soul is happiness itself. It becomes unhappy when something is the matter with its vehicle, its instrument, its tool - through which it experiences life. Care of the body, therefore, is the first and the most important principle of religion.

204. The purpose of the whole creation is fulfilled in the attainment of that perfection which is for a human being to attain. The saints, seers, sages, prophets, and Masters of humanity have all been human beings: and they have shown divine perfection in fulfilling the purpose of being human.

205. The teaching of Jesus Christ has, as its central theme, unfoldment towards a realization of immortality.

206. Vanity, in its proper place, is a great virtue. When not in its proper place, it is a great sin.

207. Every person has his life designed beforehand; and the purpose that he is born to accomplish in life - the light of that purpose has already been kindled in his soul.

208. Is not man the creator of sin? If he creates it, he can destroy it also. And if he cannot destroy it, his elder brother can.

209. The impression of sin, in metaphysical terms, may be called an illness - a mental illness, not physical. And, as the doctor is able to cure physical illness, so the doctor of the soul is able to heal spiritually.

210. In reality, no sin, no virtue can be engraved upon the

-soul-

soul - it can cover the soul. The soul is, in its essence, Divine Intelligence; and how can Divine Intelligence be impressed with either virtue or sin?

211. When the object, the purpose for which a soul is born upon Earth, is fulfilled - then there is nothing to hold it; and the soul is naturally drawn back to its source and Goal.

212. God Himself sees through the eye of man - so the eye is a road between man and God.

213. Man has neither been created to be as spiritual as an angel, nor has he been made to be as material as an animal; and when he strikes the happy medium, he will certainly tread the path which leads straight to the Goal.

214. Man by nature is good. Goodness is his real self: badness is only a cloud. But clouds are ever floating - they are sometimes here and sometimes there - and if we trust in the goodness of man, the clouds will disappear. Our very trust will disperse them.

215. The sun shines on all the trees; it does not make distinctions between this tree and that, but in accordance with their absorption of the light falling upon them and according to the response they give to the sun, they receive its light.

216. Remember, that very often a disciple is an inspiration for the Master; because it is not the Master who teaches - it is God Himself.

217. The Master is only the medium; and, as high as is the response of the disciple, so strongly does it attract the message of God.

218. The further we go, so the more our disputes and arguments cease. They fade away until there is no colour left in them; and when all the colour has gone, the white light comes which is the Light of God.

219. The one who serves, however humbly, has the privilege of serving God.

220. Cheerfulness is life: sadness is death. Life attracts: death repulses.

221. Do not let your own mind be impressed by the depression of your friend. If you do, you will have taken the germ of

-his-

his disease.

222. It is harmony, established with everyone one meets in life, which tunes one's soul with the Infinite.

223. The man conscious of his duties and obligations to his friends is more righteous than he who sits alone in the solitude.

224. The condition of God and His true lover is that either the Beloved lives or the lover - not both.

225. Whether a person feels attracted to God now or not, there will come a day when he will be attracted; for every soul has to return to God.

226. Ignorance of the self gives the fear of death. The more one learns of the true self, the less one fears death; for it is only a door through which one passes from one phase of life to another - and the other phase is much better.

227. Humour is the sign of Light from above. When that Light touches the mind, it tickles it: and it is the tickling of the mind that produces humour.

228. Renunciation is not something which we must torture ourselves to learn. It is in us, but it is buried, and it can only be dug up by our love.

229. When the sun is clouded, the light does not reach the Earth - so with the soul, which is divine and full of light. If it is covered thickly with clouds, then man does not receive the light which is in the soul itself.

230. What is rooted out in the quest of Truth, is ignorance. When it is entirely removed from his heart, man's outlook becomes wide - as wide as the eye of God.

231. Man meets with hardships in life - sometimes they seem too hard for him to stand. But often such experiences become as higher initiations in the life of the traveller on the Path.

232. Sadness comes from limitation - limitation in different forms - from lack of perception, lack of power over oneself and over conditions, and from lack of that substance which is happiness itself: which is Love.

233. The nature of Love is as the nature of water in the depth of the earth. If one does not dig deep enough, he finds mud not water; but when he digs deep, he finds pure water.

234. If there is any death, it is stillness and inactivity; and then the impulse of life comes, which breaks through the cloud of mortality and makes the soul see the daylight after the darkness of the night. And what does the soul see in this bright daylight? It sees itself living as before, having the same name and form and yet progressing.

235. Every soul is striving to attain God - God not as a Judge or as a King, but as a Beloved. And every soul seeks God, the God of Love, in the form which it is capable of imagining.

236. The soul manifests in the world in order that it may experience the different phases of manifestation: and yet not lose its way, but regain its original freedom in addition to the experience and knowledge it has gained in this world.

237. In order to be, one must pass through a stage of being nothing.

238. When Illumination comes, it seems to bring annihilation: but it is not annihilation - it is, in reality, exaltation.

239. Happiness cannot come by merely believing in God. Believing is a process. By this process the God within is awakened and made living; it is the living in God, which gives happiness.

240. It is not only the link of love and sympathy, but the belief in the hereafter to the extent of conviction, that lifts those on earth to know about their beloved ones who have passed over to the other side.

241. The soul's sustenance is the knowledge of God. It is by this knowledge that the soul lives the eternal life.

242. Man has the key of life in his own hands, if he only knew it.

243. Man is always journeying towards the Truth. He is seeking, seeking - for in his heart is the love of that which is REAL.

244. There is no such thing as mortality, except the illu-

 -sion-

sion - and the impression of that illusion which man keeps before his eyes as fear during his life-time, and still as an impression after he has passed from this earth.

Cf. Aph. 336.

245. The soul is life - it never touches death. Death is its illusion.

246. To the one who realizes ultimate Truth, time and space are of little importance; he rises above them.

247. The further one goes on the spiritual path, the more one will have to learn to play a part.

248. The spiritual man learns to answer the question of every soul at its own plane of evolution.

249. It is the ignorant soul, ignorant of his source and goal, who dreads leaving the sphere to which he has become attached. It is the soul who knows not what is beyond, who is afraid to be lifted up above the ground his feet are touching.

250. One's duty is to do now what can be done now. Nothing that one really values, does one put off till to-morrow.

251. Souls, when they start from the angelic heavens, are vibrations. They have no earthly harps; they are the harps themselves.

252. There cannot be perfection where there is duality. God alone is perfect.

253. The whole interest in life is in journeying towards perfection. If man were born perfect, there would be no joy in life.

254. In order to attain to God-consciousness, the first condition is to make God a reality so that He is no longer only an imagination.

255. The soul who develops his personality, is like the fine flower with its colour, fragrance, and delicacy.

256. The essence of spirituality and mysticism is readiness to serve the person next to us.

257. The question: "What is the purpose of manifestation?"

-may-

may be answered in one word - Satisfaction, (for the satisfaction of God).

258. Nothing in the world could give man the strength that is needed to live a life on the Earth, if there were no blessing from Heaven reaching him from time to time and of which he is so little aware.

259. The work of the spiritual man is to forget his false self and to realize the true self, which is God: and to realize this true self in his brother also.

260. It is not true that Adam was put out of the Garden of Eden. He only turned his back upon it; and so he became an exile from Heaven.

261. Every soul is born with the capacity by which it can draw all the spiritual bliss and ecstasy which is needed for its evolution.

262. Every thing and being is placed in its own place, and each is busy carrying out the work which has to be done in the whole scheme of Nature.

263. Nirvànà is not an intellectual realization; it is Life.

264. There are blessed souls living on the earth to-day to whom sacrifice gives no pain but only pleasure. In seeing another eat, their hunger is satisfied: renunciation is to them a joy; for they have gone through the cross and risen above it.

265. The better the instrument, the greater the satisfaction of the soul.

266. Truth cannot be put into words. It must be seen in the light of our own intuition.

267. That cannot be Truth which is acquired. The Truth is that which is discovered.

268. The art of personality is not a qualification - it is the purpose for which man was created. By this art, man not only satisfies himself, but he pleases God.

269. When the soul has once fought its battle with the things that make it fear and tremble and shrink, that soul has conquered life and become the master of life. It has inherited the kingdom which is its own.

270. The man who has proved in his life to be the friend of every person he meets, he in the end will prove to be the friend of God.

271. The perfection of friendship, in which there is all spiritual perfection, comes when the soul is so developed that it says: "There is not one whom I cannot bear." When it has reached that state, it has certainly passed into the ranks of those initiates whose names are written on the spiritual records.

272. Nature, in its different aspects, is the materialization of that Light which is called the Divine Spirit.

273. In prayer, the repeating of thanksgiving brings to one's soul one's own voice, and that voice echoes before the God Who is within.

274. The angels were made to sing the praises of the Lord: the genii to imagine, to dream, to meditate: but man is created to show humanity in his character.

275. It is not what Christ taught that makes his devotees love him. They dispute over these things in vain. It is what He Himself was; it is that, which is loved and admired by them.

276. Man may have rank and position and a thousand qualifications: he may possess all the goods of the Earth; but if he lacks the art of personality, he is indeed poor. It is by this art that man shows that nobility which belongs to the kingdom of God.

277. A person however learned and qualified in his life's work, in whom gratitude is absent, is void of that beauty of character which makes personality fragrant.

278. Throughout the whole journey on the spiritual path, the main thing that has to be accomplished is the forgetting of the false ego.

279. True freedom is within oneself. When the soul is free, there is nothing in this world that binds us - everywhere we find freedom, both in Heaven and Earth.

280. As the heart expands, so the horizon becomes wider, and one finds greater and greater scope in which to build the kingdom of God.

281. Joy is not something brought from outside: it belongs

-to-

to us; but it manifests to us as the result of certain actions.

282. Life is an opportunity, and the more one realizes this, the more one will make the best of the opportunity which life offers.

283. The essence of life is hope. If we hope to be better, we shall become better.

284. You are love. You come from love. You are made by love. You cannot cease to love.

285. The whole manifestation is the manifestation of love. God Himself is love. So the love which comes from the Source, returns to the Source - and the purpose of life is accomplished in this.

286. You may go to the most exalted place: a place blessed with peace and rest; but if you take sadness and unrest with you, you will find them there.

287. God's Message does not come only in words. What comes in words is small compared to the radiance the Message brings to all things and all beings. It comes in the form of a sacrament - as bread and wine. Bread and wine, when symbolically interpreted, mean love and life.

288. Renounce the good of the world: renounce the good of Heaven: renounce your highest ideal. Then renounce your renunciation.

289. The way to perfection is not limited. No one can make a rule that you can only pass by this way and none other.

290. Beauty is the watchword of the seeker.

291. Patience is a process through which a soul goes to become precious.

292. By Self-realization, a man becomes larger than the universe. The world in which he lives, becomes as a drop in the ocean of his heart.

293. In our sorrow is God's sorrow; for, if God cannot sympathise, man is greater than God.

294. Part of our sorrow, and our joy, comes from life: part we make for ourselves. Life cannot give us joy if we will not earn it.

295. The God ideal is the flower of the human race, and this flower blooms in the realization of God.

296. The mind is a world - a world that man makes: in which he will live in the hereafter as a spider lives in the web it has woven.

Cf. Aph. 39.

297. The further on the path of life's mystery a person travels, the finer he will have to become, in order to perceive and to express the mystery of life.

298. The prophetic soul is like a fruit, dropped upon the earth but still connected with the branch. The branch has bent and the fruit has touched the earth, but it has not lost connection with the stem.

299. The further we advance, our part in the symphony of life becomes more difficult and more important; and the more conscious we become of this responsibility, the more efficient we become in accomplishing our task.

300. With all the arguments for and against the divinity of Christ, no sincere believer in God can deny that God reflected Himself through the personality of the Master.

301. The prophetic soul must, of necessity, rise so high that it can hear the voice of God: and, at the same time, it must bend so low that it can hear the softest whisper of the beings on earth.

302. Even the presence of the prophet is the answer to every question - without speaking one word, the prophet gives the answer ..... The prophet is only the medium between God and man; therefore, the answer is from God. It is not true that the prophet answers the question, because he reads the mind; it is the mind of the one who asks the question, that strikes, on the inner plane, the Divine Bell which is the heart of the prophet.

303. The moment a person rises above his mind and wakens in the light of the soul, he becomes spiritual.

304. There are many facts, but only one Truth. The facts can be put into words, but not the Truth.

305. The mystic seeks God both within and without; he recognises God both in unity and in variety.

306. As one evolves spiritually, one rises above the tendency to intolerance: for the reason that one begins to see, besides oneself and the second person, God - and so one unites oneself with the other person in God.

307. The souls of all are from one and the same Source, but a soul which is unveiled, shines out. Love and light come continually from such souls: you need no proof for it, for it is living - all else is dead in comparison.

308. It is death that dies, not life.

309. The soul covers its own truth with a thousand veils from its own eyes.

310. The ideal must not be turned into the idol.

311. The soul has not come on Earth to die the death of helplessness nor continually to suffer pain and misery. The purpose of the soul is that for which the whole creation has been busied, and it is the fulfilling of that purpose which is called God-consciousness.

312. Evil is an ever-floating thing - sometimes here, sometimes there. So, evil in man is just a cloud: it comes and goes; and, if we trust in his goodness, the clouds will disappear.

313. Man's sacred duty is to strive to attain to that perfect consciousness which is his true religion.

314. By making many sacrifices and practising renunciation: by going through many tests and trials, man will attain to that consciousness which is God-consciousness - in which resides all perfection.

315. Balance is the key-note of spiritual attainment.

316. No sooner is the God Ideal brought to life, than the worshipper of God turns into Truth.

317. The depth of every soul is good. It is only belief in this doctrine that gives us reason for our belief in the goodness of God.

318. The man who shuts himself away from all men, however high spiritually he may be, will not be free in the higher spheres.

319. In order to fulfill the practical duties of life, it is not necessary to forget our ideal. We can hold the ideal in the tenderest spot of our heart, and yet fulfill our practical duties. The ideal is to illuminate our lives, not to paralyze our actions.

320. The disciple can inspire, and the disciple can shut off his inspiration. If there is no response on the part of the disciple, then the inspiration of the Master becomes closed. Just as the clouds cannot give rain when passing over the desert, so, when they come to the forest, the trees attract and the rain falls.

321. The soul, in manifestation on Earth, is not at all disconnected with the higher spheres. It lives in all spheres, but is conscious generally only on one plane. Thus it becomes deprived of the Heavenly bliss, and conscious of the troubles and limitations of life on the Earth.

322. Nirvànà means "no colour". What is "colour"? Right or wrong, sin or virtue - all this is "colour"; and, in the realm of Truth, they fade away as every colour fades in the brightness of Light. He who has realised this, has entered Nirvànà.

323. There are rays and there is Light. If the rays are the source of the souls of living beings, then the light of the Divine Sun is the spirit of the whole of Being.

324. When we develop our sense of beauty, then we are naturally critical of that which does not come up to our standard. But, when we have passed this stage, in the next cycle divine compassion is developed in our nature and we become able to add all that is lacking, and so to make up for that perfect beauty.

325. In the making of personality, God finishes His divine art.

326. As the source and goal of all creation is one, so the source and goal of all religion is one.

327. The law of God is endless and limitless as God Himself, and, once the eye of the seeker penetrates through the veil that hangs before him, hiding from his eyes the real law of life, the mystery of the whole life manifests to him: and happiness and peace become his own, for they are

-the-

the birthright of every soul.

328. The soul longs for a keen perception. The absence of such fine perception causes depression and confusion, because the inner longing is to see.

329. There comes a stage in the evolution of an illuminated soul, when he begins to see the law hidden behind Nature. To him, the whole of life reveals its secret.

330. The wider the outlook, the less are one's troubles in life. If one fixes one's eyes on the horizon as far as one can see, one is saved from troubles and trials.

331. God is the horizon, and you can neither touch the horizon nor God. The horizon is as far as you can see and even further; and so is God.

332. When we find faults and see no excuse, we are blind to the Light which can free a person from his faults and give rise to that forgiveness which is the very essence of God - to be found in the human heart.

333. Life and death, both, are contrary aspects of one thing: and that is change. Death is only passing from life on the Earth to a still greater life.

334. Wealth such as spiritual wealth, the more you give, the more it increases; what you have given, you have not lost: you have gained.

335. What is the soul? The soul is life: it never touches death. Death comes to something which the soul holds, not to itself.

336. There is no such thing as mortality, except as an illusion: and the impression of that illusion, which man holds as fear.

Cf. Aph. 244.

337. Every machine must have an engineer, and the engineer must be powerful, controller of his power - not subject to his power. If God is limited, He can no more be God.

338. Can a composer give a justification for every note written in his composition? He cannot; he can only say: "It is the stream which has risen out of my heart. I am not concerned with every single note. What I am concerned with, is the effect which is produced by my composition."

339. Is Law predominant, or Love? Law is the habit: Love is the being. Law is made: Love has existed - it was, it is, and it will be always.

340. Belief in the human soul is the bridge to belief in God.

341. By our trust in the divine beauty in every person, we develop that beauty in ourselves.

342. Worry comes from self-pity. When the self is forgotten, there is no worry. Worry comes also from fear: and fear comes from the clouds of ignorance. Light breaks the clouds.

343. The soul takes with itself into the hereafter all that it has collected in the way of impressions.

344. The teaching of the prophets is the answer to the demands of individual and collective souls.

345. To weigh, to measure, to examine, to express an opinion on a great personality, one must rise to that development first.

346. If there is any solution to our ever-rising questions, it is never by studying the law that we are satisfied. If anything will give us satisfaction, it is by diving deep into love and letting love inspire us: and that will enable us to see the law.

Cf. Aph. 53.

347. Verily, a deep-felt need is a prayer in itself.

348. There is no liberation unless one has an ideal before one. The ideal is a stepping-stone towards that attainment which is called liberation.

349. Love is the shower by which sin is purified - no stain remains. What is God? God is love. When His mercy, His compassion, His kindness are expressed through a God-realized personality, then the stains of sins, faults, and mistakes are washed away and the soul becomes clear.

350. Earthly pleasures are the shadows of happiness, because of their transitoriness. True happiness is in love, which is the stream that springs from one's soul: and he who will allow this stream to run continually in all conditions of life, in all situations, however difficult, will have a happiness which truly belongs to him - whose source is not without, but within.

351. Failure does not matter in life. To a progressive person, even a thousand failures do not matter. He has before his view success: and success is his, even after a thousand failures. The greatest pity in life is the standstill when life does not move farther; a sensible person prefers death to such a life as that.

352. Verily, Truth is all the Religion there is, and it is Truth which will save. At every step towards the final goal, man will be asked for a sacrifice; and that sacrifice will be a greater and greater one as he continues on the path. When there is nothing, whether mind, body, thought, feeling, or action, that he keeps back from sacrificing for others - by this man proves his realization of divine TRUTH.

P A R T F I V E

PHRASES.

INTRODUCTION TO PART FIVE.

The following sentences are the phrases given by Inayat Khan to many of his mureeds to be repeated for their spiritual advancement and to help solve their problems in life.

Each phrase was specifically meant for a certain person, and a desirable attitude of the mureed, the realization of the full meaning of the phrase, the number of repetitions, the emphasis on certain words and the rhythm of the sentence are of great importance for the result. Therefore they were not published before.

The main reason for publishing them now is to safeguard them for the future and to pass them on in their authentic form.

Furthermore, no doubt, many mureeds may be benefitted by them, as in these phrases also a general meaning can be found. It is, however, pointed out that only when given by an initiator to a mureed a phrase becomes a practice and as such will then attain a deeper meaning. According to the initiator's insight into the psychology of the mureed he will select a certain phrase to be given.

The phrases were taken from Inayat Khan's special notebooks with prescriptions of practices for each one of his mureeds.

The phrases given by Pir-o-Murshid Inayat Khan to his mureeds.

1. Let Thy divine blessing flow through any heart to all Thy people in the world.

2. Bless, Lord, my life with Thy divine blessings.

3. Providence has blessed me.

4. Bless my life with every bliss.

5. May my soul be unfolded, may my heart be at rest, my mind tranquil and my body in good health.
God bless me and my dear ones, every moment of life.

6. Bless my life in every way Lord and illuminate my soul.

7. Complete my life with blessing.

8. Complete my life with every blessing.

9. Providence is blessing me in abundance of all I need.

10. Bless my life with every blessing.

11. Providence has blessed me. No fear, all is well.

12. Bless my home, my life, my soul.

13. Providence bless me with abundance, abundance, abundance.

14. Bless, Lord, my life every day and in every way.

15. Bless me, inspire me and fortify me, Lord, with Thy power and wisdom.

16. Strengthen me, Lord, and inspire me and bless me, make the best of my life.

17. Providence has blessed me and is blessing me with abundance, abundance, abundance.

18. Raise me, Lord, with all the worries and anxieties of life and bless me with Thy divine Providence.

19. My life is blessed in every way by the divine light.

20. My mind is balanced, my soul is illuminated, my life is blessed.

21. Fortify me against the jarring influences and strengthen me in my struggle of life.
Bless me with providence and illuminate me with Thy divine light.

22. My soul is unfolding every day and my life is blessed in every way.

23. Bless me, Lord, in every way and unfold my soul.

24. Bless, Lord, my life and guide me on the right path.

25. Bless my body, mind and soul.

26. Divine Providence, bless me, inspire me and strengthen my faith.

27. "Fazal", bless my life from all sides in all things and every way.

28. "Fazal", bless me in all things through all conditions and in every way.

29. "Fazal", bless my life from all sides through all things in every way.

30. Bless me with light, life, health, happiness, joy and peace, that I may serve Thy divine Cause, wholeheartedly.

31. Heal my body, inspire my mind, bless my heart and illuminate my soul.

32. Bless me, Lord, and my dear ones.

33. My life is unfolding to receive Your blessing, Lord, bless me in every way, guide me on life's path.

34. "Fazal", better my condition within and without. Bless, bless, bless.

35. Bless my life and my body, heart and soul.

36. Inspire me, Lord, to Thy divine wisdom, guide me on the right path and bless my life.

37. Providence has blessed me to have all I need.

38. Bless me with all that will enable me to serve Thy divine Cause.

39. Providence bless and complete my life.

40. God's blessing is in me and around me.

41. Kindle my heart with Thy love, God, and bless my life in every way.

42. Bless my life in every way and from all sides.

43. Providence bless me through every person I meet and through every condition I go through.

44. Make my life smooth, harmonious, progressive and fruitful with every blessing.

45. Inspire my heart, illuminate my soul and bless, God, my life.

46. Bless our lives and guide us on life's path.

47. God grant all I want. Providence has blessed me.

48. Bless me amply that I may share my blessing with all.

49. Providence has blessed me, I have all I need.

50. Providence has blessed me and supplied all my needs.

51. Bless my life in every way, God, by Thy love and compassion.

52. Providence has blessed me, has bestowed upon me all I have and all I need.

53. Bless me, Lord, at every moment of my life.

54. Bless, Lord, with Thy Divine perfection.

55. Bless, Lord, my life and my child and the path which 1) tread.

Note 1): In Inayat Khan's handwriting, no pronoun was written between 'which' and 'tread'.

56. Make my life's path easy and bless me, Lord, at all times.

57. Surround me and those around me with Thy blessing.

58. Providence must bless me thousand times over.

59. I am inspired, I am guided, I am illuminated and I am blessed.

60. Bless me, inspire me and fortify my faith.

61. Bless, God, my soul, heal my body, make my life complete.

62. Providence bless me at every hour, each day, through all I meet and through all conditions I pass through. Abundance, Abundance, Abundance.

63. Bless me with all that my life needs and my soul longs for.

64. I receive Thy blessing, God, in every thing, in food, in drink, in sleep and when I am awake.

65. Bless me a thousand times over and bless me every day more and more.

66. "Fazal" - Harmony within, without, around and about one.

67. "Fazal", kindle my heart, lift up my soul and make my body healthy to give my whole life to the service of the Sufi Cause.

68. "Fazal" - open my heart, unfold my soul, fill me with Thy life and illuminate me with Thy light.

69. I hate no one -
I have grudge against no one -
I tolerate all -
I forgive all -
I love God and all His creation.

70. God is love and in Him I have my being and I have no fear.

71. Guide me toward Thy love and light through the right path.

72. Balance my life with Thy wisdom and love.

73. O Thou, the perfection of love, harmony and beauty, complete my life in every way.

74. Fill my heart, Lord, with Thy love, harmony and beauty.

75. Give me Thy love, teach me Thy harmonious way, show me Thy divine beauty, take me in Thy arms and protect me in Thy enfoldment.

76. Waken in my heart Thy divine love, Lord, and illuminate my life.

77. Fill my life with Thy love, light and life.

78. Beautify my character and kindle Thy love in my heart, and make my life happy.

79. Produce in my life, Lord, love, harmony and beauty.

80. May my life become peaceful and harmonious.

81. Harmonize my soul, Lord, with all people and with all conditions.

82. Brighten up my life with Thy light and harmonize my spirit with the peace of Thy divine Being.

83. My spirit is productive of divine Harmony.
I spread peace and keep balance.

84. Harmonize us both and bring happiness in our home.

85. Raise my consciousness to Thy harmony and peace.

86. Make my home harmonious - mind tranquil - heart at rest - soul illuminated and body at perfect rest.

87. May my influence harmonize my self and others and may my spiritual ways create harmony.

88. Be thoughtful, harmonious and peaceful.

89. Make my home harmonious and illuminated. Heart at rest and life happy.

90. May health, harmony and happiness come in my life.

91. Let my soul manifest Thy sublime beauty in art.

92. Let the vision of Thy divine beauty be reflected in my heart and be expressed in my decorative art.

93. "Muṣavir": Make my art perfect and turn my life into the art.

94. Help me to serve Thy Cause.

95. Let me become a perfect instrument to serve Thy divine Cause.
Let me become a perfect channel to deliver Thy divine Message.

96. Enable me Lord to serve Thy divine Cause.

97. Fortify and strengthen me and inspire me Lord to Thy will and to serve Thy divine Cause.

98. Enable me to fulfil my life's purpose in serving Thy divine Cause.

99. Enable me, Lord, to serve Thy divine Cause with my whole heart.

100. Give me control over my body and mind and enable me, Lord, to serve Thy divine Cause.

101. May my heart be prepared for the future guidance of Murshid.
May conditions allow me to have the association of Murshid.
May God give me the power, means and desire to serve the divine Cause.

102. Bless me, Lord, and my dear ones and illuminate my soul to serve Thy divine Cause.

103. Inspire me, strengthen me and enable me, Lord, to serve Thy divine Cause.

104. Heal my body, mind and soul, that I may best serve Thy Cause.

105. Give me wisdom and power that may enable me to serve in Thy Cause.

106. Prepare me to fulfil my life's purpose in serving Thy divine Cause.

107. Strengthen my faith, Lord, that I may serve Thy Cause for ever.

108. Make me a proper channel to serve Thy Cause.

109. Make me a proper instrument to serve Thy divine Cause.

110. Enable me, Lord, in every way to serve Thy divine Cause.

111. Grant me all that is necessary to serve Thy divine Cause.

112. Grant me every facility to serve Thy divine Cause.

113. Give me all I need to serve Thy divine Cause.

114. Make me, Lord, a worthy instrument to serve Thy divine Cause.

115. Make me a worthy instrument to serve Thy great Cause.

116. Grant me all I need to be best fitted to serve Thy Cause which is my life's purpose.

117. Prepare me to become a proper instrument to be used for the furtherance of Thy divine Cause.

118. Grant me all that is needed to serve Thy divine Cause fully.

119. Complete my life, Lord, that I may serve Thy divine Cause best.

120. Enable me to serve Thy Cause every day more and more.

121. Free my life, Lord, from all undesirable influences, make it pure and exalted to serve Thy divine Cause.

122. Enable me, Lord, to further Thy divine Cause.

123. Make me best fitted to serve Thy divine Cause. Health, Balance, Happiness.

124. Enable me, Lord, to serve Thy divine Cause: Sufi Message.

125. Thou hast healed me, strengthened me and inspired me, Lord, to serve Thee and Thy divine Cause.

126. Arrange my life so that I may serve Thy divine Cause.

127. Enable me, Lord, to serve entirely Thy Divine Cause.

128. Help me, Lord, that one day I will serve the Sufi Cause.

129. Divine beloved, reveal Thy Message through my devoted heart.

130. Make my vision clear, Lord, that I may serve Thy Message better.

131. Inspire me and enable me to serve Thy divine Message.

132. Guide me, Lord, to the path on which tread those you favour and enable me to serve Your divine Message.

133. Provide me with all I need that I may fulfil my life's purpose in serving Thy Message.

134. Enable me, Lord, to serve Thy divine Message.

135. Strengthen me, inspire me and direct me to spread Thy divine Message.

136. Inspire me, strengthen me and fortify my faith, o Lord, to serve and spread Thy divine Message.

137. Enable me, Lord, to give my whole heart to the service of Thy Divine Message.

138. Kindle my heart and illuminate my soul, Lord, that I may spread Thy divine Message.

139. Make me a channel in all Planes
to deliver Thy divine Message.

140. Awake, awake, awake to the Message of God.

141. I give all Message without saying a word.

142. I give the Message in silence.

143. Reveal Thy secret to me, Lord, through my every day experience of life.

144. I live in God, see His light, enjoy His happiness and experience His peace.

145. My body is healed, my mind is fortified and my soul is illuminated by the Grace of God.

146. My mind is at rest, my body is healed and my soul is illuminated by the grace of God.

147. I have risen above all troubles of life and am happy by the Grace of God.

148. Enable me, God, to do my life's work which .... Thy service.

149. My life is dedicated to the service of God.

150. Fortify my heart, give me a new life and new inspiration that I may see in life Thy divine eminence.

In Gd.'s handwriting: Fortify my heart. Give me a new life and new inspiration, that I may see in life Thy divine inspiration.

151. My respondent heart be still,
be still and listen to the consoling voice of God.

152. Still my heart, be still and listen to the consoling voice of God.

153. My heart is still to hear the word of God.

154. Be still, my mind, and hear the word of God that inspires and illuminates.

155. Let me seek Thy divine kingdom and let all that I sought be added into my life.

156. Reveal unto me Thy purpose and guide me towards Thy path.

157. Guide me, Lord, to the path that leads to Thy pleasure.

158. Help me to understand and obey Thy will.

159. I am well and happy in the life and light of God.

160. Heal me, Lord, by Thy all sufficient power, give me, Lord, Thine own light to see and thine own life to live.

161. God, throw on my path Thy divine light and life, that I may find sunshine all over.

162. Unfold my soul to the Divine light, Attain my soul to the Divine life.

163. I am charged by Divine Life and by Divine Light.

164. Give me, Lord, Thy light to see, Thy life to live and Thy almighty power to struggle, Thy patience to bear all and Thy divine wisdom to understand and to forgive.

165. I rise with new life, new courage, and hope to fulfil the purpose of my life for which God had created me.

166. My life is changing and taking a better turn.

167. Let my life show growth and expansion in every direction that is beneficial.

168. Ya Qadīr - right all my life's affairs.

169. Make my path in life smooth and clear.

170. Make my life rhythmic, harmonious, progressive and successful.

171. Help me, Lord, from every direction and make life easy for me.

172. Bring all the possibility of being better to be realized in my life.

173. Providence has its doors open for me everywhere.

174. I see the door of the providence open before me everywhere.

175. Providence prepairs all that I must have in my life. Abundance, abundance, abundance.

176. Providence is on my side.

177. Providence is on my side, so I attract all I need.

178. Providence has promised to grant all of need.

179. Providence, grant my mind peace and my soul illumination.
Bless our home with everything we need.

180. Providence, grant my mind rest, my heart peace, my soul illumination and bless our home with everything we need.

181. My body, heart and soul I gave Thee under Thy divine protection.

182. I am under divine protection, nothing else has power over me.

183. Fill the cup of my heart with Thy divine Spirit.

184. Quiet my mind, calm my spirit.
Surround me, Lord, with the peace of Thine own being.

185. Fear not, worry not, be not anxious, thy spirit is cured and thy body well.

186. Open, Lord, to me Thy glorious vision.

187. Enable me to see Thy divine vision, God, in all things and in every being.

188. Day by day my vision becomes clearer and clearer.

189. Make my vision clear and guide me on the right path.

190. Complete my life by the Grace of Thy perfection.

191. By the Grace of Thy divine perfection, make my life complete.

192. My body, mind and soul is healed by Murshid.
I am calm and peaceful.

193. Guide me to fulfil the purpose of my life.

194. Guide me aright to fulfil the purpose of my life.

195. Guide me to fulfil the purpose for which I am born on the earth.

196. O Spirit of Guidance, throw Thy Divine light on my path.

197. Guide me, Lord, on the right path and illuminate my soul.

198. Guide me, Lord, to do the right thing which is best for me.

199. Awake my soul to the call of the Spirit of Guidance.

200. Strengthen me, inspire me and guide me, Lord, to the road .... leads to the goal.

201. Help me, Lord, to find my self and guide me on the path of life.

202. The inner guidance leads me toward desired goal.

203. Guide me on life's path, Lord, that I may feel Your guidance every day.

204. "Ya Hādī", guide my life aright.

205. Lord, make me rich with contentment, illuminate the chamber of my heart with the light of faith, all that I need grant me without having to ask others.

206. By the divine power of God I have attained control over my self.

207. By the power of Almighty God I control my thought, speech and action.

208. Raise me above undue control.

209. By the divine power of God I am qualified enough to teach and strengthened enough to control every situation.

210. Give me new spirit of enthusiasm and courage to proceed on life's path.

211. I have strength, courage, enthusiasm and hope.

212. I live safely in the spirit of God, and I am free from depression and fear.

213. All clouds of depression are scattered away; I am joyous and I am happy.

214. I am surmounting all difficulties of life every hour and each day more and more.

215. Help me, Lord, to surmount all difficulties.

216. Relieve me, God, of all difficulties and purify my soul.

217. Release me, Lord, from my difficult situation, free my life for Thy divine path.

218. Strengthen me, God, on my path of duty.

219. I am feeling more energetic, more enthusiastic, more and more hopeful every day.

220. Give me confidence in my self, God, and faith in the providence.

221. I seek my life's happiness in God.

222. Lord, Thou art my happiness and Thou hast made my life happy.

223. Bless me, heal me and make my life happy.

224. Inspire me, guide me and lead me through the path of happiness to the divine perfection.

225. Make my life easy, Lord, for me to live happily.

226. Make my life easy and open for me the path of spiritual attainment.

227. Make me, Lord, a fountain of happiness for myself and for others.

228. Enrich my life, Lord, with all that is really good for me.

229. Grant me life, light, wisdom, power, Lord, to bring all those ..... come in my way happiness.

230. Make me a fountain of happiness for myself and others.

231. Keep us both free from all harm coming from our adversary.

232. Grant me, Lord, Thy wisdom, joy and peace.

233. God, send Thy joy and peace in my life.

234. Make my life fruitful, joy giving and progressive in every direction.

235. "Ya Ṣābir", fortify me against all attacks upon my soul with Thy divine patience.

236. Grant me to have all power and wisdom, that I may best fulfil my life's purpose.

237. Give me that wisdom and power which will enable me to influence my fellow beings to their welfare and welbeing.

238. I am purified, revivified and envigorated by the divine power of God.

239. I am purified, revivified and envigorated by Thy divine power, Ye God.

240. Providence has blessed me.
Divine light has illuminated me.
Thy almighty power has strengthened me.

241. Make me strong and fortify me, Lord, with Thy almighty power.

242. Heal me, all sufficient God, by Thy divine power.

243. Let Thy power and wisdom balance my life.

244. "Ya Ḥabīb", let Thy power and Thy wisdom guide my soul.

245. Give me, Lord, Thy power of action, that my life may become a success.

246. Surround me, God, with Thy power, glory and success.

247. Give, Lord, Thy divine power to my spirit that I may serve humanity better.

248. My heart is the receptacle of Thy divine inspiration and power.

249. "Ya Qadīr", strengthen my character and help me to progress.

250. O Thou, the Allpowerful Being, God, the Lord of heaven and the earth, give me strength from Thine own strength, give me wisdom from Thine own wisdom, to rise above the strife of life.

251. Fortify me, Lord, and strengthen my heart to make my way through life.

252. Make my vision clear, Lord, and strengthen me to face the struggle of life.

253. Give me, Lord, Thy divine influence, which may spread among my dear ones.

254. Bring Thy harmony and peace in my home.

255. Connect our lives with the blessing of marriage.

256. Connect us both in the blessing of marriage.

257. Unite our lives in the bond of marriage.

258. Raise me above all limitations.

259. Free me, Lord, from all undesirable influences and keep me safe under Your divine wings.

260. Bless me, inspire me, and draw me closer to Thy divine being.

261. Inspire me, illuminate me and make my vision clear.

262. Let my intelligence shine out as love, let my limited self expand to Thy divine Perfection.

263. Success is my birth right.

264. My success is the sure 1) by the grace of God.

Note 1): The text in Inayat Khan's handwriting should perhaps read 'secure' instead of 'the sure' or 'sure', without 'the' or with the word 'success' repeated after 'sure'.

265. All my efforts for good are being crowned with success.

266. Guide me on the right path, inspire my heart with Thine own wisdom and make my life a success.

267. Open my way to attain all I need.

268. A door is open before me leading to success.

269. Open my way in life and clear my path.
Help me to go forward in life and to attain success in every direction.

270. I erase past out of my mind, brighten the present and build a hope for the future.

271. Help me to progress, Lord, in every direction.

272. Inspire me, strengthen me and fortify my life, Lord, that I may steadily progress in every direction of life.

273. Help me to progress, Lord, in every direction of life.

274. Enable me, Lord, to progress in every way.

275. Make me progress in every direction of life.

276. Clear my way, Lord, on the path of life and help me to progress in every direction.

277. Help my life to fulfil its purpose.

278. My life proceeds towards its purpose.

279. Make to my soul clear my life's purpose.

280. People are favourable to me,
Conditions are favourable to me,
Planets are favourable to me,
Because You are favourable to me, my Lord.

281. O, Thou who are the light of heaven and earth, throw on my path in life Thy divine light.

282. Thy divine light illuminates my heart and I see in life all sunshine.

283. God, throw on my life sunshine.

284. I have Thy divine light upon my heart that I may see my way and understand life better.

285. Illuminate my soul with Thy Divine light.

286. My heart is fortified and is being filled with the light of God.

287. "Munīr", kindle my soul, that I may find my Self, its purpose and on .... 1)

Note 1): The sentence in Inayat Khan's handwriting was left unfinished.

288. No death for me.

289. My body is made of vapor, is floating through the space.

290. My mind is still, my thought is steady, my sight is keen, my life is balanced.

291. Heal my body, still my mind, illuminate my soul.

292. Heal my body, still my mind, Lord, and illuminate my soul.

293. Calm my nerves, still my mind, give my heart rest, Lord, and make my life happy.

294. Calm my nerves, still my mind, give my heart rest, Lord, and make me in life happy.

295. Make my vision clear, make my mind still.
Kindle my heart, God, and illuminate my soul.

296. My mind, free thyself from all thoughts and imaginations and all feelings and emotions, be still, be still, be still.

297. Still my mind, kindle my heart and illuminate my soul.

298. My vision is clear, my mind is still, my heart is kindled and my soul is illuminated.

299. Give my mind rest, my heart peace, and my soul illumination.

300. Let me be fearless and free from all worries and anxiety and let my mind be restful, calm and peaceful.

301. My heart is happy, my mind is rested, and my soul is illuminated by the divine power of God.

302. Heal my body, strengthen my mind and illuminate my soul.

303. Grant health to my body, peace to my heart, illumination to my soul.

304. God, heal my body, strengthen my mind and illuminate my soul.

305. Make my heart respondent, my mind capable and my body sound, that I may fulfil the purpose of my life.

306. Open my heart.

307. Open my heart that Thy spirit it may reflect.

308. My body is the Temple of God and my heart His shrine.

309. Make my heart Thy divine temple.

310. Inspire my mind, kindle my heart and illuminate my soul.

311. My body is healed, my heart is kindled and my soul is illuminated by the light of God.

312. Heal my body, kindle my heart and illuminate my soul.

313. Fortify my heart, o Lord, to withstand all in life with Thy divine patience.

314. My heart reflects Akbar, the mighty One who attracts all and inspires (?) 1) all.

Note 1): Question mark put by Inayat Khan.

315. Release my heart from all that keeps me back from Thy peace and liberate my soul.

316. My heart is unfolding toward its object in life.

317. Radiate Thou through my soul.

318. Awake, my soul, to make your way towards life's purpose and goal.

319. Awake my soul to Thy perpetual glory.

320. Let my soul seek Thee, Lord, in all things.

321. Let Thy .... run 1) through my body, let my soul merge into Your Being.

Note 1): Over the dotted line was written 'word', 'run' was cancelled and replaced by 'raise', both in Sr.'s handwriting.

322. My soul is now blossoming to bear fruit(s) ?. 1)

Note 1): Inayat Khan wrote the 's' between brackets after 'fruit', with a question mark.

323. Raise my soul that I may see the Truth.

324. Unfold my soul to expand in the spheres of freedom.

325. Unfold my soul that I may see life better.

326. May my soul unfold and Thy light give up.

327. May my soul unfold every moment of the day.

328. Unfold my soul, make my sight keen and draw me closer to Thee, my divine Beloved.

329. Unfold, my soul, and expand to perfection.

330. Unfold my soul, O Lord, that I may see Thy sunshine.

331. "Ya Waḥābo", enable my soul to expression.

332. My body, heart and soul radiate the healing spirit of God.

333. My body, soul and mind are healed.

334. "Ya Shāfī", heal Thou my breath, my thought, my word, my touch and my glance, "Ya Kāfī".

335. Bless my home with providence, health, harmony and peace.

336. In Thee I seek my health, comfort, balance and peace.

337. Heal Thou, Lord, through my glance, through my touch and through my words and atmosphere, Thou Almighty and Allsufficient.

338. Let my glance touch and breath have Thy healing power and let me serve, Lord, Thy divine Cause.

339. Heal me, o all sufficient God.

340. By Thy healing power, Lord, I am healed.

341. My body, mind and soul are healed by the divine power of God.

342. My body, heart and soul are healed by the divine power of God.

343. Heal my body, fill my heart with joy and elevate my soul.

344. God, complete my life in bringing me my better half.

345. Open the spring of my heart from which rises Thy healing power.

346. Health, harmony, happiness and bring in my home peace.

347. By the divine power of God my body is free from all illness.

348. Health, power and happiness.

349. Let Thy divine power of healing passing through my being heal me and those whom I heal.

350. Your health is sound by the grace of the divine Perfection.

351. My body, heart and soul are healed by the divine spirit, nothing is the matter with me.

352. Ye shall, o divine Healer, with Thy mercy and grace heal my husband, Thou art all Sufficient.

353. I feel healthy, happy and vigorous by the divine power of God.

354. Heal me, Lord, giving me strength out of Thy Almighty power.

355. "Shāfi", heal my body, heart and soul.
"Kāfi", give me sufficient strength, joy and peace.

356. "Shāfi", divine Healer, heal my body, heart and soul.
"Kāfi", Thou art all sufficient.

357. I am quite well.

358. Behind my activity there is Divine Impulse.

359. My soul is made free from jealousy, anger, depression and fear.

360. My balance is secure in the hands of God.

361. My balance is secure in divine hands.

362. Balance my life that I may know and act aright.

363. Almighty God, Lord of heaven and earth,
give me the power to control my self and balance my life.

364. Free me from the captivity of my life's condition.

365. Complete my life with all I need and with all that is best for me.

366. Beloved Lord, Almighty God, make my life complete.

367. Make us both united, make our life complete.

368. Complete my life with all I need.

369. Send me, God, the other part of my soul and complete my life.

370. Make my life happy and complete.

EXPLANATION OF FOREIGN WORDS AND NAMES.

The following signs have been used:

´ to indicate the primal stress;
¯ to indicate a long vowel;
kh to indicate a sound as the 'ch' in the German word 'Dach';
ẓ to indicate a sound as the English 'th' in the English word 'the';
' before 'a' and 'i' to indicate a vowel sound, similar to a sound in the throat as a very short cough.

A.	Akbar	-great; Mogul emperor of India, 1542-1605.
H.	'Ārif	-knowing, wise, pious, devout; a holy man, a saint.
A.	Bárzakh	-interval, partition, bar, the interval of time.
	Beethoven	-Ludwig van -, German composer, 1770-1827.
P.	Bēgum	-lady, queen, a title of Mogul ladies.
S.	Bōdhisáttva	-the one whose being is light; the one who becomes a Buddha.
S.	Buddha	-an enlightened one. Here is meant Gautama Siddhārtha.
S.	Chaitanya	-consciousness, intelligence. Sufi terminology: the Spirit or Light of God.
A.	Faṇā	-destruction, death; Sufi terminology: annihilation.
A.	Faẓl	-excellence, virtue, grace, favour, superiority, wisdom.
A.	Fikr	-thought, reflection; Sufi terminology: a Sufi practice.
S.	Gángā	-The Ganges - main river of North India considered sacred by the Hindus.
A.	Habīb	-beloved, friend; the Divine Beloved.
A.	Hādī	-guide.
	Judaism	-the profession or the practice of the Jewish religion; the religious system or polity of the Jews.
A.	Kāfī	-sufficient, all-pervading life of God, the All-Sufficient (a name of God).
S.	Kármā	-act, work, result; Sufi terminology: the rhythm of past actions.
S.	Krishna	-dark, black; Messenger of God said to be the eighth avatāra of Vishnu.
S.	Láya	-absorption, destruction, annihilation; also a musical term.
S.	Maitrḗya	-the friend of God, the Rassul; the next human Buddha to come.
A. H.	Málakūt	-spirits, angels, the angelic world; Sufi terminology: sphere of thought and imagination.

Note: The origin of a word is indicated by S. - Sanskrit, A. - Arabic, P. - Persian, H. - Hindustani, Hb. - Hebrew.

S.	Māyā	-delusion, supernatural power, illusion, cosmic illusion which makes the One appear as a multitude.
P.	Místī, Mástī	-drunkenness, intoxication, lust.
A.	Munīr	-brilliant, shining.
A. P.	Murēed	-follower, disciple of a Murshid.
A. P.	Múrshid	-spiritual teacher.
A.	Musáwwir	-fashioner, designer, painter, sculptor.
	Napoleon	-Napoleon I Bonaparte, Emperor of France, 1769-1821.
	Narciss	-Narkissos, son of the rivergod Kephisos and the nymph Leiriope. (Greek Mythology).
S.	Nirvāna	-extinction of the consciousness of a separate existence. Sufi terminology: realizing the soul's freedom.
A.	Nūr	-light, splendour; ether, the first of the five elements.
P.	Ōmar Khayyām	-Famous Persian mathematician, astronomer, free-thinker and poet of the 11th/12th century.
A.	Qādir	-powerful, having legal power, the capable.
A.	Qadīr	-powerful, the Almighty.
A.	Rassūl	-Apostle, Messenger, Prophet.
A.	Rissālat	-Apostleship, state of being a Rassūl, divine mission.
A.	Sābir	-patient, resigned.
A.	Salāt	-prayer, blessing, benediction, the first duty of a Moslim; the second prayer in the Sufi Universal Worship.
S.	Sangatha	-meeting-place, centre, confluence.
S.	Sangita	-music, symphony, song of many voices.
P.	Sâki	-see Sāqī.
P.	Sāqī	-pourer of wine, in Persian Sufi poetry; the giver of ecstasy; the symbol of God wishing to reveal Himself.
A.	Saum	-fasting; the first prayer in the Sufi Universal Worship.
A.	Shāfī	-healing, the healing power of God.
	Shakespeare	-William -, English poet and play-wright, 1564-1616.
S.	Vairāgya	-freedom of all worldly desires, indifference.
A.	Vilādat Day	-birthday. The birthday of Pīr-o-Murshid Ināyat Khān on July 5th, celebrated by his followers.
	Wagner	-Richard, German composer and writer, 1813-1883.

A.	Wahhābo	-the Bestower of blessings to his creatures.
A.	Yā Habīb	-oh Beloved, oh Friend.
A.	Yā Hādī	-oh Guide.
A.	Yā Kāfī	-oh All-Sufficient One.
A.	Yā Quadīr	-oh Almighty.
A.	Yā Sābir	-oh Patient One.
A.	Yā Shāfī	-oh Healer, oh All-Healing Power.
Hb.	Yavéh	-God.

Note: The following dictionaries have been consulted:
M. Monnier-Williams Sanskrit-English;
Al Faraid Arabic-English;
J.F. Platt's Hindustani-English dictionary (for Persian and Hindi words);
Duncan Forbes's Hindustani-English dictionary;
Rubab Monna's Short Dictionary of Foreign Words in Hazrat 'Inayat Khan's Teachings, 1982, East-West Publications, London and The Hague.

INDEX

B.o.S. = Part One: "The Bowl of Sâki".
U.S. = Part Two and Part Three: "Hitherto Unpublished Sayings" and "Additional Sayings and Words".
Aph. = Part Four: "Aphorisms".
Phr. = Part Five: "Phrases".

- - - - -